PAULA DIPERNA

PRICING THE PRICELESS

The Financial Transformation to VALUE THE PLANET, SOLVE THE CLIMATE CRISIS, AND PROTECT OUR MOST PRECIOUS ASSETS

WILEY

Published by John Wiley & Sons, Inc., Hoboken, New Jersey.
Published simultaneously in Canada.

ISBNs: 9781119913801 (Cloth), 9781119913825 (ePDF), 9781119913818 (ePub)

For general information on our other products and services or for technical support, please contact our Customer Care Department within the United States at (800) 762-2974, outside the United States at (317) 572-3993 or fax (317) 572-4002.

Wiley also publishes its books in a variety of electronic formats. Some content that appears in print may not be available in electronic formats. For more information about Wiley products, visit our web site at www.wiley.com.

Library of Congress Control Number:

Cover design: Paul McCarthy
Cover image: © Getty Images: Eyeem

SKY10046158_042023

To the hope that we may repay the patience of our wondrous planet

Contents

Preface

"One of the World's Coldest Places Is Now the Warmest It's Been in 1,000 Years,"

Scientists Say

Such was a news headline greeting the new year of 2023, but how to respond, how to process, absorb, take it in? As is said in French, the news was *bouleversant* (roughly, enough to turn you over).

"Ice in Greenland, one of the planet's refrigerators, is defrosting, leading to melting events that could raise sea levels 20 inches by the end of the century."

Incomprehensible, ungraspable—information and the oceans, over the rim of the cup. And yet, facts like these will be ever present, their own tick-tock. The climate crisis is not only a crisis of science, but of contemplation.

Facts collect and compound, and the question is whether they accelerate or paralyze our ability to act to address climate change. We have a need to know, but because solutions are elusive and costly, we tend to emphasize our quest for knowledge, as if that were action in itself.

Rachel Carson, author of the long ago *Silent Spring*, meticulously collected facts for her landmark book illuminating the impact of toxic insecticides that were disrupting many natural cycles, killing invisibly until we finally saw the corpses of birds and bees.

Carson's work triggered a ban on DDT and a revamp of how pesticides were used, leading to reforms within the chemical industry for which we can be grateful to this day, even as our knowledge and will to avoid the problems Carson cited has increased.

However, Carson's contribution transcended the science she put forward. She enabled us to see what we couldn't see before our eyes, what was far away, what we thought couldn't or wouldn't happen in the world we knew. She reminded us how easily nature could get out of balance while we weren't looking and then, oops, too late.

Climate change is of the same stealthy quality, happening at a distance until it comes home. For decades, climate science has brought us facts, but these too seemed to describe incidents and places beyond ourselves, not about us. Until the now of things.

Climate change, so quickly it seems, is proximate, notably in the extremes of weather that no longer qualify as odd. Victims of climate change seem close, even if there is no bulletin board making the connection. We hear more often of people we know losing their houses to fire, or flooding, or crazy wild storms, like the nightmare snow in the winter of 2023 in Buffalo, New York, where hundreds were stranded and shocked, or the chain of wildfires plaguing the world. Maybe we cannot tie all this rashness of weather inarguably to climate change, but common sense suspects the relationship. The ring of impacts touches us more personally each day.

We can also read climate change in our instincts. Gradually some years ago, I began to be aware of more wind around me—more breezes, more light warm wind coming off the earth, more treetops swaying, more wind in a common rainstorm. Then one day as it rained and blew, my neighbors lost a sturdy oak it had seemed no wind could topple, falling awfully close to their roof. Was that fall climate-change related? It happened only once, but once would have been enough if they'd been standing too near. I put the incident aside. Not every errant event can be blamed on climate change.

Later, though, I came to learn that maybe my instincts on the wind were borne out. Wind, I was told by an astrophysicist devoted to wind research, plays a critical role in mediating temperature extremes and so my hunch of more wind around perhaps correlated with subtle changes in temperature patterns. Cause and effect? It will be a while before we can say for sure, but is certainty our best friend?

As examples in this book demonstrate, extreme weather events are becoming more frequent and we are not bystanders. We can feel it as earthly temperatures vary wildly, sometimes within the safe confines of the four seasons we all recognize—the four seasons of composer Antonio Vivaldi and every other artist in any culture who has ever contemplated seasons and for which every language has a word. And sometimes the extreme highs and lows, wetness and dryness occur within the familiar four. But, more of late, the extremes rearrange our experience, creating even a fifth season that has no resemblance to the others and occurs outside of any calendar.

I wonder if any language yet has a word for this alien time of year.

To an extent, climate change information may have reached a point of diminishing returns—we don't need to know much more before we put addressing climate change at the heart of our economic efforts and open our eyes to the rewards. Climate change has become the hub of our wheel.

Yes, changing climate presents a vast engineering problem, but also equally vast jobs creation potential for people with every level of skill. There is so much to redesign, retrofit, rehab, reinvent, and reconstruct—an exciting expansive reconception of how we organize our energy and energies. A thrilling recast, in fact, driven by the need to avert and stem risks, convert the invaluable to value, and invest a steady devotion to the precious.

I worked closely with French ocean explorer Jacques-Yves Cousteau, who opened my eyes originally to the absurdities of our pricing systems relative to the stewardship of invaluable resources.

In the United States, vast oil reserves were discovered in Alaska and brought to market via a network of feeder pipelines from Prudhoe Bay to be loaded on to oil tankers and shipped to points around the world. Estimates were that Prudhoe's reserves would last about 25 years and serve as a "bridge" fuel to the next era of energy supply, perhaps even renewables that at the time were drawing research attention.

When the *Exxon Valdez* infamously ran aground in Alaska in 1989, causing the largest oil spill in US history at the time, hundreds of activists headed to Prince William Sound, where the oil tanker lay stricken and seabirds and sea mammals, especially otters, swam into dank pools of heavy crude. Emergency animal welfare centers were set up, and heartbreaking images of soiled and dying cormorants, gulls, otters, and other sickened animals flooded the airwaves.

Cousteau, however, seemed remote from the impact of the event and so I asked him, "Why aren't you upset about this tragedy?" He quickly responded, "I am upset, but the real tragedy is taking that oil out of the ground at today's prices."

Oil was oozing on the sea, as wasted there as it might have been when it reached its destination. America's profligate energy consumption was made possible by undervaluing nature and a sense of limitless rights of use.

In the public narrative, the running aground of the *Exxon Valdez* was a wildlife story, not an oil story, and soon the ship underwent a name change to leave the shame of the accident behind, and all went on as before.

Since Cousteau's remarks about the tragedy of undervalue, though, I've tried to keep close to the price questions, not to debase the more metaphysical aspects of nature but because—for reasons I outline in this book—underpricing indicates disrespect. What is free, we take, and we take to an extreme.

We have tended to demonize fossil fuels as our woes about climate change have intensified, as if the fuels themselves were the villains, whispering "Burn me" seductively in our ears. Yet fossil fuels, too, have been victims of our failure to account for the irreplaceable in our pricing and accounting systems. Fossil fuels have also suffered our disrespect. Now we seek to banish them even as we truly have no coherent plan to fairly and efficiently distribute their replacements. And even though this book venerates the billions, even trillions, of dollars worth of unpaid labor provided by nature, I surely know that people cannot eat "ecosystem services" or pour those values into gas tanks, or use them to heat homes or boil water. The gap between theory and practice closes, but too slowly.

Perhaps this is the charge of leadership for the foreseeable future?

We fell into a belief that sustainability was a plateau point and a forever construct, if only we could reach it, but we haven't yet.

Part of the climate crisis is that our sense of cause and effect is too stretched, and our target dates too far away. Science projects impacts to the end of the century, or 2050, even 2030. But those dates outrun the stamina we have today.

The climate crisis is outsized, too large for our psyches. The planet's resilience has been our illusion.

Perhaps instead of living in fear that we must catch up with a crisis, to fend it off, we can transform our fear into animated compulsion to create a beautiful and inspiring counterforce, that collects our best and most brilliant beliefs in the answers at hand, infuses the hopes of all people as the propulsion, and then off we go in manageable bursts of forward motion.

Greenland, of course, is far to the planetary north—but is it only Greenlanders who can hear the ice of ages melting into cups of slushie?

If we can put meeting the climate change challenge at the center of our lives and imagination, especially our economic and financial decision-making for five years, then another five, and so on, we will gradually tilt the earth toward resolution.

1

Michelangelo's Finger: The Pope and the Atmosphere

There was no hush when Pope Francis entered the Sala Clementina in the private Apostolic Palace in Rome. Instead, we flew to our feet in a standing ovation—some even hooted and cheered as if for a baseball hero who had hit it out of the park. But if this was not the standard decorum for the occasion, the pope did not seem to mind. He broke into a broad smile, walked across the room to greet his cardinals, and then took his place.

The pope does not usually grant audiences in July, we were told, but he was making an exception because of his stirring commitment to the topic at hand: climate change and its deleterious impacts especially on the poor, the core theme of his landmark environmental encyclical, *Laudato Si,* issued in 2015 just before a pivotal UN Climate Change Conference to be held in Paris. The encyclical placed the pope at the forefront of leadership on insisting that governments address the care of our common home, planet earth. The encyclical was not static, and the pope seemed intent on keeping it topical and in the public eye.

This meeting with him marked the third anniversary of *Laudato Si,* and we had all been invited to the Vatican to make suggestions for advancing the statement's meaning and impact.

My trip to Rome began in London, where I had flown from New York so I could spend the night and continue on reasonably rested first thing the next morning. I left my hotel so early that the lone night porter had to let me out, lifting the heavy brass bar bolted across the antique wooden lobby door.

Nearly alone on the city streets, the taxi driver peppered the trip with curious chitchat.

"Where are you flying?" he asked.

"To Rome," I replied.

"And what's that for, dearie?" he probed. "Vacation?"

I could not resist. "Believe it or not, I have an audience with the pope."

"Well, that's a big one, isn't it?" he said. Then, speechless for barely a second, he let out the long tale of how he had happened to get married twice. We all have our priorities, I thought.

Gatwick Airport was wide awake, its serpentine gallery of duty-free shops chock-full of dallying passengers, as if planes were no longer the point of airports.

At last I got to my gate, the zigzag aluminum boarding ramp shaking like a portable dock on a summer lake—no carved marble masterpiece staircases leading into grand Vatican meeting rooms quite yet.

But in Rome, American Express was keen to let us know where we'd arrived. "Don't tackle tagliatelle without it," warned the billboard in the customs hall.

I entered the joyful state of listening to Italian, trotting out my basic version. I had chosen a hotel just outside the Vatican, thinking I had better be a stone's throw from the action.

The driver knew the street but not the specific address. "Is it on the right or the left side of Concilazione?" he wondered. "If we knew, I could avoid a lot of turns." I didn't know and neither did his GPS.

We pushed on. The driver took a second to point out the Castel'Sant Angelo in full view nearby, and then said, "So signora, let's take a guess. What do you think—left or right?"

Life is always some sort of gamble in Italy, some aspect of a pursuit of the artful. "What would Tosca say?" I teased him back, knowing he'd get the Puccini opera reference for sure as we passed 'Sant'Angelo, site of the opera's last scene. He burst out laughing.

"Let's try right," said I.

That was wrong, but the driver gave me a stately bow as he dropped me on the nearest corner. My hotel was just a few suitcase rolls away, and so was St. Peter's Cathedral, icon of multitudes but that day, off-season, standing alone in silent gleaming white marble perfection. I had only to raise my eyes to take it all in.

In the morning, I found a Daily Gospel under my door. It turned out that the hotel doubled as the home base of the Salvatorians, a monastic order founded in the 1880s. I left the gospel on my desk and headed out.

Above, a sky-diving unbroken blue sky, and Rome's summer heat was very present. At the vaulted entrance to the square, homeless men were still curled up inside their overnight cardboard boxes, and trash was tucked between bricks as if treasured possessions left for future generations to find. In the street, a woman draped in black bent herself into a right angle like a bracket holding up a shelf, whispering her misery in such a choked yet audible voice, she might have been cast by Shakespeare to play a pauper hag to break our hearts.

Security guards and carabinieri were everywhere, and I could feel the eyes of the police on my back as I bent to tie my shoe, heading for the private Uffizi gate entrance.

What was I doing here, I, who had left the practice of Catholicism years ago? For one thing, I had a lifelong fear of all things Church dating back to my First Communion days, when the nuns commanded that we keep our heads down while the priests did their magic on the altar, turning bread and wine into the body and blood of Christ. Ask no questions, we were told, and so I peeked often, widening my fingers just enough to see if I alone was sneaking a look, thinking I was flirting with going to hell. In this cradle of obedience where rigid authority ruled, popes were beyond us all, out of imagination and out of reach.

But this new pope, the former cardinal from Argentina named Jorge Mario Bergoglio, elected Pope Francis in 2013, was close to real life, venturing directly into the concerns of real people wrestling with complexities and ambiguities. After all, when he declared shortly after becoming pope, "Who am I to judge?" about gay people of goodwill seeking their god, he stunned the world with his thoughtful grasp of the boundaries between theory and practice, and I welcomed with relief and admiration his astonishing rejection of dogma.

The pope was also bringing his moral authority to knotty environmental and economic issues, such as climate change, which have festered for decades without resolution because they, like some social issues, have also been prisoners of dogma and preconception. The major environmental problems that plague us today have defied resolution mostly because they defy certainty and easy rules.

The sweeping *Laudato Si,* published to global acclaim in the buildup to the UN conference in Paris, was intended to add the weight of the pope's voice to the impending international negotiations and clearly stated that nature is a common inheritance of all people equally. The pope urged all nations to once and for all accept the science of climate change as irrefutable and all environmental problems as a universal responsibility.

Still, on the subject of tactics and what to actually do, I felt obliged to challenge a few misguided but influential paragraphs in the pope's encyclical that would not help the cause. Refreshingly flexible on social issues, the pope seemed stuck like many with a tired, rigid mantra when it came to climate change and environment—that money, capitalism, and markets were the root of environmental evils. Specifically, the pope had too roundly reproached carbon markets and "carbon credits" as false, mere reflections of commercialism and permitting what he termed "the guise of a certain commitment to the environment."

However, I believed that when properly designed, monitored, and implemented, carbon markets were vital to implementing the pope's best hopes for *Laudato Si.* They are integral to the vital idea of "putting a price on carbon," for one thing, and so may be one of the very few effective economic means to reckon with global environmental urgency.

Pricing carbon means attaching a clear financial cost to emitting deleterious carbon dioxide and other greenhouse gases (GHGs) into the atmosphere from the burning of fossil fuels, otherwise a cost-free act of pollution. "Pricing carbon," a goal of environmental advocacy for decades, has never quite established itself in the financial mainstream because carbon markets have been set up in fits and starts in a patchwork of inconsistent policies, nation to nation.

Then, just as carbon markets had a chance to be accepted and coalesce globally, scheduled to be a high-priority discussion at the impending Paris conference, the pope was condemning them. So, to try to avoid this setback, I wrote the pope a letter to seek a change in his view. The subject line was "Laudato Si and 'Carbon Credits'—observations and possibly useful advice."

Dear Holy Father, it is in the spirit of mutual dedication and belief that I humbly bring to your attention some references in the Laudato Si that may benefit from reflection and modification and which may have resulted in advice that did not have the benefit of complete information on the topic, namely, environmental markets . . . that have tended to undermine confidence in useful tools . . . and the policy relative to a "price on carbon," an unfortunate shorthand that oversimplifies a complex matter. . . .

First, I would like to provide some philosophical and moral context for my views. As you well know, all of time stands still in Michelangelo's "Creation of Adam" on the ceiling of the Sistine Chapel, perhaps one of the most famous paintings ever known. And, in the painting, all divine power sparks not as two fingers touch, but as they come only close to touching. The power seems to live rather in the space between Adam's finger and the finger of the god who is reaching out. That space between them is invisible, intangible, limited yet omnipotent and, of course, priceless. Earth's atmosphere is also as fragile, as limited as this space. Thus, we must protect it, by discouraging gluttonous use and abuse of this ineffable rarity. . . .

Carbon markets do not privatize or exonerate. They are simply accounting systems like any other that assign value where the failure to assign value to date has led to obscene denigration of that which we have considered ours to use freely, at no cost. . . . I put myself at your disposal. I would travel to Rome, if desired, to discuss the topic. With my gratitude and any blessing a humble searching soul such as I may convey from my being to yours,

Most sincerely,

To have a chance of the letter actually reaching the pope, I first ran it by a Vatican diplomat at the UN office of the Holy See, who read and cleared it, and even promised to put it in the diplomatic pouch he sent weekly to Rome. The letter found its way to the desk of Cardinal Peter Appiah Turkson of Ghana, then the pope's key advisor on *Laudato Si* and Prefect for the Dicastery for Promoting Integral Human Development, who sent me a polite thank-you note. But seeing the phone number next to the cardinal's name, I immediately called and, through the goodwill of the cardinal's personal secretary, booked a follow-up for some weeks later to flesh out the topic with Cardinal Turkson. At the appointed hour, the affable cardinal and I batted around the issue of carbon markets for a bit, and he acceded to my visiting him in Rome to speak further in person.

Perhaps he didn't expect me actually to do it, but I made the trip that fall. We met at the Palazzo San Callisto, an open hexagon of pink stucco with palm trees swaying in the garden. In the homey salon, the cardinal and his assistant Father Josh Kureethadam and I chatted about the

paragraphs on carbon markets including "carbon credits" in *Laudato Si*
I had questioned. I further made my case, understanding that the pope
could not retract opinions expressed in his original *Laudato Si*, but suggesting that perhaps the pope could issue a clarifying addendum or editorial in *L'Osservatore Romano*, the Vatican newspaper.

I went so far as to suggest that the Vatican declare a plan for all its
operations in Rome to become "carbon neutral," which would mean the
Vatican could directly test out the workings of carbon markets, including buying "carbon credits," also known as "offsets." These are derived
from environmental projects such as reforestation intended to neutralize
a metric ton of greenhouse gas emitted in one setting by capturing it, or
"offsetting" it elsewhere. Interpreted by some as relieving the burden on
major emitters of greenhouse gases to directly reduce their own actual
emissions, offsets courted controversy and what the pope himself had
termed the "guise" of action. A carbon-neutral Vatican would require the
Vatican to try to reduce the fossil fuels it burned and purchase carbon
credits equal to the emissions it could not eliminate. I suggested that
surely countless committed enterprises in the world would cover any
associated costs, to spare the Vatican budget and support the demonstration. The Vatican would set a monumental example, I suggested, of
how carbon pricing can work, including the constructive role of carbon
credits, especially since critics of carbon credits tarnished them with
comparison to indulgence letters once sold by clerical leaders, including
popes, in return for forgiveness of sins. Cardinal Turkson said he would
consider my views, and Father Josh gently saw me out.

That Christmas, I perched a tiny bright red feathery cardinal in the
pine wreath on my door and sent a photo of it to Cardinal Turkson as
a Christmas card. I heard nothing for several months. But the following
spring when I checked in again with Father Josh, he let me know our
discussion had not been forgotten. I was invited to a forthcoming special
conference in Rome of environmental and theological leaders to discuss
my points and several others that were being proposed to deepen and
extend the reach of *Laudato Si*.

And so began my journey to the inner sanctums of the Vatican and
beyond, tracking the radical transformation under way in finance, in
which carbon markets are but one part.

Old ideas about money—what it's worth, how it operates, and what
backs it up—are becoming useless and obsolete because of a gaping
flaw in our financial systems no longer possible to ignore: failure to
financially value and price the priceless, the ineffable elements of life,

especially our atmosphere, on which our environmental and social stability now increasingly depend. The result? Intangible yet indispensable natural assets taken financially for granted, and therefore essentially laid waste.

Reversing this reality is neither fringe nor naïve, but a necessary seismic shift.

From the pope to mega-investor Larry Fink, who heads Blackrock, perennially the world's largest financial asset manager, to Swedish teenager Greta Thunberg, who squatted outside her school to protest climate change and triggered a global movement, to mainstream bankers and oil company barons in China, and everyday people everywhere, our world hears multiple unconnected voices coming together in the same global chorus proclaiming that our financial systems have fallen far short of protecting the planet and that capitalism needs to change its priorities to avoid catastrophic environmental and social detriment.

Though once fresh, these calls for what has been termed reimagined, more inclusive, or stakeholder-led capitalism have become their own drumbeat, stuck between wishful thinking and real-world practice. No matter how loud or widespread they become, they can never gain traction without the missing piece, the tool of pricing the priceless—experimental, at times controversial, but upending and inevitable.

It seemed to me that dismissing capitalism and the drive to make money as irredeemably in conflict with environmental stewardship is another rigid sweeping dogma whose time has gone. At the least, we cannot merely continue to complain about the excesses of the past. Suppose, instead, we could use money and its language—the language of price—to protect the priceless elements of living and social cohesion that we cherish, rather than sabotage them?

And what if a quiet revolution has occurred among the money changers and lenders, and the Wall Streets of the world—such distrusted entities—were evolving from dens of suspected villainy into incubators of noble ideas that can be used to advance the greater good, such as protecting the atmosphere?

Carbon markets, carbon pricing, and other financial innovations (including new forms of insurance, bonds, investment funds, and indices) are part of this revolution and a simultaneous reprogramming of the financial workings of the world so that inanimate black-red ink balance sheets no longer function in an isolated arena undefined and unscrutinized by the needs of people and the planet. At the heart of this rebooting process is price.

Capitalism and finance are nothing more than the motor systems of pricing and valuing—who pays for what and how much based on a perceived value, or, in simplistic terms, "The value of a thing is what it will bring."

Now though, as we face expanding environmental and social risks, there is a paramount need to use price to value and shield the assets that invisibly, for the most part, underpin our well-being. Pricing makes an asset visible, illuminating the value of saving and protecting it, and the cost of losing it. Either we come to terms with the actual chain of value of natural resources and other intangible essentials and account for them literally and figuratively in our economic system, or they will slip away because we undervalue them, allowing them to be spent by the lowest bidder for lack of appropriate financial recognition.

In short, we may have to accept that there is a financial price to be assigned to the so-called "nonfinancial goods" we love and need most, and that it is neither immoral nor shameful to do so. On the contrary, pricing the priceless may be the only practical solution to resolve increasingly unfathomable contradictions.

For example, why do our capital markets value companies such as Uber, which offer merely on-demand service we can live without, in the billions of dollars, but our atmosphere, on which all life depends, at zero?

Why do we place an unbridled financial premium on ocean-view property but treat the coral reefs that protect that property from catastrophic storms as financially worthless?

Why do we value our infinitely scarce freshwater so low that we are free to blast and contaminate it as we force it underground to release natural gas in the hydrofracking process, only to then burn the gas with scandalous energy inefficiency?

Only pricing the priceless can redress these destructive patterns by transferring bookable financial value away from what is mostly extractive or exploitative and toward what is vital, and irreplaceable. This move redefines the essence of profit and loss and brings to light what truly supports reliable and worthwhile economic investment: natural assets.

In turn, if capital markets reward coherent risk management and resource stewardship of those assets in higher credit ratings for public entities, for example, then those entities are in turn recognized as more financially and reputationally sound, able to perhaps borrow favorably to meet other pressing needs, or even reinvest in natural asset protection.

In this sequence, pricing the priceless translates the natural capital of clean water or standing forest into bankable collateral, as compared to short-term raw material. If clean water and other natural resources enter the financial ledgers of public budgets as vital assets, then by extension public funds can be commanded to care for and protect those assets commensurately. After all, assets are generally treated as prized and nonexpendable.

Once these assets have a notable value, protecting them becomes logical and better understood by taxpayers, who might otherwise think of environmental protection as dispensable, a costly frill that can be put off because its value comes tomorrow, not today. Pricing the priceless captures financial prominence for natural assets that are otherwise mere footnotes on the books.

Moreover, momentum is with us as disparate forces converge to confront and disrupt enshrined financial presumptions. First is the evolution in the global economy away from traditionally valued tangible goods, such as manufactured products, to the valuation of intangible goods, such as brands, apps, intellectual property, service industries, and basic research and development. This transition reset the econometric comfort level that intangibles can be expressed in tangible pricing and serve acceptably as wellsprings to economic growth.

Second is the intensifying skepticism that conventional economic practice works for the general good. There is heightening awareness of economic inequality with plenty of backup data, thrown into stark relief by the COVID-19 pandemic that exposed just how many people live at the economic precipice. Public yearning for justice and credible institutions feels ready to combust and increasingly does, typified by the "yellow vest" protestors who set fires to grand boulevard cafes in Paris in 2018 to vent anger at higher taxes, including carbon taxes. In 2022, according to the Carnegie Endowment for International Peace, economic protests "soared" worldwide, largely driven by inflation and recession worries.

Third, there is compounding evidence and increasing recognition that environmental problems are urgent, especially climate change. Numerous polls, surveys, and voting patterns worldwide confirm that people, especially those under 40, want action on climate change, clean energy, and social progress. The annual UN conference on climate change held in November 2021 in Glasgow, COP26, was nearly brought to a standstill by activist protestors pressing for governments to act more decisively. In November 2022, the host government of COP27, Egypt, cancelled some public programs due to security worries.

Meanwhile, extreme weather events continue, and communities are left alone to cope; for example, in the United States in 2021, the failure to prepare was so blatant that the whole city of New Orleans lost power after a single catastrophic storm, and extreme monsoons in Pakistan in 2022 left most of the low-lying country underwater with no rescue plan. Global anxiety mounts.

Fourth is the emergence of alternative ideas about what backs up money as legal tender. Seemingly overnight, there is expanding use and consideration of intangible, even libertarian, digital currencies such as Bitcoin, Ether, iWallet, Alipay, NFTs, digital yuan, maybe even digital US greenbacks, not quite dismissed by the sitting head of the US Federal Reserve in 2022, Lewis Powell. If transactions of once-esoteric home-made digital currencies are credible and acceptable, why not a water bond or carbon credit resting on the underlying value of lasting environmental health?

Fifth is a surprisingly broad wake-up among mainstream asset managers, bankers, and asset owners to environmental, social, and governance (ESG) risks as financial risks and, on the other hand, that money can be made, not lost, by investing to minimize them. Global uptake of ESG investing concepts proceeds rapidly, and new metrics and investment vehicles are being invented, tested, and applied.

Sixth, there is a tidal wave of money seeking purpose, accompanied by huge intergenerational turnover in wealth and attitude. By 2030, according to Wealth X, about $18 trillion will change hands, about 60% of that in North America alone. Research firm Cerulli estimates global transfer as high as $84 trillion by 2045. In 2020, research by Barclays Private Bank reported that "investing for both financial returns and with consideration for its impact on the world has been gaining momentum for some time. . . . This is led by the children who are positively influencing their parents on ethical and social investment matters . . . most of the patriarchs and matriarchs of high net worth families (59% of 40–60 year olds and 68% of over 60 year olds) say that their children have taken the lead on ethical and social investment matters for the family." In 2022, the Schwab Modern Wealth Survey found that 79% of millennials, 82% of Gen Z, and 70% of Gen X used "personal values" to guide their investment decisions. The 2022 Bank of America Private Bank Study of Wealthy Americans found that investment in ESG vehicles had doubled in 2018, with 73% growth among millennials.

Finally, these tendencies amount to major financial genre blur, to match so many other genre blurs rippling through society. For-profit and nonprofit financial motivation are gradually resembling each other, and stewards of capital can no longer be proud to brag about raw financial gain alone.

So, taken together, these trends will catalyze a significant financial disruption where outdated models and economic presumptions are wholly replaced. No longer just a matter of personal moral stance or choice, the need to examine why and how money is applied grows encompassing.

The social, environmental, and economic challenges are complex, with evident moral and even spiritual dimensions. Yet they have no chance of solution without fresh credible and productive new scrutiny of what we value as assets.

The stakes are vast and high. Estimates of the unbooked value of nature in conventional global economic ledgers have been as high as $125 trillion per year—more than global gross domestic product (GDP). In other words, unpriced priceless assets can lead to astronomical value squandered because we are blind to it.

Achieving the new dynamic of pricing the priceless taps both philosophical and practical concerns. But what does that mean?

Nature and natural resources do essential physical work for us but do not get paid a penny, like lowly free laborers. Trees and grasses hold the surface of the earth together but have been valued almost only when cut down as lumber for products and building. Crops are grown year after year and sold, but the soil that makes agriculture possible is paid nothing. Coral reefs slow down the waves of the sea to protect the coasts, but earn no direct value recognition themselves. Swampy wetlands filter poisons and dirt from our water, also for no fee.

Since nature provides these and myriad other services at no cost, we have become used to a take-what-you-can approach. Result? Pollution, degradation, climate change, and a false security that nature's services will never cease to function no matter how much insult we deliver.

Yet in the end, all financial profit depends on these priceless services, termed "ecosystem services," invisible, quiet, and now in trouble, because without these services, economies cannot function with predictability or foresight, and goods cannot be produced.

But how to pay nature, and who will pay?

The most cosmic free laborer of all is our delicate and exceedingly thin atmosphere, providing not only all our breathable air, but also hosting our weather patterns and deflecting the burning heat of the sun, overall making life on earth possible. Yet our financial systems place no value on atmospheric functions. As a result, we have indifferently crowded our atmosphere with greenhouse gas emissions, unavoidable by-products of burning the fossil fuels like oil, gas, and coal—themselves incomparable natural assets—that made modern industrialization possible. But, on the way, the buildup of fossil fuel emissions trapped solar heat and catalyzed major climate disruptions to wreak havoc.

To try to reverse this process and better value the atmosphere, carbon markets put a price on using increasingly rare space in the atmosphere for greenhouse gas pollution, The more space you occupy with pollutants, the more you pay, in theory, so the incentive develops to take up less space (i.e. pollute less). But this simple carbon market premise has been suspect because it treats the atmosphere like real estate and because of the long-prevailing view that capital and the methods of capitalism cannot have the greater good at heart. That is why Pope Francis found carbon markets distasteful.

Indeed, pricing the priceless can be morally risky, for it can also demean our most revered invaluables, labeling them as mere commodities, subject to fluctuation, speculation, gouging, or cheating.

Because there can never be sufficient money to buy back a priceless item once it is gone, any pricing system intended to protect the priceless can never truly set the price high enough. So how do we price what is beyond price?

Such is the vexing and inescapable paradox of our current economic lives. Addressing climate change is entwined in that paradox. It requires that we assign a tangible value to those intangibles that make up the aptly named global commons, the transcending intangible of our time. Reconciling these irreconcilables fairly for all people is perhaps the emerging purpose of the economy itself. Are we up to it?

Capitalism is a dogma, but anti-capitalism can be equally dogmatic. To stem climate change and other problems, we must perhaps suspend moral judgments even as we are compelled by moral commitment. At least until miracles happen.

We can keep faith with preconceptions, or we can throw them off.

I am no apologist for capitalism, for its ugly ills and ill results are as visible in human history as pricelessness is invisible. In some ways, contemporary capitalism has become a caricature of itself, spreading as much poverty as wealth, directing investment to the reckless extraction of minerals and fuels, rampant shearing of forests, paving over of wetlands, and countless other dubious projects. Yet it is also possible that capitalism can right its wrongs, and I am open to optimism instead of complaint and despair.

Also, finance should not be an exclusive province. Perhaps the fact that finance has been left only to financiers to interpret accounts for public doubt that finance serves other than to make the rich richer, all the more in the aftermath of the ostentatious and self-centered Trump era in the United States that left the idea of common good in shambles.

People across all social groups and ages are in a tailspin, wondering where they fit in the economic engine. Still, most do not realize that a main cause of our distress is that intangible priceless assets have had no champion in our economy. Greed is easy to blame for waste and ineq-uities, but we can get beyond that fallback to the root and remediable causes—faulty measurement and valuation.

There are trillions of dollars sloshing around in our world looking for useful application, and we can capture them for the betterment of all. However, this requires a clean lens: a vigilant lowering of our doubts and raising our tolerance for ambiguity. The idea of pricing the priceless will influence where tides of money flow, with the potential to convert massive amounts of capital from "bad" uses to "good."

To price the priceless is to bridge the tangible and intangible and embark on a breakthrough that will dictate the prosperity and well-being of everyone, everywhere—a brand-new look at what we value and how.

The titanic battle is not merely between the politics of left and right, or free markets and their alternatives, but between private and public interest more broadly, a battle expressed in pricing.

Pricing the priceless answers a critical question of rising personal and social inspiration: in our tense and cherished world, what is money for?

2

Marooned: The Island of Wrong Things Measured

I am writing this in the sun, because I want to. I crave the warmth and the angle of view to the vast glassine lake below.

I am not alone. Smoke rises from a brushfire not far away, set by a worker clearing away dried leaves from a garden that is otherwise perfectly groomed. It is a brushfire to create both food and beauty.

Bells ring bronzed tones from belfries of stone churches built by hand at least five centuries ago.

Ferry boats cruise like toys on the blue water, up and down between towns and villages, carrying people of all ages and races to work or holiday in a rhythmic medley of busy human transaction. The boats glide on the surface of the deep lake, gouged by retreating glaciers about 10,000 years ago, the ice claw instigators of everything I see.

What is it worth? The beauty, the enterprise, the time in evolution, labor, and human history, the fuel spent in the boats, the drinkability of the water, the sweeping panorama of the lake, the water held in the flowers and the soil, the seeds carried by the birds who land here from all over and fly all over too, the snow on the peaks melting and giving water back, the pleasure of it all? I can run out of time and space listing what I see in just one sitting, starting with the fact that I came outside for the warmth.

Did the sun start it all, this cascade of value that nevertheless has known no price?

Maybe if we could price the sun, that would cover all the rest, and we would not have to price the other details, down to each fuel tank and tourist trinket sold, to come up with a dollar value of all the elements of nature in my view, so many things that for too long have been left out of conventional calculations of value and cost, considered external to the core.

What is that sun worth?

If we knew that value, would we pay for it? Could we? Conventional economic study cannot answer these questions, even though its very purpose is to measure and express the value of objects and ideas in monetary terms all can understand.

And perhaps so much the better, for that which makes us human is precisely that we do not reduce ourselves to tangible measurable components, that we can embark on the uncertain voyages of living that we value but cannot say why or how much, such as falling in love, having a child, taking walks or a deep breath, or listening to the reassuring sound of our own heart beating.

Indeed, what does priceless really mean? We all may have our definitions, but surely something priceless cannot be re-created as it was originally, once it is gone. Something rare and easily lost, a loss the depth of which we can never accept, that goes on forever. Something that defies the familiar expressions of money. And something of which we might take little notice because there is no price on it. All that money cannot buy?

To be human is to live by the beacon of pricelessness, even as the forces of economics, bankers, and capitalism have pressed to reduce all of living to the short-term formula of tangible costs and profit, captured in the wholly inadequate symbol of price. This conventional view of ascribing value has most especially left out the value of the forces and gifts of nature, for the value of the planet has also been beyond our capacity to express, given all the services it provides us in phenomenal forces, resources, magisterial beauties, and countless mysteries, the stripes of the zebra, the perfect petals of the rose. What amount would we deposit in a bank to pay for all this? There are no banks, bills, or price tags sufficient for the job.

That earthly delights come mostly free of charge has been their undoing, and for decades new-thinking economists have tried to redress this pricing dilemma and take integrated account of environmental costs and benefits in the fundamental formulas, balance sheets, and calculations of economic value. Despite repeated effort, though, moving from theory to practice has been plodding and slow. Too anomalous, and outlandish, even outsider, literally.

"Externalities," economists have had to call these things for which there has been no accounting and no clear method to conventionally price. Booking the unbooked, in fact, has been the raison d'être of the field of environmental economics; even the US National Academy of Sciences had examined prospects for national environmental accounting in 1999 in the ambitious report "Nature's Numbers," but nothing came of it.

Given new environmental urgency, in spring 2021 the UN announced an updated framework to value unexploited natural resources in the UN's official System of Environmental Economic Accounting, referenced by about 90 nations to supplement other national economic measurements. In the United States, the Biden administration catalyzed a similar resurrected effort, with results announced in January 2023. But 15 more years of work were projected by the highly detailed analysis involving all US government departments, including the US Office of Management and Budget. The report concluded, "By 2036 there is high expectation both domestically and internationally that the United States will incorporate the environment and nature into economic decision making."

At this pace, far-sighted efforts remain frozen policy abstractions, distant from the public's day-to-day understanding of why such changes matter and still truly external to the actual national econometric planning and budgeting that determine how public money is spent. The direct and indirect benefits of clean air and water, especially the atmosphere, have been the quintessential externalities.

To this list of environmental assets we can add good health, social coherence and harmony, educational advancement, safe streets, reliable fire departments, arts, and culture. These are the services and supports the so-called nonprofit sector provides that keep the rest of the world whole and functioning. They add meaning and pleasure to living, reinforcing it all, but are still so easy to label as extra, dispensable items to starve for funding when time comes to decide public budgets and allocate tax dollars.

What would happen if we could at last bring these so-called "externalities" into the countinghouse of our economic system and make them visible in quantitative terms, so we could better gauge their true worth, heighten their value, and shield them from trivialization and harm? This disruption of the financial status quo would be heroic, sparked by the idea of pricing the priceless.

Otherwise, we risk just getting more accurate at tracking planetary resource demise, and we ought not be so slow at improving our economic decision-making that we can no longer benefit from those improvements. The transition should be well within our modern economic know-how, since we have jumped from the industrial age to the IT age in a flash, able to ascribe enormous cash and market value to much we cannot see or touch, as examples such as Uber make vivid.

When the new car service was just barely up and running, I was in San Francisco with colleagues eager to show me Bay Area hospitality. After lunch al fresco, they offered me an Uber ride to my next stop. Zip. They gleefully tap-tapped their iPhones and ordered a car. Zip, zip. "Do you want to watch it coming?"

The polished phone screen presented the now familiar miniature perfectly delineated streetscape and, clearly threading along, the little bug icon of a car, headed to the A spot on the map—me. Countdown: 9 minutes, 8, 7—be there soon. Then, whoosh. The cyber-bug car reached "A" just as the real car swung into the real street and I was off in my Uber.

Soon enough, Uber, the company, was a darling of the world's financial markets, expanding globally and raising fistfuls of capital. Uber already had a market capitalization at its outset in 2015 of about $60 billion, in the same realm as the market value of General Motors, which actually produces cars and other material goods.

Yet the value of Uber, like that of WeWork and other shared-economy new-model IT businesses, is largely the perceived value of disrupting legacy pre-IT-age systems, and consumer demand for novelty. Uber creates nothing new, embodies a digital nothingness, produces little but right-now satisfaction, and is indirectly subsidized by its drivers, who use their own cars driving. Yet in late 2020, fueled in part by the results of a referendum in California that exonerated Uber from complying with various protective labor laws, another form of indirect subsidy, the value of Uber had climbed to $78 billion.

Our atmosphere, by contrast? Zero has been the cash value of the atmosphere by any current means of bookkeeping or conventional economic theory, even though life on our planet would be impossible without this premier omnipotent intangible.

No money can buy the atmosphere or re-create it. It is so rare and limited that an American astronaut reportedly said that seen from the space shuttle far above, the thin halo of atmosphere was in the same relationship to the earth as peach fuzz to the peach.

The value of our atmosphere lies outside any chance of pricing it, so we became atmospheric gluttons. It is this wild consumption that has brought us face to face with the ubiquitous challenge of climate change, seemingly intractable.

As we know, climate change is triggered by the buildup in the atmosphere of notorious greenhouse gases, heat-trapping by-products of combustion of coal, oil, and gas. These easy-burning fossil fuels made the Industrial Revolution and industrial wealth possible, powering factories, cars, motorbikes, ships, planes, anything that runs on electricity or gasoline, and virtually every aspect of modern economic progress anywhere.

All enterprises cause emissions directly and indirectly, and so does meeting most human needs and desires. We became enthralled with fossil fuels, and we cannot be blamed for that, for there they were, decaying primeval organic material loaded with carbon, underground for millennia in Jurassic pools and rock formations, as if waiting there for us to find one day. The fuels were so plentiful and expedient to burn that the richer countries indulged themselves lavishly for the last half a century or so and then all poorer countries began to do the same.

People cannot escape poverty without using energy, and fossil fuels have been the easiest fuels to use. The awful irony of our modern industrial world, though, is that its success has rested on converting our natural endowment of carbon-based substances from safe to unsafe. Almost all modern economic progress derives from tearing out those substances from deep below, forcing them to the surface, blazing them willy-nilly, letting their gaseous by-products waft into the air such that they now must be removed from that air, perhaps even injected as gases underground again where the cycle started in the first place.

Preposterous but true—all our industrial economic growth has depended on our putting up into the atmosphere that which we now must bring down.

Spending nature madly, we must now un-spend it.

That society is not necessarily fated to overspend nature and, on the contrary, that people innately understand the importance of managing shared resources were key and pioneering research themes of political scientist Elinor Ostrom, the first woman to win the Nobel Prize in Economics. In 2009, she was recognized along with social scientist Oliver E. Williamson for her work on economic governance of common resources and her lifelong cross-cutting study of how communities can protect resources they understand and perceive to be of common benefit. In fact, Ostrom's early book *Governing the Commons: The Evolution of Institutions for Collective Action,* published in 1990, directly challenged the more pessimistic view of "the tragedy of the commons," which suggested that because resources are finite, people would be bound to act in their self-interest rather than the common interest, leading to resource exhaustion.

In her Nobel lecture, Ostrom reflected, saying, "The most important lesson for public policy analysis derived from the intellectual journey I have outlined is that humans have a more complex motivational structure and more capability to solve social dilemmas than posited in earlier rational-choice theory. . . . I argue that a core goal of public policy should be to facilitate the development of institutions that bring out the best in humans."

Ostrom spent decades in empirical and field research to support her conclusions, though of course problems such as water scarcity, which Ostrom studied extensively, have generally worsened, perhaps even despite best community efforts. Environmental complexities mount, likely made more demanding because our financial and economic systems have so long held environmental realities at arm's length.

To bring those realities closer to economic measurement and accounting systems has been the founding preoccupation of the field of environmental economics and, here again, pioneering women have led the challenge, notably an informal international triumvirate: Marilyn Waring, Vandana Shiva, and Hazel Henderson.

Waring, a political economist and academic who also served in the New Zealand Parliament, wrote *If Women Counted: A New Feminist Economics,* published in 1988. The landmark work pointed out that the denial of nature's work as economically valuable was no surprise, given the denial in conventional economics of women's work in child-rearing or other "nonproductive" activities. The book offered a scathing review of standard national accounting systems, and the construct that, for example, "a cool breeze is of no value, but cool air produced through an air-conditioner is." Of course, a breeze was considered valueless then, but with modern wind energy demands, a breeze is now nearly golden.

Still, the value of actual wind to the wind energy's economic heft remains an external.

Vandana Shiva, a philosopher and physicist, founded the Research Foundation for Science, Technology, and Natural Resource Policy in India in 1982, a think tank that questioned traditional economic planning in international development assistance. In one of her earliest books, *Staying Alive: Women, Ecology and Development,* published in 1989, Shiva strictly criticized development experts who "decided that indigenous knowledge was worthless and unscientific and proceeded to destroy the diversity of indigenous species by replacing them with row after row of eucalyptus seedlings and polythene bags in government nurseries. Nature's locally available seeds were laid waste. . . . Trees as a living resource maintaining the life of the soil and water of local people were replaced by trees whose dead wood went straight to a pulp factory hundreds of miles away. . . . Women's work linking the trees to the crops disappeared and was replaced by the work of brokers and middle men who brought the eucalyptus tree on behalf of industry."

Hazel Henderson, who died in 2022 at the age of 89, devoted most of her life to environmental activism, achieving global stature for her early work in reshaping economic theory, including framing out formative concepts of a "green economy." Among her most influential books was the far-sighted *The Politics of the Solar Age: Alternatives to Economics,* published in 1988, in which she wrote, "For years economists have used the concept of 'externalities' to explain those social costs of production that they did not want to include in their balance sheets and accounting. I always like to call the concept of 'externalities' a Freudian slip because it shows so clearly the economists' own logic and mindset. Now we have come to the realization that these 'externalities'—the social costs of a polluted environment, disrupted communities, disrupted family life, and eroded primary relationships may be the only part of our GNP that is growing."

Another chief architect of environmental economics was Professor Herman Daly, who consistently illuminated the imbalanced and statistical shortcomings of economic systems, notably in his much-heralded prescient farewell speech to the World Bank, in January 1994, when he resigned from his post as senior economist in the Environment Department.

Warning that globalization could weaken national authority to steward natural resources, Daly offered some prescriptions that went to the heart of the mismatch of how natural resources, also called "natural capital," are accounted for in economic activity. Among his directives to the economic community:

> Stop counting the consumption of natural capital as income. Income is by definition the maximum amount that a society can consume this year and still be able to consume the same amount next year. . . . But the productive capacity that must be maintained intact has traditionally been thought of as manmade capital only, excluding natural capital. We have habitually counted natural capital as a free good. This might have been justified in yesterday's empty world, but in today's full world, it is anti–economic.

In an interview with the *New York Times* in 2022 shortly before his death, Daly put it this way: "What I call the empty world was full of natural resources that had not been exploited. What I call the full world is now full of people that exploit those resources, and it is empty of the resources that have been depleted and the spaces that have been polluted. So it's a question of empty of what and full of what. Is it empty of benefits and full of cost? Or full of benefits and empty of cost? That gets to that point of paying attention to the costs of growth."

In other words, the depletion of our natural resources is not fully charged to users or accounted for in national and global economic analyses, and, if it were, gross domestic product (GDP) ledgers, which are intended to record all economic activity, might be seas of red ink. Moreover, all this under–accounting codified in the GDP accounts of the world has made it easy to ignore the prices and costs of environmental indifference, parasitically riding along.

Oil spills classically exemplify the failure of GDP to take into account environmental insults, where loss of fish and fisheries due to suffocation from oil spreading across the sea does not appear in national economic accounting, but the expenditures to clean up the spill, equipment purchased, and wages paid to cleanup workers would appear as productive expenditure that feeds into economic growth. As Henderson commented in *The Politics of the Solar Age,* "We are so confused that we add these social costs into the GNP as if they were real useful products. We have no idea whether we are going forward or backward or how much of the GNP is social costs and how much of it is useful production that we intended. We need a complete restructuring of economics and of all the statistical illusions by which we are trying to manage this abstraction called 'the economy.' We must include all kinds of data from many other disciplines including psychology, biology and physics. Economists must learn this or simply be swept away."

Because activity is what the GDP intends to sum, no matter what kind, the GDP has no way to account for leaving resources alone.

Nobel Laureate in Economics Dr. Amartya Sen embarked on a major assessment of the failures of the GDP with economist Joseph Stiglitz, also a Nobel Laureate in Economics, and the French economist Jean-Paul Fitoussi in 2008. They reviewed the relevance of the GDP as part of the Commission of Economic Performance and Social Progress convened by then-president of France, Nicolas Sarkozy.

In their extensive "Report by the Commission on the Measurement of Economic Performance and Social Progress," the economists wrote, "Indeed, for a long time there have been concerns about the adequacy of current measures of economic performance, in particular those solely based on GDP. . . . Moreover, it has long been clear that GDP is an inadequate metric to gauge well-being over time particularly in its economic, environmental, and social dimensions, some aspects of which are often referred to as *sustainability*."

A year later, at the height of the global economic depression triggered by the crash of the US housing market and the infamous "housing bubble," the commission revisited its GDP work, highlighting even further that one of the most vivid problems that traditional economics presents for people is the issue of valuation and what is valued:

> The current crisis highlights the problem of relying on market prices for the valuation of wealth. Net wealth as measured was increasing in periods prior to the crisis, but that was the consequence of a market failure. Private debt was increasing, but according to the market, asset prices were increasing at a faster pace. A reliance on market prices would have led to the conclusion that the high levels of pre-crisis consumption in many countries were sustainable. The revaluation of wealth that occurred subsequently showed that they were not . . . even ardent advocates of markets have lost faith in their valuations, at least in the short run. The difficulty is finding an alternative.

Over the years, many academic theorists have tried, launching efforts at a "Green CDP" or the Physical Quality of Life Index (PQLI), or the UN's Human Development Index, and numerous others.

One of the first of these experiments took place in the tiny mountain kingdom of Bhutan, hemmed in by the Himalayas and a long-standing monarchy. The Gross National Happiness Index (GNHI), introduced in 1972 by the Fourth Dragon King, Jigme Singye Wangchuck, when Bhutan was rarely visited by outsiders, aimed to do just what the name suggests: put a numerical weighting on the subjectivity of well-being.

The index tried to measure nontraditional parameters that lie outside classical economic metrics, but which people need and feel, examining nine noneconomic domains: living standards, education, health, environment, community vitality, time use, psychological well-being, good governance, and cultural resilience. These received equal weight in the overall calculations, and the people of Bhutan were surveyed on various subcategories, such as literacy and whether they felt a sense of inclusion. All intangibles. "Environmental diversity and resilience," which covered wildlife damage, urban issues, and responsibility toward ecological issues, was also one of the subsets in the nine basic parameters used to evaluate and weigh happiness.

Is this nonsense?

Bhutan's Happiness Index is a clear alternative to the GDP, but was often dismissed as idealized, impractical, and unworkable at a global scale. Happiness is, after all, as subjective and intangible as love. A vapor. Not measurable.

Perhaps.

The GDP, or gross national product (GNP), the formulation used in the United States, came into being in roughly 1937 in the United States to do a particular job: provide the United States with reliable data on income and production, as a response to the utter lack of such reliable data at the time. This absence led to the wild financial swings and crashes of the Great Depression and also hampered economic recovery plans. Nobel Laureate Simon Kuznets, an economist then working at the US Bureau of Economic Analysis (BEA), was assigned the task of designing a system for gathering data needed to keep better track of the health of the economy. He proposed the GDP, along with a framework of other basic elements for a system of national economic accounts in his report "National Income, 1919–1935."

Of course, this was a half century before any general awareness of environmental fragility. The invention of the GDP was one of a long cavalcade of firsts and other inventions that gradually became the integrated architecture of the world's financial system, synthesizing into what we know as global capitalism, for better or worse.

Alas, though, there has been no concomitant coherent, practical, and systematized effort to "reinvent the invention" for new circumstances. We have been generally unable to move good new ideas to the nitty-gritty of current annual economic accounting, which is where it needs to be.

How do we advance, and in time? Presumably the shift to valuing nature cannot be harder than the shift made to value research and development as investments—that took long enough.

In 2002, the beginning of a breakthrough occurred, quietly and on the side, a whisper on the stage. Two economists from the US Bureau of Economic Analysis (BEA), Dr. Barbara Fraumeni and Dr. Sumiye Okubo, took a new look at how the GDP handled research and development investments, classically intangible and classically left out. In a paper entitled "R&D in the National Income and Product Accounts," they wrote:

> A country's national accounts ideally provide measures of the composition and growth of its economic activity. To the extent that the economic accounts do not include all economic activities or classify some expenditures as intermediate when they actually represent a final use, the accounts are an incomplete basis for measuring a country's growth. In particular, not taking into account R&D investment and other types of intangible capital such as education embodied in human capital, understates investment, net wealth, and national savings. This understatement is larger if intangible capital has risen in importance in the U.S. economy over the past decade, as some have argued.

Not sexy, for sure, but the work of Fraumeni and Okubo radically changed what goes into the GDP basket—a first step to translate and properly account for intangibles in the system of national accounts.

This first work led to a sea change in how US economic activity was reported, which came in 2013, the first major change since 1999, called "Comprehensive Revision of the National Income and Product Accounts" and intended to "more accurately portray the evolving U.S. economy and to provide for consistent comparisons with data for the economies of other nations."

The BEA defined research and development as "creative work undertaken on a systematic basis to increase the stock of knowledge, and use of this stock of knowledge for the purpose of discovering or developing new products, including improved versions or qualities of existing products, or discovering or developing new or more efficient processes of production." As of the Revision, the BEA declared, "Investment in R&D will be presented along with investment in software and in entertainment, literary, and artistic originals in a new asset category entitled 'intellectual property products,' beginning with 1929. . . . The recognition of R&D as investment will improve BEA's measures of fixed investment, allow users to better measure the effects of innovation and intangible assets on the economy."

In other words, by recognizing private and government research and development as investment, the statistics of the economy were catching up with the transformational shifts that were occurring in what and how we value, and where investors wanted to place capital.

And how much did the inclusion of research and development add to the economic value of the country? According to the BEA in a July 2013 recap, $396.7 billion, including $74 billion for "capitalization of entertainment, literary and artistic originals"—and no small change at the time.

By 2015, 80% of US productivity already derived from intangible goods and services. In its "Annual Study of Intangible Asset Market Value," Ocean Tomo, a leading intellectual capital valuation firm, put it this way: "The components of S&P market value data from the start of 2015 reveals the implied intangible asset value of the S&P 500 grew to an average 84% by January 1, 2015, a growth of four percentage points over ten years."

By Ocean Tomo's next update in 2020, intangibles made up 90% of market value of the S&P 500 and 75% of the S&P 350 in Europe, with growth in major Asian regions. With its next update due in 2025, Ocean Tomo concluded that, at least for the United States where 25 years of data existed, "the economy is inverting from one where value was measured by 'touch' to one where value is driven by thought."

The integration of research and development—intangibles—in the GDP did not foresee an eventual need to also include the intangible values of natural capital and other missing environmental considerations asserted by early environmental economists such as Daly, Henderson, and others, but the ultimate effect of the inclusion is quite related.

If the economy and the GDP could officially start to take account of the intangibles such as the brain power that goes into a new patent, or artistic creation, or any of the "soft stuff" that eventually leads to a breakthrough in the so-called "knowledge economy," then accounting for the intangible benefits of nature, that have gradually come to be known as "ecosystem services," could no longer be called impossible.

Opening up national economic accounts to the reality and value of intangibles was like pouring acid on a knot—a great problem might be untied. And if we could translate the intangibles of "R&D" into the GDP relatively easily and without fanfare, and move from "touch" to "thought," why not an equally smooth and efficient translation of the value of natural resources, or their depletion? And if so, then what? Is that a Pandora's box of troubles, or answers?

The most comprehensive attempt of the 21st century to sort out answers has been "The Economics of Biodiversity: Dasgupta Review," an independent global review published in February 2021, and authored by renowned economist and professor emeritus at Cambridge University Sir Partha Dasgupta, along with an extensive team. The encyclopedic work was commissioned by Her Majesty's Treasury of the UK government in 2019, and strings together the detailed plot of economic measurement and environmental degradation since the appearance of homo sapiens on earth, emphasizing the bridge between environmental and social well-being.

Dasgupta credits his exposure to the idea of "social capital" and its connection to ecology to his work with Ismail Serageldin, another key visionary, who served as the World Bank's first vice president for Environmentally and Socially Sustainable Development. This role was created by then-president of the bank Lewis Preston, after the inspirational Earth Summit, convened by the UN in Rio de Janeiro in 1992, then the largest gathering of heads of state in history and expressly intended to prioritize care for the environment as an economic imperative.

Serageldin set up an advisory board, including Dasgupta and even Amartya Sen, not yet a Nobel Laureate, because the Earth Summit had clearly called out the shortcomings of economic measurements as key culprits in environmental degradation. Regularly, the board convened in inspirational locations not far from Washington, D.C., such as overlooking the expansive harbor of Baltimore, attempting to come to terms with the most succinct principle enshrined at Rio, that economic progress and environmental health were indivisible. But how to express this encompassing unity with economic tools that were fragmented and narrow?

The Dasgupta Review, 30 years later, summarized key research from the four corners of the globe, and again exposed the shortcomings of the GDP, calling instead for the concept of inclusive wealth, defined as "the sum of the accounting values of produced capital, human capital and natural capital."

Easy to demand, but not easy, even with so many years of academic effort, to implement. According to Dasgupta, natural resources continue to escape practical expression of value because their individual contributions to the stability of our lives are mobile, so they may not fall under a specific jurisdictional protection; silent, so they do not complain when abused; and invisible, so they are easy to ignore. But, Dasgupta says, "Nature is more than a mere economic good. Nature nurtures and nourishes us, so we will think of assets as durable entities that not only have use value but may also have intrinsic worth. Once we make that extension, the economics of biodiversity becomes a study in portfolio management."

Natural capital is core to the portfolio, and as Dasgupta notes, "It is convenient (even natural) to create a two-way classification of natural capital in terms of whether the assets are *renewable* such as fisheries (we will use the term 'self-regenerative') or *nonrenewable* (fossil fuels, minerals)." He says that living systems are considered self-regenerative, unless "they have been degraded beyond repair."

As Dasgupta explains, "The view that the biosphere is a mosaic of self-regenerative assets also covers its role as a sink for pollution . . . the waste we create has to be discharged somewhere. The discharge contributes to the depreciation of the biosphere. More generally, we may view pollution as the depreciation of capital assets. Acid rains damage forests; carbon emissions in the atmosphere trap heat; industrial seepage and discharge reduce water quality in streams and underground reservoirs; sulfur emissions corrode structures and harm human health, and so on. The damage inflicted on each type of asset (buildings, forests, fisheries, human health) should be interpreted as depreciation."

By this reasoning, all around us, in the same way that a brand-new automobile begins to depreciate in value as soon as we start driving it, as we draw upon nature, nature is simultaneously depreciating. In fact, as Dasgupta reminds us, "GDP does not include the depreciation of assets, for example the degradation of the natural environment." He goes so far as to conclude, "in recent decades eroding natural capital has been precisely the means the world economy has deployed for enjoying what is routinely celebrated as 'economic growth.'"

Once this reality sinks in, all efforts at environmental protection then are efforts to catch up with that depreciation, or at the least to keep it in check, but, as we know from automobiles, holding off financial depreciation is nearly impossible unless we take fastidious care.

With a car, or any purchased priced asset, at least we have a semblance of value based on what we paid in the first place. With our planet, we have to grapple.

One of the first to try, Professor Robert Costanza, a key figure in ecological economics at University College London, and colleagues in 1997 calculated the value of 17 services nature provides for free, from water filtration to pollination, climate regulation, soil formation, and more. In groundbreaking analysis, they estimated that value to be $33 trillion a year in 1995 dollars, $46 trillion in 2007 dollars, noting the figure was likely to be an underestimate. The paper, published in the journal *Nature,* referenced that global GNP was around $18 trillion per year at the time, meaning that nature's real value was 1.8 times larger. Costanza and team wrote: "One way to look at this comparison is that if one were to try to replace the services of ecosystem services at the current margin, one would need to increase global GNP by at least $33 trillion partly to cover services already captured in existing GNP and partly to cover services that are not. . . . This impossible task would lead to no increase in welfare because we would only be replacing existing services and it ignores the fact that many ecosystem services are literally irreplaceable."

This research attracted critique, including by Dasgupta much later in his review; he disliked the idea of trying to impute to nature an absolute purely monetary value, as a case of "misplaced quantification."

In 2014, Costanza had updated his work and earlier methods, publishing further touchstone research in the journal *Global Environmental Change.* Costanza now put the value of global ecosystem services at value at $125 trillion, given various ups and downs in the physical state of resources. That figure, calculated in US 2007 dollars, has been much cited ever since, often without footnote.

In further work in 2017 Costanza concluded that future value of ecosystem services could decline by $51 trillion a year or increase by $30 trillion, depending on scenarios. Since global GDP for 2022–23 hovered at roughly $100 trillion, with sluggish growth and inflation projected, exacerbated by the Russian invasion of Ukraine and the ensuing war that plunged the global economy into shortage, confusion, and fear, Costanza's 2014 estimate of $125 trillion still placed the value of earth's free labor well above all industrial goods and services produced on earth.

These total value figures can be quibbled with, notably by Dasgupta's review. But mincing no words, in December 2022, the Task Force on Nature Markets, a group of environmental financial leaders, said crisply in their "Global Nature Markets Landscaping Study," "One hundred percent of the economy is dependent on nature but not all of nature's value is recognized as economic activity. Some of nature is priced in the economy via policies and markets, although not necessarily correctly."

Are these calculations accurate, or even knowable? This is likely a question whose answer we can only approach. Meanwhile, though, sticking mostly to conventional ideas of profit and loss, failing to reflect the value of externalities and the costs of doing nothing maroons us all on an island of wrong things measured.

The time has come to leave this island behind. Uber cannot be worth more than the atmosphere. Pricing use of the rarity of the atmosphere is a necessary expedient.

Adam and Eve, by succumbing to temptation in a world that freely provided them ecstasy, probably paid the world's first price for anything, let alone a priceless intangible. The bite of the apple? Trivial and beneath price. But all the pleasures of Eden? Incalculable. Even from the beginning, price has been inadequate to the task when the stakes climb high.

Since Paradise, apples have become a common commodity. But for Adam and Eve and the rest of us too, sadly, of their particular apple, there was only one.

3

One of a Kind: The Gamble of Rarity and Price

Adam and Eve, of course, could not have known the sheer magnificence of their apple—and that the fruit was actually an apple is not specified in the tale—for they had no point of reference in Eden, no "comparable values." Paradise had neither peer nor apparent limits and so Adam and Eve took what was so readily available all around them, literally for the picking, their curiosity needing no restraint. The apple was just another blissful temptation in a garden overflowing with pleasures.

Not knowing what they risked, nor that embodied in that fruit was the foundation of stable civilization, they bit. An item of priceless value had appeared on a branch, but the mythical protagonists had no way to appreciate either its paramount quality or the chaos that would ensue once that tree had been violated. In fact, until they bit, Adam and Eve could have had no idea of price whatsoever, Eden being living proof, as it were, of the cliché that the best things in life are free.

The idea of Eden encapsulates what French economist Lucien Karpik calls "the economics of singularities." In his landmark book, *Valuing the Unique*, he writes that singularities are "incommensurable products" that by definition cannot be compared or blended with the value of other products.

Of course, most products do not rise to the heights of incommensurable. Price tags, and pricing, came into existence understandably, as Karpik writes, to standardize values and make it possible to compare like items so we can decide whether to buy or sell and to represent values that buyer and seller can recognize and agree upon. In *Valuing the Unique*, he says, "we must lend visibility and intelligibility to the relationship between qualities and prices and, more specifically, we must verify the general principle that states, the greater the qualities, the higher the prices. . . . There exists no tool that can be taken as the common criterion for ordering the general qualities of the singularities. And so we must look for the actual procedures that have been and still are being used by the economic actors. And then we must assess their consistency and make sure they are effective, which implies that they are socially valid."

In this sequence and as a functional matter, pricing is inseparable from accounting, the organized actual procedure of communicating money in and money out, money earned and money spent. Derided as "bean counting," accounting is nevertheless an essential financial invention that permits coherent understanding of assets, value, and financial position. In fact, the march of financial progress was built from the human urge to keep track, perhaps starting with the Lebombo bone, found in a cave in Swaziland and dating from 35,000 BC, the oldest known physical counting artifact made by humans—29 orderly notches scratched into the fibula of a baboon.

What was being counted, no one knows. Perhaps days, full moons, successful hunts, pebbles worth a Lebombo fortune? Regardless, as we know, as civilizations and trade evolved from bone age to Stone Age, Iron Age to Gilded Age and all the ages of empires, rarities commanded respect as price, from metals like gold, silver, and copper to spices, silks, and cocoa pods.

How to comply, without argument or confusion? How can we be efficient in transaction across cultural diversities, national borders, and generations?

The quest is always to have common understandings and reference points to fix, determine, record, transfer, or nail down value, itself fluctuating and wily.

Take the cowrie shell (*Cypraea moneta*), a shiny mollusk plentiful in the seas of India, Asia, and West Africa, though now suffering depletion along with almost all ocean creatures. Exquisite, easy to handle, and mostly uniform in size, cowries could be assigned a value on a per-shell basis and conveniently laced onto strings in groups when many cowries were needed to seal a purchase or conveniently put aside as savings. Records on the use of cowrie shells as money date back to the first century BC.

Coinage was a radical invention when it began to appear in the seventh century BC, and the fastidious study of numismatics tracks the trail of human thought in a way, offering glimpse after glimpse of national and empirical portraits, maps, and emblems pressed and embossed into metal, ceramics, and stones—weighty in authority, the promise of payment and weight itself.

Paper money, of course, even more radical, eliminated the burden of stockpiling and transacting with sacks of coins, easing exchange exponentially, especially across distances, and was first introduced in China during the Tang dynasty in roughly the eighth century AD. Notes conveyed the promise to pay the bearer on demand the agreed printed worth, reliable stand-ins for payments due, tradeable and fungible based on fiscal trust. Paper currency also projected national self-worth in elegant linen-threaded papers and watermarks designed to impress— yuan, yen, mark, franc, drachma, dollar, pound, forint, cruzeiro, dinar, rupees, rands, rials, and so on—a tapestry of individualized financial expressions of the prideful identity and the supposed reliability of the issuer's full faith and credit.

The invention of money led logically to the invention of methods of recording monetary transactions. As one of the fathers of modern accounting put it, the Muslim scholar Muḥammad ibn Mūsā al-Khwārizmī (born around AD 750) in the signature work *The Compendious Book on Calculation by Completion and Balancing,* "When I considered what people generally want in calculating, I found that it always is a number."

From the point of view of capturing nature's price and wrestling pricelessness into visible worldly terms, numbers appear in plain-old double-entry accounting, an ancient tool that nevertheless could be flexible enough to grow into the contemporary pricing the priceless task.

While the cognoscenti of Renaissance Venice, particularly the Franciscan friar Luca Pacioli, receive much credit for establishing robust accounting systems to support the cravings of global commerce, double-entry accounting is far more universal and ancient in origin. In fact, the financial world has little deviated from accounting ideas formulated in ancient Mesopotamia over 7,000 years ago, traveling across Africa, India, and Iraq, and finally reaching the west only when key Islamic and Hindi documents were translated into Latin in the 12th century.

Al-Khwārizmī's work became vital, bringing algebra to the world and through the emphasis on balanced equations, also related accounting principles, not to mention that his name was anglicized to give us the digital era's inescapable word "algorithm."

Al-Khwārizmī described his *Compendious Book* as "a short work on Calculating by (the rules of) Completion and Reduction, confining it to what is easiest and most useful in arithmetic, such as men constantly require in cases of inheritance, legacies, partition, lawsuits, and trade, and in all their dealings with one another, or where the measuring of lands, the digging of canals, geometrical computation, and other objects of various sorts and kinds are concerned."

The book became a kind of blueprint for commercial and cultural expansion, according to Professor of Information and Decision Sciences J. Christopher Westland, who is also a certified public accountant, of the University of Illinois at Chicago. In a personal correspondence in 2022, he wrote that al-Khwārizmī extended the administrative use of Arabic script to "mathematics and accounting, and his 'double-entry' system became entrenched . . . from most of southern Europe to Indonesia. This is why you see double entry systems in the Tang Dynasty (eighth century) and the Tangs influenced the Japanese, then the Koreans in the coming centuries, and ultimately the Mongols through Kublai Khan (largely through his wife Chaba). . . . Pacioli wrote about these systems 600 years after their invention."

The friar Pacioli, born in Sansepolcro, Italy in roughly 1447, is widely recognized as the first to compile and collate the basics of the double-entry accounting system for day-to-day business in his no-nonsense user's manual, *Particularis de Computis et Scripturis* (Accounting Books and Records), published in 1494. The accounting handbook was included in his larger work compiling known mathematical principles entitled *Summa de Arithmetica, Geometria, Proportioni et Proportionalita*.

Pacioli's accounting manual, directly addressed to merchants so they could "keep all their accounts and books in good order" and written in sparing vernacular Italian, handholds the user through the fundamentals of double-entry—where a debit has a concomitant credit within the same tracking system. Step-by-step, Pacioli lays out the virtues of inventories, ledgers, journals, profit-and-loss statements, trial balance sheets, year-end closing procedures, even document retention recommendations. Above all a stickler for balance, Pacioli wrote, "The very day a debit is born, it has a twin credit. So it is quite natural for them to always go together in your books."

Even though accounting practices were not standardized, and accounts were closely guarded by their keepers, Pacioli's methodical recitations came down to the premise that accurate financial knowledge depends on accurate bookkeeping so that consolidated financial statements can provide a credible snapshot of assets, liabilities, earnings, and working capital.

The only reference to natural capital of a sort in Pacioli's treatise appears in his model inventory listing of kid and fox skins as "fine skins for lining," and seal skins as "thick skins," no purpose specified.

A fast-forward in the accounting story takes us to the dramatic opposite of the meticulous methods Pacioli lauded, the infamous Depression of the 1930s, and the crash of global stock markets, also financial inventions, due to fraudulent and inflated valuations conveyed in misleading accounts, leaving the global economy resting on quicksand. The tide went out, economic ruin spread across the world, jobs and livelihoods evaporated, and underlying capital values wisped into ether.

In the United States, to reform the deceptive practices that hollowed out the nation, the US Congress established the Securities and Exchange Commission (SEC) in 1934 to oversee the stock market, along with the office of the chief accountant. The American Institute of Accountants also promulgated core standards, recognized as generally accepted accounting principles (GAAP), with counterparts in Europe and worldwide.

GAAP represents the universal language of financial transparency, and the ethics and procedures that should apply. GAAP means that financial statements make sense around the world, reader to investor to regulator. Without GAAP, financial statements would be the Tower of Babel. Yet the GAAP has never sought to capture values for environmental assets, depreciation, or losses. Nor was the GAAP designed to capture environmental dynamics of a given activity, nor to translate implications of environmental circumstances in any sense.

In 2010, a pioneer in environmental advocacy and business, Jochen Zeitz, inserted an unprecedented environmental dimension into the practice of GAAP. He was then CEO of PUMA, a leading brand of high-end apparel, running shoes, and other fashionable accessories. Using PUMA's actual global business activities as his canvas, Zeitz introduced the world's first environmental profit and loss statement (P&L), where "profit" was defined as "activities that benefit the environment" and "loss" as "activities that adversely impact the environment."

In the foreword, Zeitz wrote, "While nature is much more to us as humans than a mere 'business,' the simple question I put forward was if our planet was a business, how much would it ask to be paid for the services it provides to a company in order to operate? I decided it only made sense to utilize the essence of our accounting framework when monetizing PUMA's environmental impacts so that it would read like a traditional Profit and Loss Account."

PUMA examined all direct and indirect aspects of its business, going well beyond outright manufacturing to include business travel; conversion of land from agriculture to grow raw materials for PUMA products, such as cotton or rubber, or to raise cattle for leather; loss of habitat for animal species as a result, and more. The environmental P&L captured a vivid panoply of entangled impacts negative enough to make you never want to buy another sneaker, hardly the goal of the exercise.

The environmental P&L did not seek to establish "environmental profit" (i.e. environmental benefit) and did not show any. On the contrary, if the environmental tally had been a traditionally audited statement used to gauge the company's financial health and profits, PUMA would have been in irremediable red-ink debt to nature and its services of €145 million, the aggregate environmental costs, a whopping cut into that year's reported net earnings of €202 million. What would Pacioli, the advocate of daily balancing of books, have made of that overly risky extension and unreported heavy negative carriage?

To arrive at an instructive result, no matter how negative, PUMA had commissioned extensive best-in-class research on how to cost-out environmental inputs and effluents, carefully pairing each classic business line item cost with its environmental parameter, covering what PUMA termed "all significant environmental impacts from the production of raw materials right through to the point of sale, a scope sometimes referred to as 'cradle to gate.'"

Metrics used to quantify PUMA's environmental impacts were for worsening climate change, metric tons of GHG emissions; worsening water scarcity, volume of water used; loss of biodiversity, area of land, and ecosystem converted to PUMA purposes; adding to smog and acid rain, metric tons of noxious particulates and other air pollutants; increasing solid waste problem, leachate, and metric tons of waste generated for disposal or incineration. Then, incorporating weighted averages and regional variations, the P&L assigned financial costs to the impacts based on knowable market levies and going prices.

For example, for land use changes, PUMA charged itself an average of €347, based on comparison with land values far-ranging regionally from €63 per hectare for grassland changes in Pakistan, to €18,653 for changes to coastal wetlands in the United States. Also, apropos of carbon pricing, still fledgling at the time, PUMA assigned itself a cost of €66 ($87 US) per ton of greenhouse gas emissions, well above the average market price of €14 of the year before. The PUMA carbon price also included various projected indirect costs of climate change, such as reduced crop yields.

The financial statement of PUMA's negative environmental impact, Zeitz wrote, "provides us with a wake-up call and the urgent need to act upon it." By that he meant trying to convince PUMA's myriad suppliers and others in the production and sales chain, who accounted for 85% of the negative impacts, to improve their processes, a tall order considering that most suppliers were outside PUMA's direct control and themselves subject to widely varying practice and competitive forces.

Still PUMA continued to try to squeeze out negative inputs and impacts from its business lines, and its parent company, Kering, also began issuing environmental profit and loss statements. These were profoundly bold efforts, but illustrations only, standing alone outside convention.

GAAP still reigns as the general set of principles, with environmental and other debts and impacts still a sideshow nice to have.

A proponent of a standardized remedy to fill the gap in the GAAP, so to speak, has been Sir Ronald Cohen, a pioneer of the venture capital field. He advocates adding more expansive accounting approach standards called "impact weighted accounts," and a potential set of globally accepted impact principles (GAIP). As Cohen put it in his 2020 book *Impact*;

> To arrive at impact weighted accounts, it is necessary to give a monetary value to businesses' social and environmental impacts. This monetization of impact pushes portfolio theory to the next level, allowing investors to optimize risk-return impact in the same way that they already optimize risk and return. . . . Impact weighted accounts will apply impact coefficients to the various lines of a company's profit and loss statement—sales, employment costs, costs of goods sold—to arrive at an impact-weighted profit line, which reflects the impact a company has on the environment. . . . They will similarly apply weighting to the assets that appear on a company's balance sheet.

As to the relationship of GAIP to GAAP, Cohen writes, "These impact coefficients would be set by an impact accounting board, similar to the ones we already have for financial accounting," and that the GAIP would "sit alongside" the GAAP and "make it possible for companies to publish impact-weighted accounts in the same form as their financial ones, allowing us to judge impact and profit in a familiar way when making decisions."

To advance the GAIP approach an "Impact Weighted Account Framework" was incubated by the Impact Economy Foundation, and developed by Harvard Business School, Singapore Management University, and Rotterdam School of Management and Impact Institute. The framework was put out for public consultation that closed in September 2022.

In terms of priceless assets and environmental implications of economic activities, moving from GAAP to GAIP would be a transformation equivalent to moving from cowrie shells to paper money. Whether the GAIP framework formalizes, as Cohen and others envision, remains a long shot in uncertain economic times.

In the meantime, as sophisticated as our pricing, accounting, and financial architecture have become, enabling trillions of dollars to be transacted each day, most of these transactions still ignore the value in our daily lives of environmentally and socially intangible priceless components.

Numbers do speak, but coming to terms with environmental values also requires acceptance of qualitative ambiguity, a sense of accuracy beyond numbers as new concrete practices and tools evolve—a balance of productive imagination.

Perhaps it is only in the art market where we have some practical edifying experience with this ambiguity, with price and pricelessness spilling into each other day in and day out. Dealers bargain, and values fluctuate wildly as the market tries to nail "the value of the thing." When it comes to art, personal preferences, tastes, beliefs, and motives strongly influence buying, selling, and why, long before sales figures get recorded by GAAP, let alone GAIP.

Values in the art market often defy rhyme or reason, but that ambiguity can power significant decisions and choices. In fact, ambiguity in value can actually catalyze further inestimable value, including to buttress a great American city, as would happen when Detroit faced financial ruin.

4

Art in a Box: Pricelessness Saves Detroit

Frederic Church, the acclaimed 19th-century American painter, once went to Italy to shop for art bargains. He was busy buying art by others for his mansion at home, Olana, an architectural confection of arches, parapets, and panoramic porches overlooking the snaking Hudson River in upstate New York like a dream palace settled on a cloud.

Church bought dozens of artworks by known and unknown Italian artists on that visit, trekked the paintings back to America, and hung them on the four walls of his dining room, one picture crowding the next like postcards on a rack.

But Church kept the prices he paid secret from everyone except a best friend. And even to that friend he revealed in a letter only that he had paid between $1 and $20 for each of the paintings he'd brought home. He wrote that he believed that his guests and visitors would respect his choice only if they thought them costly.

Paintings by Church commanded princely sums at the time, so keeping the Italian prices secret was also shrewd business for Church, enabling him to avoid eroding his own value in the eyes of his regular clientele and friends at home.

Church's work was powerful, whether landscapes of his beloved Hudson Valley or other exotic places. He threw color on the canvas before him as if spinning clay on a potter's wheel. Swirling reds and pinks and lavenders—Church's colors confound any sense of flaming sunset other than fire itself.

Church's *Heart of the Andes,* first exhibited in 1859, a few years before the trip to Italy, had sold for $10,000, the highest price yet paid in the United States for a painting by a living artist. As both creator and collector, Church personified the vagaries of price.

Meanwhile, at the time Church was painting and busy decorating Olana, the economy of America pushed inevitably west, a mishmash of expanding agricultural and upstart industrial businesses. The manufacture of tangible industrial goods, and mass production, were about to transform the nation.

The economic explosion came in 1903, when Henry Ford, who had been tinkering with gadgets and machinery most of his life, founded his motor company, introducing the groundbreaking Model T in 1908.

Detroit, then a modest midwestern town, burgeoned into an industrial hub when Ford became the world's leading captain of industry and based his rapidly expanding automobile business there. Thousands came to Detroit from the poor rural south seeking jobs.

Even before Detroit's industrial wake-up, the city already had a formidable art museum. The Detroit Institute of the Arts (DIA) had been founded in 1885 by Detroit civic leaders, including James Scripps, scion of a newspaper empire, who, like Church, had traveled to Europe, sampling its pleasures and collecting. He understood the importance of great art and donated 70 paintings to the new Detroit Museum in 1889, setting it on course to become a preeminent cultural showplace.

DIA became significantly grander in 1927 when it moved to a fabulous Beaux Arts palace more in keeping with Detroit's growing stature and wealth, and dead center downtown. Art was becoming a complementary statement to the economic reputation of Detroit overall.

When DIA got its new home, in an administrative move that would prove fateful some 80 years later, the museum's trustees changed the governance structure. DIA became a department of the city government, meaning that the city of Detroit would meet all operating costs, with the trustees and other civic notables providing funds to acquire art. To make sure that DIA's prestige and holdings continued to grow, the trustees named a celebrated European scholar and collector, Wilhelm Valentiner, to lead the ambitious institution. Buoyed with support, Valentiner set to work building DIA's collection into one of the foremost in the world at the time, including in 1922 acquiring the first van Gogh bought by a museum in the United States, *Self-Portrait,* and also the first Matisse, *The Window.*

Meanwhile, Detroit spun off fancy satellite suburbs such as Grosse Pointe, which would become synonymous with the wealth being generated by the car industry, but also tracked with the city's increasing racial divisions. Where money flowed, racism generally kept Black families out.

Though starkly socially and economically divided, Detroit marched ahead, until the market crash of 1929, when the air went out of America's balloon. In 1931, when DIA's Valentiner traveled to California, where he met the Mexican artist Diego Rivera, America's unemployment rate was nearly 16%; it would climb to 25% just two years later.

Still the guests no doubt mingled merrily when the two artistic visionaries found themselves at the same cocktail party in San Francisco. By then, Rivera enjoyed such fame worldwide that he was due to have a retrospective of his work at the Museum of Modern Art in New York— only Henri Matisse had been so honored before. Rivera was working on his latest commission, a mural for the Pacific Stock Exchange Luncheon Club to be called *Allegory of California.*

Valentiner wrote in an unfinished memoir, "I soon discovered that Rivera's interest in economic and industrial development was at least as great as his interest in nature, if not greater. He wanted to hear all that I knew about industry in Detroit and explained that he had a great desire to see that city and study its extraordinary growth. . . . I had always hoped to have on my museum walls a series of frescoes by a painter of our time—since where could one find a building nowadays that would last as long as a museum? The likelihood was that it would outlast hotels, factories, private houses, and even churches." And so it would be, by far.

Valentiner pitched the idea of commissioning Rivera to do a mural for DIA to Edsel Ford, Henry Ford's art aficionado son, who immediately agreed, also agreeing to cover Rivera's $10,000 fee. Rivera was a known communist, which forced Valentiner to lobby hard to hire him, winning his case with the Detroit city commissioners only because of Edsel Ford's support and pledge on the fee.

As to subject matter, Valentiner gave Rivera only gentle guidance: "The Arts Commission would be pleased if you could find something out of the history of Detroit, or some motif suggesting the development of industry in this town. But, in the end, they decided to leave it entirely to you."

Rivera threw himself into the monumental project, a series of 27 fresco wall panels that he chose to base on the sights, sounds, and raw materials that came and went from the Ford Motor Company's Rouge River assembly plant. The mural would be named *Detroit Industry* and arranged high above an inner court of the museum.

Rivera painted in his shirt sleeves, a tall barrel of man with the rippling arms of a laborer. Alone on his wooden scaffold, he worked steadily on his masterpiece. The work depicted every step and stage in the making of cars, ranging from the origins of metals deep in the earth, represented by a sumptuous infant coiled in a fetal ball inside an underground plant bulb encased in minerals, to rubber trees and raw red iron ore, to the pounding thump of vacuum pumps, the incessant *zizz* of drills, and countless hefty workers on assembly lines wielding tools and fielding auto parts. There are fighter jets and fertility goddesses, and ominous hints at the dangers of the workplace, such as a cluster of workers who, instead of whistling while they work, wear protective gas masks, looking like giant worried bugs.

Workers punch time clocks and roll out molten steel, dodging conveyor belts and flywheels. Symbolism is everywhere, with squared-jawed machines looking like Aztec deities. Rivera also painted wry cameos here and there. He tucked himself in, as well as Valentiner and Edsel Ford, his patrons. And art scholars claim that the nurse in a clinic vaccination tableau is actually a portrait of Jean Harlow, the sauciest starlet of that age, centered like the Madonna in a macabre Nativity scene.

Rivera visited the Ford Rouge plant over and over again and took hundreds of photographs, from which he then drew freehand outlines for his frescoes, paintings made in wet plaster that, as they dry, become the very walls on which they appear. Rivera's several assistants mixed and spread the plaster on the walls, and then laid out Rivera's huge drawings like blueprints over the thick paste, punching holes through the paper along the drawn lines. They then dusted the whole with charcoal before removing the tracing paper, leaving a trail that Rivera could follow when he painted.

According to museum reports, Rivera fed his already fiery verve for the work by waiting until the plaster was nearly dry before he began painting. That meant his every stroke raced against time, a technique no doubt nerve-wracking for all, but which surely imbued the mural with its pulsing life and three-dimensional dynamic.

According to an account by Graham W. J. Beal, former director of DIA, only Rivera himself applied paint to the walls, after the legwork done by his assistants, some of whom had come to work for him direct from the communist party or riot prison. According to Beal, a worker named Paul Meier Davis "had been in jail for being part of some labor riots in Pennsylvania after which he changed his name to Pablo Davis, jumped on a train with 60 cents in his pocket and came to work for Rivera."

As for price and value in 1931 terms, Rivera's fee translated to about $100 a square foot for his talent, plus cost of materials covered by the museum.

The murals throb with the raw muscle power of human labor and the steam power of machines. Rivera's passion for paint and belief in solidarity with the working class came together with the reverberation of cymbals crashing. Through Rivera, factory work had acquired cultural sweep and worldly scope, and nothing like his murals had ever been seen in America.

But when the completed *Detroit Industry* was unveiled, critical mayhem ensued as civic stalwarts complained that Rivera's hero worship of workers was too radical, and Catholics and other religious leaders deemed that insinuations of the Holy Family in the vaccination panel and other allegories were blasphemous and racy, what with bare breasts and baby bottoms.

The editorial board of the *Detroit News* condemned the work as "un-American" and "foolishly vulgar." The editorial also said that the work "bears no relation to the soul of the community, to the room, to the building or to the general purpose of Detroit's Institute of Arts. . . . This is not a fair picture of the man who works short hours, must be quick in action, alert of mind, who works in a factory where there is plenty of space for movement. The best thing to do would be to whitewash the entire work [and] completely return the court to its original beauty."

Rivera was shocked by the reaction, and when asked to comment by the media on the protest, he read from a letter of praise he had received from a wood carver named Louis Gluck, who wrote to him, " Please give me the permission to express my grateful thanks for the greatness of your feeling and understanding in all your great work this, your own creation, as I stand here and see it with my old eyes that labored for 45 years for others with no other recognition in this corrupt society than just to be called a 'hand.'"

According to Beal's history, Edsel Ford, the showman and patron, may also have fueled the media storm around Rivera on the theory that all press is good press. The Ford family needed public recognition to counteract growing labor unrest and violence. At the time, as the

Depression took hold, wages of auto workers had been cut 50%, and auto production had dropped from around 5 million cars in 1929 to just a million or so in 1931. Half the workers in Detroit were then unemployed, and a third of all households had no cash income.

In fact, just a few weeks before Rivera had arrived to begin the mural work, angry workers had staged a hunger march just outside the Rouge plant. The workers intended to present a sheaf of demands to Henry Ford, including calls for rehiring the laid-off workers, the right to unionize, and no discrimination against Blacks in the hiring process. "We want bread not crumbs," read some of the placards, but city police and private Ford security guards turned tear gas and fire hoses on the assembly and four marchers were killed. A few days later, 60,000 workers marched right past DIA to attend the funeral.

So it was a welcome antidote for Edsel Ford when respected civic leaders defended the Rivera murals, including the city's most famous industrial architect, Albert Kahn, the very designer of the Rouge plant, who said, "There is nothing new in these attacks by churchmen. Michelangelo portrayed as devils the churchmen who tried to interfere with him when he was doing the Sistine Chapel. Rembrandt was just as guilty of the charges of sacrilege as Rivera. But who throws stones at Rembrandt today?"

In the first month the Rivera murals were on view, 100,000 visitors came to see them, and the draw of what had become known as the Rivera Court helped Edsel Ford with funding for DIA. During the lean Depression years, the city had cut back its museum spending, so Ford had been paying the salaries of museum staff from his own pocket. The headlines on Rivera brought DIA prestige, and so the city revived its funding, taking the pressure off Edsel, the patron.

This resurrection of Rivera's reputation and renown would be only the first example of the magic of pricelessness to transform art into cash in Detroit. In a few decades, that pricelessness would be the desperate city's sole bargaining chip, called upon to ride to the rescue as once-mighty Detroit lurched toward financial catastrophe.

As the 1960s rolled into the 1970s and 1980s, and the fortunes of the automobile industry ebbed and flowed, social strife and civic mismanagement further hit Detroit. Inklings of bankruptcy began to appear in 2005. At that time, the city of Detroit issued $1.4 billion in new debt, in the form of pension obligation certificates of participation (COPs), to fund the city's retirement systems and pensions. These certificates of borrow were then refloated in a risky swap design, engineered with the

Bank of America and UBS, where the city accepted a variable interest rate on the next tier of debt built upon the COPs, rather than a fixed rate.

If interest rates rose, that premium flowed to the city, but if interest rates dropped, Detroit agreed to cover the gap to the new owners of the COPs. In 2008, interest rates did indeed fall, and Detroit was on the hook. In 2009, Detroit pledged its casino tax revenues to mollify creditors.

Meanwhile, land values in the city kept dropping, likewise tax rolls, and city workers were right to worry that the pensions they had expected to live on would be vaporized by the financial mismanagement of the city's elected officials.

In 2011, the state of Michigan examined Detroit's precarious finances—the report noted severe municipal financial distress. The state won limited oversight of the city's finances in early 2012, buying the city more time, but another financial review the following year declared the situation a "financial emergency." An emergency manager, Kevyn Orr, was appointed in March.

An ugly stew was on the stove.

Detroit had essentially no cash and no cash flow. It faced $18 billion in accrued obligations, and 4 out of every 10 dollars were due to be paid out on either pension contributions for the city's workers or interest on debt.

Orr sought to file an official declaration of bankruptcy. The governor of Michigan had to approve the petition, and his endorsement letter is a pathetic litany of failed governance: "This decision comes in the wake of 60 years of decline for the City, a period in which reality was often ignored. . . . We must face the fact that the City cannot and is not paying its debts as they become due, and is insolvent."

Among debilitating Detroit realities, the governor recited:

- An unemployment rate double the national average, up 200% since 2000
- Population decline of 60% since 1950
- Income tax revenue decline of 40% since 2000
- A wait on average of 58 minutes for the police to respond to a call, compared to a national average of 11 minutes
- Police, fire trucks, and ambulances so old that "Breakdowns make it impossible to keep up the fleet or properly carry out their roles."
- 40% of street lights not functioning in the first quarter of 2013

Plus that Mount Everest of borrowing debt and pending obligations.

Orr filed for Chapter 9 bankruptcy protection for the city of Detroit on July 18, 2013. Once bankruptcy proceedings began, so did the scrambling by creditors, who began pressing to be paid immediately or went into court to hold off bankruptcy protections. Those to whom money was owed—banks, bond holders, reinsurers, and the most vulnerable, the city's pensioners and workers—quaked. Pension shortfalls were estimated at $3.5 billion; the water and sewerage department owed $5.8 billion in bonds. Another $5.7 billion loomed in unfunded healthcare costs for city workers.

Detroit had to look everywhere for ways to pay and so it was inevitable that the DIA collection, practically the city's only unsullied asset, presumed highly valuable, would become fair game.

According to the *Detroit Free Press* chronicle of the DIA events, one of the city's attorneys, Bruce Bennett, had set up an urgent call on April 19, 2013, even before the bankruptcy filing, convening DIA's chairman, director, and chief operating officer, who dutifully called in from airports and hotel lobbies. Nerves jangled. Bennett threw out the casual question, "what is that Van Gogh self-portrait worth?"

Later, Bennett even told the museum officials that, in theory, the city's emergency manager could simply seize the collection by cancelling the museum's arrangement with the city, citing emergency powers. Emergency indeed.

And even though the Michigan state attorney general in June 2013 issued a legal opinion that the museum's art collection was held in public trust on behalf of the people of the state and so could not be sold, the legal sway this declaration would hold in a municipal bankruptcy procedure was not at all clear.

DIA certainly offered a treasure trove of assets that could theoretically help bail out the city, because the collection had become one of the most important in the United States, if not the world. In addition to the Rivera murals, by the time the city declared bankruptcy there were 66,000 works in the DIA collection, including not only the early van Gogh and Matisse purchases, now recognized worldwide as masterpieces, but also many other famous and revered works by such artists as Rembrandt, van Eyck, Parmigianino, Bellini, Bruegel, Fra Angelico, Perugino, Gozzoli, Degas, Cézanne, Monet, Renoir, and many more.

But their worth in bankruptcy court? No one knew. Like most museums, DIA kept an accession list of holdings for insurance purposes, but the insured value of art can be dwarfed by market value and, as a rule, museums do not track the market value of their collections. Their assumption is they will not deaccession or sell off holdings, since deaccessioning is generally anathema to art museums.

Despite the declaration by the state that the DIA collection could not be sold, Emergency Manager Orr ordered an appraisal anyway. He turned to the auction experts Christie's for a fee of $200,000. Meanwhile, ripples of shock tore through the art and philanthropic community. Could the city really just sell its art to pay its bills?

Christie's proceeded.

The city and Orr began to split hairs, at first taking the legal position that the city could potentially sell only the artwork for which the city itself had paid with municipal funds, and which had been purchased after 1919, the year the city took ownership of the DIA building and its collection, excluding all major gifts. This limited the scope of Christie's appraisal to only about 5% of the collection, or about 2,700 works. The remit to Christie's from the city was to conduct a fair market value (FMV) appraisal for these works (i.e. what a willing seller would accept from a willing buyer).

Christie's appraisal officially put the value of the art purchases of the city of Detroit at a low of $452 million and a high of $866 million—not even a billion. However, most of this value came from only 11 works, including the liltingly vivid *The Wedding Dance* by Peter Bruegel the Elder, painted around 1566, considered the prime exponent of the artist and his period. Christie's had valued this painting alone at between $100 million and $200 million, the highest value of any single piece of art on the list.

Christie's excluded from its appraisal the Rivera murals and many other major masterpieces because the city itself had not spent city money to buy them; donors and patrons, such as Edsel Ford, had made those gifts.

The Christie's appraisal seemed like a lowball. Creditors were askance, especially bond insurer Syncora Guarantee, Inc. In the teetering house that had become Detroit's finances, Syncora sat stuck under a large looming rafter. Syncora faced $400 million in losses if the city of Detroit defaulted, since it had guaranteed that portion of the city's original $1.4 billion bond debt. The hotter Detroit's debt became, the more risk to Syncora. When it seemed as though the DIA collection was not worth as much as Syncora hoped, Syncora retained the Winston Art Group to undertake a new assessment, sparking the cycle of dueling appraisals.

Winston's report, published in March 2014, totaled the value of the collection at $1.75 billion, based on appraisal of 582 selected pieces, including those it said were most valuable. This triggered another critique from other creditors, now alert to the art collection and how it might help cover their losses. The creditors clamored for an appraisal of the whole collection.

The city of Detroit obliged, along with DIA itself, retaining the firm Artvest for the appraisal, in the hope of quelling creditor objections to bargaining on debt repayment.

But Artvest's report took the debate both forward and back. First, Artvest did capture the essence of the pricelessness at stake:

> A collection of the quality and range of art in the DIA would be impossible to recreate in current times. Given the fierce competition from Private Collectors and the level of today's prices, it would be impossible for the City of Detroit, or any institution in the world, to recreate the quality and scope of the DIA collection.

The valuation Artvest ascribed to the entire collection ranged from a low of $2.76 billion to a high of $4.6 billion.

On the other hand, the report said, the museum could not realistically expect to reap those amounts in a sale, since sufficient buyers and markets did not exist to absorb the volume of work involved. Sale of DIA's holdings would simply flood the market. Artvest said, "Liquidating the DIA collection in a timely manner is unlikely, given the multiple levels of legal challenges as well as the financial risks and uncertain auction outcomes."

Assuming legal challenges and delays, Artvest reduced the potential sale value of the collection to a worst-case scenario of "recovery of $850 million to $1.3 billion." Further complicating that low-ball figure, Artvest had been stymied in trying to evaluate some works that it said simply could not be valued credibly because no comparable works had come on the market in decades, and probably never would. Among the incomparables, Artvest cited Bruegel's "Wedding Dance," though Christie's had priced it, as well as the ancient glazed terracotta panels of the snake-dragon section of the Ishtar Gate of Babylon, dating to the seventh century BC.

So, Artvest seemed to conclude, the collection to be appraised was incomparable, and even if priced it could not be productively sold. It seemed the collection's value was frozen by virtue of existing at all. And

Artvest did not even attempt to appraise the centerpiece Diego Rivera murals; on top of being incomparable, Arvest said they were immovable:

> While these are incredibly rare, historic and significant works of art, they are frescos applied directly to the walls, so they cannot be removed without cutting them off the wall and inflicting serious damage and incurring significant cost. Additionally, as they were recently designated a National Historic Landmark in April of this year, it is hard to imagine how such removal could be done without serious backlash.

Artvest added, "the works would be destroyed if they were removed from the building, therefore the value is 0 [zero] OR the value of the real estate." In other words, do not even try to sell these.

What seemed like an ironclad case against the sale or liquidation of the collection from Artvest still didn't satisfy creditors. Another creditor, the Financial Guaranty Insurance Corporation, hired yet another appraiser, Victor Weiner and Associates. Financial Guaranty stood to lose significantly more than Syncora on the city's bond debt, since it had insured the lion's share: $1.1 billion of the $1.4 billion.

Weiner's appraisal raised the stakes considerably, stating that the "total value of the collection is $8,149,232,354 and probably more than that," double Artvest's high estimate. Weiner also propounded that the collection could be worthy collateral for a loan that could in turn be used to pay off creditors such as Financial Guaranty.

Weiner's appraisal also made some "extraordinary assertions," that is, suppositions that are permitted in appraisals but which, if they turn out to be wrong, can unravel the entire finding. Directly castigating Artvest, Weiner wrote, "One of the most egregious errors in the Artvest Report is the treatment of Diego Rivera's *Detroit Industry* frescoes," stating that they "can be removed successfully . . . by highly trained technicians with specialization in the removal of wall paintings."

As to the cost of the lift and replace, Weiner estimated $1 million to $3 million as a "transaction cost," though he did not back up that estimate with a comparable example of such a work being safely relocated. Weiner further asserted that the historic landmark designation of Rivera's work "does not shield the property from ownership changes or prevent an owner from making any other changes they wish." Weiner concluded that "the reconstruction of Rivera's masterful frescoes in a comparable museum is entirely plausible."

He derided the Artvest report for excluding the murals, disagreeing strongly with the Artvest conclusion that the fixed nature of the works meant their value was essentially nil. Au contraire, stated Weiner, "these works, major masterpieces by the most important Mexican artist in history, have a value far in excess of zero. And since, as discussed above, the Rivera murals are of a class of property that can be relocated with relative ease, their value is not the value of the real estate."

However, on the heart of the matter, the potential market value of Rivera's *Detroit Industry* murals in themselves, Weiner too was silent. Pricing Rivera seemed to defy all attempts, and the search to nail the ultimate value of DIA's collection flowed on.

Weiner's appraisal of the collection was the highest, but that backfired a bit, since the city feared his estimate would only encourage creditors to hold out for higher settlements. Eager to move beyond the bankruptcy filing to a workable restructuring plan, the city tried to exclude Weiner's appraisal from the proceedings, dismissing it as rushed and unreliable.

The city chastised Weiner's methods and conclusions throughout, for example: "Many of Mr. Wiener's appraisals are outliers that diverge dramatically from the appraisals performed by other testifiers in the case . . . a number of Mr. Wiener's estimates are simply off the charts."

Meanwhile, financial fires flamed. Lawsuits multiplied and creditors still needed to be fended off. Detroit was under severe pressure to present its restructuring intentions. The DIA collection, still neither credibly valued nor appraised, remained an asset in suspended animation.

Then, as it would turn out, Weiner's appraisal became moot.

The Grand Bargain discussion emerged, immortalized in "the Doodle" that became known as Art in the Box. In November 2013, Judge Gerald Rosen, the mediator in Detroit's bankruptcy case, had called a meeting of Detroit's civic leaders and some leading national figures in philanthropy to discuss the city's crisis. He wrote the word "Art" on a piece of paper and drew a box around it. He proposed that the city's leaders, including the trustees of DIA, put the art in a box, so to speak.

This meant finding a way to use the art and its presumed but yet-to-be-stipulated and agreed value—in other words, its pricelessness—to raise money that would then be passed on directly to the city. These proceeds would be earmarked to lighten the cuts in public pensions, thereby alleviating a major reason the city hoped to sell the art. He challenged those present—especially philanthropic institutions—to raise hundreds of millions, private money to pay off public debt. In return, donors to the Grand Bargain would be guaranteed that the DIA collection would never again be at risk of hostage. It was a "how much do you love me?" question.

Rosen's idea was unheard of, untried, and, at first glance, preposterous. Foundations are generally lumbering organizations, careful to preserve their endowments, operating close to the line, and rarely straying from their preset grant-making guidelines. Foundations especially do not keep pots of cash on hand in case of extraordinary circumstance such as Detroit faced.

Or so Darren Walker, president of the Ford Foundation (founded by Edsel Ford in 1936) and a leading figure in philanthropy, had said at first. According to the *Detroit Free Press,* even before Judge Rosen's plan had been circulated, Beal, DIA's director, and Annmarie Erickson, its chief operating officer, had made a supplicant's journey to New York City to meet with Walker, hoping for help. Walker reportedly told them then that "foundations don't pay for the mistakes of the past." Still, Walker would come around.

Coincidence also played a card. In September that year, with summer ending and fiscal fears intensifying, Judge Rosen was in a deli in Detroit and bumped into Miriam Noland, president of the Community Foundation for Southeast Michigan. They discussed the city's bleak prognosis, and Noland asked Rosen to assemble some foundation peers, since Rosen lacked the contacts to take his Art in a Box idea forward. Noland hit the phones and email chains.

The next weeks were a flurry of dinners, debates, hours of calls, taxi rides, cajoling, foundation board meetings, arm twisting, pressuring, and pleading. Finally, Rosen's Art in the Box plan prevailed. Thanks to Noland's pursuit of a critical mass of potential donors, and the basic brilliance and inevitability of Rosen's idea, a handful of leaders in philanthropy who had the power to move money to a problem actually did it, like medics at last on the scene to wrap a hemorrhage with towels. It would have been so much easier to say no.

That a major city like Detroit might have been left to its own devices, and its art collection sold at a fire sale to pay off bad debts, did seem a debacle at direct odds with the meaning of philanthropy.

As to what the DIA collection was actually quantitatively "worth," we still don't truly know. What we know is that, in the end, the Ford Foundation committed $125 million; Kresge Foundation, $100 million; Knight Foundation, $30 million; and Kellogg Foundation, $40 million; and other foundations stepped up as well, including $10 million from the Ford Motor Company fund. To that, DIA itself pledged $100 million, to be raised in a superhuman plea to its donor base, and the state of Michigan pledged another $350 million.

Ultimately, an $816 million Grand Bargain package was assembled, to be provided and disbursed from the donors over 20 years and earmarked to reduce the bite of the cuts to pensions and benefits that would still have to be made. Even the Grand Bargain could not wipe out all the accumulated years of budget shortfall in Detroit.

Quid pro quo for the funds into the Grand Bargain was a legal commitment from the city of Detroit that it would allow DIA to become a separate, independent and irrevocable trust, and transfer all ownership to that trust. The entire DIA art collection would no longer be an asset of city government, and could never again face possible liquidation, sale, loan, or another financial jeopardy.

In what it accomplished, the Grand Bargain epitomized a public purpose for money, even if malfeasance and inept financial management had been at the root of the need for rescue. And though the city's pension funds had originally tried to block the bankruptcy proceedings along with the other creditors, seeing that the Grand Bargain offered them at least some guarantees, they accepted the deal as well. It was bitter medicine, given cuts to their hard-won pension payments due to dubious financial deals made by city officials. The pensioners were the least to blame for their predicament, but they had the most to gain by going along.

Once the Grand Bargain was in in place, it triggered other crucial momentum. With the pension debts addressed, and the art definitively off the table, Syncora and Financial Guaranty Insurance Company had no choice but to secure what settlement they could.

All creditors, including the pensions, took a "haircut," settling for lesser payoffs because they had little choice, accepting between 14 and 75 cents on the dollars owed them.

For the city's pensioners, the Grand Bargain cash infusion meant that planned cuts to pension benefits for general retirees would be 4.5%, rather than the projected 34%, and for the police and firefighters, no cuts at all. Cuts to cost-of-living adjustments were also reduced. The financial pain was far less than originally required.

Syncora ended up with about 26 cents on the dollar, in the form of $25 million from the city in cash and credits to use to purchase downtown real estate, plus a 20-year lease extension on its lease to operate the Detroit-Windsor Tunnel, and a 30-year lease on the city's Grand Circus parking lot, preferred parking for two major sports centers.

Financial Guaranty settled for $74 million in cash, plus $20 million in real estate credits, city notes worth $146 million, plus the uncontestable rights to develop a hotel, shopping center, and condominium at the Joe Louis Arena, home of Detroit's hockey team, the Red Wings, stemming their announced plan to move out of the city in 2017. Rights to redevelop the valuable riverfront site had significantly sweetened the deal for Financial Guaranty, even though agreement with Financial Guaranty was an 11th-hour affair reached the night before Victor Wiener was due to testify on his appraisal and its methods.

So, indirectly, the never truly specified value of the DIA art collection translated into a whole range of other expressions of value: for private financial companies, art values transferred into highly prized parking lot and real estate deals; for pensioners, art values cushioned their retirement payments and safety net from disaster; and for future generations worldwide, the art values of DIA created a sacred trust forever, with priceless art never again to be subjected to a demeaning cavalcade of conflicting self-interested opinion.

Detroit's official exit from bankruptcy protection occurred in December 2014, and it remained to be seen whether the city could manage itself as the restructuring terms rolled out.

The Grand Bargain made all the difference, and had DIA's art collection not existed, and not commanded both the tangible financial expression of known values and intangible unknowns that no appraiser could quite capture to everyone's satisfaction, Detroit likely would have dissolved financially. The inexpressible value of art became the linchpin because of the common compact held about its pricelessness. As Artvest had said, the collection could never be re-created, a one-off that lit the way out of a financial nightmare.

As for Frederic Church, the genius of landscape and panorama who wanted to keep prices he paid for his trinket Italian art a secret, his own monumental masterpiece in the DIA collection, *Cotopaxi,* which depicts the exploding volcano in Ecuador spewing smoke and ash in the moonlight, was valued by Weiner at a high of $90 million.

And what, in the end, of Rivera's murals? Just when the world's greatest placers of art value had a historic opportunity and need to price them at last, they could not. The Rivera murals encapsulated the pricelessness all around, the whole DIA-Detroit saga crystallizing Lucien Karpik's economics of singularities and his advocacy that we put aside what he called a "blind spot" that "in the end, excludes all differential features but price."

In *Valuing the Unique,* Karpik also writes that "inalienable things, whether tangible or intangible, cannot be the object of a commercial transaction that would necessarily downgrade them . . . the unity of this universe, often designated by the generic term culture, resides nowhere else than in the human person. This connection singularizes, whereas commerce leads to the system of equivalences." He writes that "singularity" is "preserved in culture and lost in the market."

In other words, singularity dances on the head of a pin, inexpressible yet accepted, accepted yet untouchable, perceived and held aloft by all, and brought down to earth only now and then in a passing moment of price understanding and a price tag, only to be questioned and rise again out of reach.

The Rivera murals defied all notions of price, but their existence suffused the success of the Grand Bargain, thanks to which there would be no fire sale in Detroit. It was as if all the people of the city could sleep peacefully with the art under their pillows forever.

In 1932, Edsel Ford refused to bow to pressure to remove Rivera's works, so the cycle of events had begun. At the time Ford had said, "I am thoroughly convinced that the day will come when Detroit will be proud to have this work in its midst. In the years to come, they will be ranked among the truly great art treasures of America."

He could never have foreseen that those treasures and the paradox of price and value would one day save his city. In Detroit, only pricelessness could guarantee a future.

5

Mangroves and Money: All of Nature Is an Economic Machine

W hen I first arrived in Myanmar there were no ATMs at the airport in Yangon. In 2014, the country formerly known as Burma was barely out of the clouds of dictatorship and years of isolation as a pariah state. We visitors were funneled through immigration queues, visa check queues, hotel and car queues, but where a bank or ATM machine should have been so we could get busy spending money, there were none. International banking sanctions led by the United States had frozen out Myanmar for 25 years, and the only way to secure local cash was to exchange brand-new, perfectly crisp, never-before-used US dollars, the only paper currency then accepted by Burmese banks and money changers for mountains of the local kyat—the exchange rate being about K1000 to one US dollar. The kyat was valueless outside of Myanmar, but it worked smoothly inside the country, if you could get your hands on some.

Once in a while a money changer would accept a US bill with a fold or a tear or an ink mark, but anyone who arrived without an ample supply of pristine US greenbacks would be unable to buy even a crust of bread. Credit cards too were alien items, pointless and worthless—swipe and tap still far off—until the banking world connected its dots with Myanmar.

ATMs are just another financial invention, as it turns out, moving from rare to ubiquitous. According to the Automated Teller Association, there were about 3 million ATMs worldwide as of 2021, or about 40 per 100,000 people, though that number feels low considering ATMs seem to be everywhere. Still, around my arrival, according to the World Bank, Myanmar had 1.5 ATMs per 100,000 people.

The first ATMs appeared worldwide in the late 1960s, upending the banking industry by turning it into a 24/7 retail rush where customers came to expect cash day or night from any grocery store, street corner, or dingy gas station Most amazingly, we were willing to pay inordinate fees to access our own money.

Happy with these flowing fees, banks could lay off human tellers and shrink their personnel costs. Many banks condensed their names to mere acronyms, leaving almost no bank with the word "trust" in its brand. Bank buildings became ghosts of their former impressive selves, their hefty arcades rich with plush carpet now gone. The once stately Citibank branch on Fifth Avenue and 51st Street in New York City, for example, was converted into an emporium to sell designer sports garb, the bank itself reduced to a small hall of empty desks and an ATM array.

Who could resist cash dispensed from the wall? ATMs made cash not only convenient but also handy, literally, and perhaps mundane. That cash came into our hands so quickly might have made it even easier to ignore the underlying assets on which the credibility of cash is based. The wall seemed to be printing the money.

The main virtue of cash is that we accept it without question when we receive it, regardless of who gives it to us. Cash has inherent credibility. Even as digital currencies proliferate and threaten to kill off legacy banking once and for all, cash commands our faith. We may move to digital wallets as paper notes and coins disappear, but the premise of cash remains indelible, and it all aims at consumption.

But what if, instead of feeling flush when we resupply with cash, we were reminded of our debt? Supposing instead of bills being spewed from the wall, we got a handful of IOUs? What if instead of ATMs there were millions of debt machines? Would we be in such a hurry to insert our ATM cards, day or night? What if, instead of replenishing our purchasing power, those bills were just a record of the value of the natural resources spent to generate the cash—a $10 note representing $10 of expended natural resources?

In fact, if we believe that all economic activity rests on natural resources of some kind, then in fact every banknote is indeed an IOU issued by the environment; we just have not yet seen things that way. In a sense, the global economy is coasting along on checking plus issued by nature—the full faith and credit of the earth.

If that fistful of bills from the ATM really did take environmental debt into account, most of us would be economically ruined. And so, obviously, ATMs will never be debt machines. But ignoring environmental debt is not viable either.

Myanmar in 2014, when it was trying to cast off the militarism and human rights violations that had isolated it from the world community for so long, was thought to be one of the countries that could take a lead on understanding the financial value of nature, to skip ahead and be the beneficiary of so many prior years of the world's trying to integrate environmental and economic trends.

I wanted to take a firsthand look at how Myanmar, then the latest undiscovered tourist destination and investment market, was trying to value a paragon natural asset—its extensive coastal mangroves. The natural resources of newly beckoning Myanmar were being eyed by the rapacious, especially outside companies seeking access to prime pristine land holdings.

Mangrove forests are thick, tangled, and sturdy. The roots of mangrove trees dig down into mud and silt like forks, holding fast for decades, keeping the earth in place. Mangroves resist the sea in a storm or tsunami, natural buffers that take fierce wave energy head on, so the force weakens as it spreads up through the mangrove tangle.

Mangroves are also a rich habitat. Fish pick at mangrove roots for food and lay eggs in still mangrove waters. Various studies in Myanmar found that mangrove-dependent species contributed an average of 90% of inshore and offshore prawn and crustacean catch, 60% of inshore catch, and 30% of offshore catch. Mangroves, if nothing else, are replenishing nurseries for marine species worldwide.

From the air, mangroves look like skirts of green jeweled trim on the coast. Verdant and vital though they are, lacking sandy sweeps and easy real estate value, mangroves have been stripped and bulldozed out to make way for roads, artificial beaches at hotels, and so-called other coastal improvements, as if a mangrove forest were a wasteland. Poor people also cut down mangroves to meet various needs, especially for firewood and making charcoal to sell.

Myanmar had only 20% of its original mangrove cover left when I visited, most of it hacked or burned away, and there I was, having a look at some mangrove expanses soon to be protected, it was hoped.

Even in a four-wheel drive jeep, it took us an hour to travel 15 miles up the coast on the Andaman Sea, our car clinging to slopes at 45-degree angles, passing and being passed by all manner of other vehicles, including three-wheelers with no hoods over the motors so they look like motorized pistons pulling the driver along and not the other way around. When we at last reached the edge of the mangrove maze, I was swooped off into a hand-carved canoe by our hosts, local scientists aiming to develop a national mangrove park and fishermen who lived in the area.

We motored across the little inlet to a tiny island, diamond sunlight dappling the surface, where we picked up our guide who was known as "the smoking woman," meaning the woman who smokes cigarettes. An inch or so of cigarette butt clung to her lips, and her skin was the color of cooked caramel, cracked from the sun and worry, or maybe sun and laughter. Anyway, we piled in with lifejackets and sunhats. I tried to macho it out without the flouncy sunhat I was offered, but in the searing sun, I soon had my sunhat on just like everyone else.

Off we went into the channels through the mangroves—mangroves as far as the eye could see, a prehistoric panorama of dark green entanglement. It was reassuring to think that the smoking woman knew the way because all was indistinguishable, and after one or two turns we were deep into the labyrinth with no mobile signal and no spare gas.

Our little craft began leaking and the fishermen took turns baling with an ex-Clorox plastic bottle that had been cut in half and fitted with a handle of sturdy mangrove root attached with nails. Nothing here was wasted because, so far from towns or shops, almost nothing could be replaced.

At the charcoal ovens, the charred centerpiece of a small village, a single mango tree stood, and the villagers told us that when there was a lot of early fruit, they knew they might soon have to abandon the settlement for higher ground because many mangos on a tree ahead of mango season was a sign that lots of rain was coming, so they say. There were many children there who had nothing—no shoes, no school, and who knew what else they would have to live without if their parents were doomed to make charcoal in this place. There were 45 families living in the vicinity, also with no health clinic.

We put-putted back out, one lagoon after the other, until thanks to the smoking woman's keen eyes and memory, we were safely back out into the main channel, out of a green world and into the dust of the road. We retraced our path and reached a newly washed-out section along the coast, made passable by railroad ties placed strategically in the sand. We got out of the van to lighten the weight, and the driver, who'd been masterful the entire journey, worked his magic again and somehow aligned each tire perfectly on each plank of wood, so that the car could cross the deep sand yearning to swallow the wheels.

At a strategic fork in the road, a little boy had positioned himself so he could get paid to warn people to take the detour, pointing the way to the safe route, earning the equivalent of about 20 cents for his advice. I wondered what kind of advice he gave to those who refused to pay. A nice little business, but no work for a schoolboy.

We reached the main road, so to speak, which was being improved, but this was the Stone Age, and road building meant workers broke rocks with pick and axe. We passed squads of road crews, mostly women, all hacking and banging and breaking the stones and layering them like gravel driveways waiting for the paving machine to come one day soon to pour low-grade macadam over the gravel layer and call it a finished road.

The poverty was sharp. Charcoal making was a main reason Myanmar had so little original mangrove cover left, and it is one of the dirtiest, most dangerous, and underpaid jobs on earth. A woman who baked charcoal for a living earned about a dollar a day, supplementing that pittance by also cutting bamboo for the souvenir umbrella trade. The woman cut and cleaned the bamboo like a sugar cane worker hacks and trims sugar, her body shushing into the sweltering bamboo groves, machete in hand, stalks cut and then leaves sliced off in a single swipe to leave an umbrella stem primed in back-breaking moments. She earned about 100 kyat for each bamboo stalk she cut and cleaned—10 US cents. By the time that bamboo stalk became a tourist's must-have sunshade or souvenir, the retail price multiplied to about US $5.

Umbrellas are far from the highest and best use of bamboo, any more than charcoal is the highest and best use of mangroves. Mangroves in Myanmar also played an influential political role. In 2008, Cyclone Nargis barreled down on the Irrawaddy region in Myanmar, ravaging its coasts and killing nearly 140,000 people, many from drowning, according to the UN and other reports. About 2.5 million people were displaced and in some way affected, including about 1 million left homeless. Costs to the economy ranged from US $4 billion to $12 billion, including 65% of the nation's vital rice paddies sea-logged. Many remained unplantable due to salt penetration, and the price of rice for local people skyrocketed, leaving many destitute for sustenance. When Nargis hit, there had been almost no holding back the scream of the sea surge; the mangroves that could have broken the force were long since cut away.

The military government, which had ruled Myanmar repressively and viciously for several decades, proved impotent. Preparations for Nargis had been nonexistent, as was rescue and recovery assistance. People were left to fend for themselves, even to dig out their own dead. Public disgust with the government rose.

Feeling threatened, the ruling junta relaxed their hold on power a bit, paving the way for gradual normalization with the outside world. Eventually this included the junta's release of long-standing political dissident and global human rights icon Aung San Suu Kyi, who had been under house arrest since 1989, made to forsake visiting her dying husband and children in the UK in order to maintain her Burmese passport and citizenship, and so beloved by her people they called her "The Lady." Her return to public life, and her nation's political leadership stage, directly resulted from the government's inability to deal with a sweep of ocean waves, largely due to mangrove deforestation.

But what next? Myanmar had been following the classic model for resource-rich, low-income countries, meaning foreign and domestic cronies often secured insider contracts, took what they could from nature, sold it, and moved on to the next exploitation. But because of economic sanctions, trade with the outside world was still somewhat limited, in turn mass limiting environmental degradation to some extent.

As trade was poised to open on a major scale, though, how could exceedingly poor Myanmar model a new economy for itself that did not undervalue assets like mangroves, while still generating income to feed people, educate and nurture children, and move beyond the manual breaking of stones when it came to roads and engineering infrastructure?

A thoughtful group of local researchers and policy leaders, eager to protect Myanmar's extensive tropical forests now that trade sanctions were being lifted, undertook a revolutionary study in 2009, "The Economic Value of Forest Ecosystem Services in Myanmar and Options for Sustainable Financing." Funded with support from the EU, it was the very first assessment in Myanmar of the potential financial value of its forests, including mangroves, and not only the obvious uses, like cutting teak trees, legally and illegally, to make tables and trinkets.

The study examined known commercial prices paid for commodities, such as wood and fish if sold directly to a buyer, and then compared those prices to what the resources contributed to the general economy indirectly. If these indirect benefits could be valued, then in theory resources would not just be sold off or contracted out to the first convenient bidder at low prices, if exploited at all.

The study was exceptionally detailed for its time, examining multiple uses of the forests, such as use of wood and forests for energy, wild foods, local value of the water held in the ground by trees and plants, value of holding back storm rages such as Nargis in 2008, value of habitat for bees that pollinate, and birds carrying seeds of tropical fruits and trees in their beaks and feces, dropping nuggets all over and thereby helping expand and refresh the forests. The study even priced the log-hauling work performed by elephants. The report was an inaugural ledger account to express what the natural forests of Myanmar were worth "used" and "unused" to the leaders and people of the nation.

Of course, the most prevalent use of forest products is logging and shipping trees to sawmills. The study found that Myanmar exported about 45% of its logs, representing about US $700 million in direct sales but meaning that much added value of Myanmar's forest was being reaped outside of Myanmar. Raw log exports generally translate to invaluable trees sold on low-common-denominator terms, and lower jobs creation at home.

The study then examined other "Industrial wood production" in Myanmar, including the local use of charcoal for fuel heating by local people, finding a value of US $582 million—could the dollar a day paid to the woman I met at the charcoal oven be any further away?

Elephants depend on forests for habit, and forestry depended on them in Myanmar. Elephants performed significant work, notably pulling the most valuable logs, like teak, out of the forest one at a time to avoid the broad forest scarring that comes with clear-cutting and industrial machinery. The study of the value of elephant labor compared the costs of caring for healthy elephants to the costs of buying and maintaining skidders, plus cutting the trails that are needed to bring in machinery. The study found that, net, the value of elephant pulling power each year to the forest economy was about US $21 million. Presumably expressing this value would help protect elephant habitat.

The study then attempted to put a value on protecting the watershed, that is, "services" performed by standing forests that help preserve water flow and water quality. Standing trees, roots, leaves, and branches trap rainfall, which can be tempestuous in Myanmar, so that soil is not washed away. Holding soil is a high-value ecosystem service, stemming erosion and siltation, all of which can foul drinking water and clog up plumbing where it does exist, as well as water flow needed for hydropower plants, especially important to avoid fossil fuel burning and which contributed nearly 60% of Myanmar's electricity at the time. Also, the stronger the forest bulwark, the less likely heavy rainfall can turn into unfettered raging random rushes, then into devastating downstream floods.

Weighing and calculating all these watershed benefits, the Ministry of Forestry in Myanmar concluded a baseline value for watershed services provided annually by its terrestrial forests at US $721 million, meaning that the forests contributed at least this value each year, for which no one accounted and for which loss no one was held responsible if trees are randomly cut down.

Far from constituting wastelands, mangroves contributed even more unseen and unheralded value. Some calculations:

- Non-forest and non–fish mangrove products, such as seeds, flowers and fruits: $20 million
- Natural coastal protection bulwark services, such as that which might have held off Nargis: $707 million, as compared to the $4 billion to $12 billion estimated costs after the fact
- Capturing greenhouse gases, combined with terrestrial forests, assuming a carbon market, based on the guesstimate of US $5 per ton: $890 million
- Nursery for fish breeding and maintaining breeding habitat: $1.1 billion

All in all, the study, far ahead of its time, showed that the highest vocation of the forests and mangroves was to nurture and protect ongoing ecosystem services, which could be calculated even with many variables.

Unfortunately, in 2021, Myanmar turned upside down again. As democracy grew, led by Aung San Suu Kyi and her political party, the military clamped down, unsettled by the freedoms people expected. Then, astonishing the world, The Lady herself seemed to switch coats, siding with repressive civic measures and unwilling to condemn the military's slaughter of the Rohingya Muslim minority, only to have the tables turn once again. As of the end of 2022, Aung San Suu Kyi had been arrested, sentenced to 33 years in prison on questionable corruption charges likely intended to keep her incarcerated and out of circulation for the rest of her life.

The enlightened ecosystem work Myanmar had undertaken in the heyday of the junta's end could barely advance in the country's shifting politics, but it was an exemplary try. Since then, much research has occurred on mangroves, summed up in the massive 2021 World Bank report, "The Changing Wealth of Nations," that like the expansive Dasgupta Review also frames measures of national wealth, including both renewable and nonrenewable capital, as indispensable companions to the GDP. The report draws on data from 146 countries from 1995 to 2018 to present what it calls "the world's most comprehensive accounts to date of the wealth of nations."

The report says that the world has lost about 4% of its mangrove expanse from 1996 to 2015, and other science including aerial mapping has concluded that the earth has lost 20–35% of its mangrove cover in the last 50 years. Mangrove elimination has come mostly from deforestation, developing coastal areas for human settlement and "produced capital," including aquaculture pool and oil palm plantations. Sea level rise and extreme cycles, à la Nargis and many since, also eat away at mangrove cover.

Yet far from being wasteland, mangroves keep bestowing their value. According to "The Changing Wealth of Nations":

> [O]verall value for coastal protection has increased substantially because of sharp increases in coastal flood risk driven by the growth in coastal populations and wealth. From 1995 to 2018 the number of people directly affected by flooding in mangrove areas grew by 66% and capital stock damages grew by 268%. Without mangroves, increased flood damage would have been even greater. In 2018 mangroves protected more than 6 million people from annual flooding and prevented additional annual losses of $US 24 billion of produced capital . . . the annual benefit of mangroves per hectare more than doubled between 1995 and 2018 from a global average of US$643 to US$ 1689 per hectare.

So, for example, in environmental P&L statements similar to the pioneering work of PUMA, a company that had caused mangroves to be eliminated would have to consider charging itself that per-hectare figure in order to be honest about its environmental negative impacts. And, at that rate of lost mangrove value, would the company's theoretical product have been cost-effective to produce, or would it have been a losing proposition if negative mangrove impacts figured into the financial statement? This is the nub of the decision, when ecosystem services come into play.

To insert ecosystem service dynamics directly into the bedrock valuation of public equities, the Intrinsic Exchange Group (IEG), based in New York, hoped to launch what it calls "natural asset companies" (NACs), aimed at stewarding natural capital, in partnership with the New York Stock Exchange (NYSE). In this potentially catalytic advance, NACs would be built on classical corporate start-up structures, but diverge radically in terms of what constitutes start-up value. The initial investable corpus of an NAC would derive from ecosystem services the NAC sought to protect and a credible business plan.

NACs would synthesize, at last, the elusive multiple intangible values attributed to ecosystem services into a single and instantly recognizable metric: stock price. By gathering immeasureables into this, an unequivocally familiar measurement, NACs could take the subjectivity out of ecosystem service math, expressing nature's value in objective terms so that nature can be constructively, productively, and equitably priced. Standardizing the value of natural capital in this manner could also reassure investors who, after all, need to justify their choices quantitatively, and so might feed streams of new capital to nature's protection.

Once successfully formed and listed, an NAC would be managed as any standard company, with an executive and governance structure consistent with established operating and oversight procedures for companies. Conceived by Douglas Eger, an entrepreneur with long-time environmental leanings, by 2024–25, equities in NACs could be listed and traded on the NYSE as any other stock.

NACs at first would focus on large parcels of land owned by governments or individuals that had significant conservation potential or need. Investors would not own the land itself, but rather invest in the rights to the ecosystem services the land generates.

The initial public offering (IPO) would raise the NAC's initial capital, and offering proceeds would generate revenue to maintain the ecosystem services of the land (i.e. maintain the land itself), so the value of protecting the parcel favorably competes with its value heavily developed or exploited. For example, an NAC could be created to support preservation of large tracts of forest or wetlands that would otherwise be vulnerable to extractive development or sale for commercial purposes.

An NAC would earn revenue as it monetized ecosystem services through various existing pricing mechanisms, such as carbon markets, or from revenue earned by environmentally conscientious business activities the NAC might undertake. For example, an NAC might engage in selective forestry or agricultural production that did not draw down the value of the ecosystem services being provided—in short, no sapping, or devaluing what the Dasgupta Review calls the "intrinsic worth" of nature, the worth the Intrinsic Exchange seeks to enshrine.

Underlying NAC capital value would depend on the "performance" of the ecosystem services intrinsic to a given NAC, assessed scientifically. Ongoing NAC performance would be reported to shareholders and capital markets through annual reports, regular investor engagement, and the usual data providers covering the outlook of companies listed on the NYSE and, potentially, beyond.

Ideally, investors would be drawn to the conservation intent, but also the economic potential inherent in the services nature provides on its own, on seasonal schedule, predictable and not—far from what traditional economy theory tends to call "improvements."

Investors, including public pension funds, university endowments, and private individuals, could buy, sell, or hold shares in a listed NAC just as they might buy shares in any company offered to shareholders wherever in the world.

The IEG framework to accurately account for ecosystem service values would conform to GAAP principles and, in 2023, IEG intended to submit its valuation proposal to the US SEC for approval so that public offerings and listings could proceed. The IEG approach attracted support from the Rockefeller Foundation, the Inter-American Development Bank, and others. Pilot projects were under way in 2023, with the first NAC to be launched potentially in cooperation with the government of Costa Rica, once fiduciary approvals were secured.

The NAC concept can draw arrows, its chief virtue also its chief vulnerability perhaps—that it reduces the innumerable roles that nature plays to a single number, force fitting in a sense nature's mystery into a commonplace metric. On the other hand, NACs would at last situate the health of nature as a transparent economic indicator, as investors tracked the vacillations of a given NAC on a stock exchange. Just as daily readouts proclaim the ups and downs of capital value in the language of traditional capitalism (e.g. "the S&P 500 is up or down today so many points"), if NACs were to flourish, we might hear "today's NAC index was up or down," putting natural capital value on a par with classic financial capital, mainstreamed and public.

A big-idea try to internalize externalities, NACs' ultimate yardstick is pricelessness. Through NACs, the pricelessness of nature could be traceable by the minute, hour, and day, and the state of its guardianship inescapable from public view.

Countless ecosystem services studies of the type that could under-pin the NAC concept or similar innovations have been undertaken in the last decade or so, touching on all of the planet's natural features. In fact, the extensive Ecosystem Services Valuation Database, funded by numerous international organizations, was updated and relaunched in 2021. By 2023, its repository contained more than 5,000 ecosystem ser-vice valuation studies from around the world, including in high-income nations that are not at all immune to environmental degradation and the mounting costs of climate change, with more research on the way.

Yet such studies still founder, struggling to seep into the real world of general civic, public, and commercial decision-making where the logic of ecosystem services must, in the end, be applied. "The Changing Wealth of Nations" explains the persistent gap between practice and theory, first noting that its "balance sheet approach to asset valuation . . . allows ministries of finance and national treasuries to consider monetary trade-offs and the important role for asset accumulation across natural capital, human capital and produced capital. . . . For some assets, par-ticularly natural assets, this monetary value can help ensure they get an appropriate level of economic policy consideration."

However, the report admits, "few of these assets are accounted for in the national balance sheets and hence appear invisible or worthless to policymakers."

So what does it matter what forests and mangroves are worth in aca-demic calculation if the practical world cannot acknowledge and protect that worth?

As the original 2009 Myanmar study humbly said, "The figures pre-sented in this report . . . should be seen as a broad indication of what *might* occur under different forest management futures, rather than a definitive statement of what *will* happen."

Events careened ahead and as "The Changing Wealth of Nations" notes, "The emergence of multiple global crises, such as biodiversity loss, climate change, and ocean pollution, is a strong wake-up call about the limits to replacing critical ecosystem services with human-made substitutes."

A simplistic view of ecosystem service valuations would seem to expect a "do nothing to nature" consensus.

But with so many people needing to work and earn, how do they convert this "doing nothing" into cash in their pockets? Why is it the responsibility of the poor charcoal farmer or bamboo umbrella maker to forsake earning 100 kyat? What are the alternatives, especially in the 26 "low-income" countries referenced in "The Changing Wealth of Nations," where land and ecosystems are vital, "comprising around 23 percent of their total wealth"?

How to translate these new econometrics and ecosystem service valuation into cash for the poor, or tax revenue for common good public budgets, so recognition for nature's value actually infuses the economy in practice and dubious plans to exploit natural resources do not go forward?

Crass as it sounds, all of nature is an economic machine constantly generating benefits, but without price tags. In terms of "The Changing Wealth of Nations," there have been great improvements in measuring ecosystem conditions and services based on rapid advances in remote sensing, but identifying and quantifying potential tipping points in the context of national wealth accounts still remains highly uncertain.

The daunting truths hover, even as they grow more accurate, but must we go to the tipping point? Suppose, instead, we came dramatically down to earth. Suppose that for every dollar withdrawn via an ATM, a penny was added to cover the costs of reforestation of an area where trees are being cut down, tracked by a global digital big data accounting system, with satellite feeds worldwide?

Those eyes in the sky could spot where trees were being cut down without replacement, make an instant calculation, and zap the cost of reforestation to all the world's banks in a kind of SWIFT system (Society for Worldwide Interbank Financial Telecommunication) for transferring environmental information. This would then tag a reforestation fee onto every ATM user, per transaction. And what if we added a fee to cover other environmental costs, such as a minuscule percentage per ATM user of the costs of flood recovery or water purification, plus the tons of greenhouse gas emissions needed to run the electricity that runs the ATM itself, and poof, suddenly, the $100 has been spent before being cashed. The $100 bill in hand is no longer cash, but an invoice of environmental costs incurred to create $100 of so-called "cash value."

On the other hand, what if the enviro-SWIFT zapped reforestation fees directly to national budgets, at the rate of ATM use, charging not necessarily the ATM user but a forestry-dependent industry? Or what if some of these fees exacted by the environmental ATM system went back to the mangrove charcoal makers, through a direct link to the mobile phone cash wallets in a kind of "ecosystem services" Zelle credit? That would be easy and fair and would perhaps gradually generate income sufficient for the charcoal makers to leave that dismal work behind forever.

Such a sharing concept is along the same lines as the "buy one, give one" model, where a company donates to a charity one of its products— say shoes—for every pair it sells. Some of the price paid by the buyer of the first pair of shoes is applied to cover the costs of the donated pair of shoes, making the first pair more expensive, but also making it viable to give a pair of shoes away. In the economic machine of nature, we could say that for every dollar of environmental service value we receive, we will have to give back at least one, somewhere, somehow, to someone. Double-entry.

But for now, we have no such system and ATMs do not spread around environmental costs or help contain the depletion of scarcities. To date, only carbon markets and other tools offer anything close.

6

The Cosmic Penthouse: Carbon Pricing, Carbon Markets

T he sluggish pace of infusing ecosystem service accounting and environmental economics into actual financial practice is the central cause of
our climate change crisis. Carbon markets, controversial and bold,
attempt to achieve the needed real-world valuation by tagging the cost
of atmospheric pollution through the fundamental concept of supply-
and-demand—value and cost of demand to use the atmosphere goes up
as supply of atmosphere goes down.

We are not accustomed to considering our atmosphere in terms of
supply, but once we do, we behold its actual scarcity with awe.

Fortunately, thanks to science, we can be humbled by the meager
width of our wealth—from the edge of the atmosphere that caresses the
earth to the edge that meets outer space, only about 100 kilometers, or
60 miles. This remarkable thin wafer provides all the air we breathe and
all the protection we have from the deadly intensity of the sun's radiation and heat.

Beyond that, the remaining ring of main atmospheric layers—
troposphere, stratosphere, thermosphere, and mesosphere—totals only
about 480 kilometers, or 300 miles, before we enter nothingness.

So precious is our atmosphere, it has no counterpart in all of space, on no other planet known, seen or conjured. Yet in this, earth's glorious unique and cosmic penthouse, we have been blithely storing the economic equivalent of dirty diapers—greenhouse gases—since the dawn of industry.

We have gotten away with this because we pay no storage fees. Use of our atmospheric penthouse has been free to us, to meet our every need and desire. While our financial systems can price the rarity of any minor or major penthouse suite atop any spear of building on the planet, they cannot capture the value of the rarest space of all, our narrow atmospheric halo. Invisible as it saves our lives, the atmosphere has counted for nothing financially, ever.

Carbon markets reject this precedent, by recognizing the sanctity of atmospheric limits, and conveying the economic yet ineluctable value of atmospheric functions. Pricing carbon makes it increasingly untenable to store the dirty diapers.

The most ubiquitous greenhouse gas is carbon dioxide (CO_2). There are five main others: methane (CH_4), nitrous oxide (N_2O), sulfur hexafluoride (SF_6), hydrofluorocarbons (HFCs), and perfluorocarbons (PFCs). Measured in metric tons, these six culprits—all emitted when we burn fossil fuels for nearly all our routine economic activities—have become known by the collective shorthand of "carbon pollution." The gases can each be physically measured; to take CO_2 alone, we can visualize a single metric ton as a "cube almost as tall, wide, and long as a telephone pole," according to the Massachusetts Institute of Technology (MIT).

The gases vary in their capacity to harm the atmosphere, expressed as CO_2 equivalent (CO_2e) per metric ton, which communicates the heat-trapping level of each gas, known as global warming potential (GWP). For example, a metric ton of SF_6, which is used for purposes ranging from insulating electrical transmission wires to inflating tennis balls, is highly potent: 1 ton of SF_6 emissions has a global warming potential equivalent of roughly 23 tons of CO_2. The higher the CO_2e per ton of greenhouse gas, the worse for us. Converting calculations of quantities of fossil fuel burned to atmospheric CO_2e is akin to converting a mixed menu of food intake to the universal metric of calories.

The more tons of fossil fuel burned, the more tons of CO_2e emitted to the atmosphere, where they cannot escape. As the gases accumulate, they in turn hold in the intense solar radiation that reaches the earth's surface, preventing that heat from bouncing back off the planet and safely away into space. Once called the "greenhouse effect," this transforms our protective atmosphere into a heat blanket the earth cannot kick off.

This also entirely disrupts the earth's critical water cycle. Warmer oceans mean more evaporation and moisture in the clouds, a key cause of torrential bursts of rain and ensuing flooding for which almost no human communities are prepared.

The trapped heat must make itself room in the tight space of the atmosphere, so it shoves wind, water vapor, and clouds around the earth like a bag of rags, wreaking havoc with established weather patterns, triggering wild storms, drought, extreme weather swings, and other frightful unpredictable breakdowns of the seasons. The worst of climate change remains unknown, but meanwhile the first of climate change impacts are already under way worldwide, raising the odds that catastrophic events will occur more frequently.

Carbon dioxide buildup in the atmosphere and its relationship to water vapor and climate variations was deemed suspicious as early as 1896, by Swedish chemist Svante Arrhenius. His inquiries were inconclusive, but they indicate just how long climate science and climate change concern have been ahead of public policy and financial practice, especially as we project objectives of vanquishing the dangers of greenhouse gas emissions by the far-off date of 2050. Decades have been spent in climate change study and worry, with clear warnings put before our eyes.

In 1958, environmental chemist and oceanographer Dr. Charles Keeling suspected accumulating CO_2 in the atmosphere. To check his hunch, he installed the world's first system to track CO_2 concentrations globally at the Moana Loa Observatory in Hawaii, operated by the US National Oceanic and Atmospheric Administration (NOAA). The system showed CO_2 only going up, plotted irrefutably in what became known as the Keeling Curve. In a paper published in 1970 by the American Philosophical Society, Keeling warned that escalating CO_2 levels could one day disrupt earth's climate even if science was still, comparatively speaking, not dead sure.

Keeling stated, "we are left without a clear prediction. Nevertheless I believe that no atmospheric scientist doubts that a sufficiently large change in atmospheric CO_2 would change the climate. We just do not yet know what increase in CO_2 the Earth's atmosphere will accept without warming noticeably."

Referring to students of college age at the time, Keeling concluded:

> I predict that they will be the first generation to feel such strong concerns for man's future that they will discover means of effective action. This action may be less pleasant and rational than the corrective measures that we promote today, but 30 years from now, if present trends are any sign, mankind's world, I judge, will be in greater immediate danger than it is today and immediate corrective measures if such exist will be closer at hand. If the human race survives into the 21st century the people living then . . . along with their other troubles may also face the threat of climatic change brought about by an uncontrolled increase in atmospheric CO_2 from fossil fuels.

In 2002, President George W. Bush awarded Keeling the US Medal of Science.

Predictive climate change modeling was pioneered by Dr. Warren Washington in the 1960s and 1970s, beginning with his graduate student research for the US Navy to better understand how fluctuating climate could affect naval operations. Washington was one of the first climatologists in America to combine the study of physics and meteorology. He went on to advise six US presidents on climate change, including George W. Bush and his father, George H. W. Bush, to be a member of the Intergovernmental Panel on Climate Change (IPCC), which won the Nobel Prize for its work in 2007, and in 2019 was awarded the US Medal of Science by President Barack Obama.

As early as 1977, President Jimmy Carter commissioned the "Global 2000 Report to the President" to help long-term US environmental policies. Admitting its picture "can be painted only in broad strokes," the report nevertheless accurately flagged climate change: "Rising CO_2 concentrations are of concern because of their potential for causing a warming of the earth. Scientific opinion differs on the possible consequences but a widely held view is that highly disruptive effects on world agriculture could occur before the middle of the 21st century."

Dismissed as too gloomy, "Global 2000" ignited no action, Carter was a one-term president and climate change action in the United States stood still.

Dr. James Hansen, a climate scientist and former director of NASA's Goddard Institute for Space Studies, is widely credited with providing the first warning straight to the US Congress. At a farsighted hearing on climate change at the US Senate in 1988, Hansen dramatically summarized his testimony: "I would like to draw three main conclusions. Number one, the earth is warmer in 1988 than at any time in the history of instrumental measurements. Number two, the global warming is now large enough that we can ascribe with a high degree of confidence a cause and effect relationship to the greenhouse effect. And number three, our computer climate simulations indicate that the greenhouse effect is already large enough to begin to affect the probability of extreme events such as summer heat waves." That same year, the UN set up the IPCC to dig into climate science in more detail and report regularly to the world's governments, which it has done ever since.

On balance, at the international policy level, through mostly the UN system, nations have been promising to try to wrestle with climate change and the rise of greenhouse gases for at least three decades—on the mark, get set, go—most notably and officially since the UN's 1992 Earth Summit in Rio de Janeiro. Attended by 108 heads of state, the summit was the first such gathering of heads of state to address environmental problems.

Every eight minutes, one at a time, presidents, prime ministers, and premiers entered the innermost sanctum of the sprawling conference compound where a leather-bound volume, the "Framework Convention on Climate Change," sat open on a podium flanked by sumptuous potted palms and an honor guard standing at stiff attention. Leaders signed their names to the book, an official United Nations treaty, pledging their nations to reduce greenhouse gases, if not right then, soon enough, the fine nib points of their engraved golden fountain pens scratching across the paper.

Their signatures, including that of US President George H. W. Bush, confirmed their commitment to the convention, which set a goal of holding greenhouse gas emissions to 1990 levels by the year 2000, developed countries acting first, with less developed countries following on an unspecified schedule.

Yet those solemn promises delivered no action at the scale required. The Rio political consensus lacked stamina and broke down as leadership turned over, activists aged out, the ambitious emissions stabilization goals disintegrated as too hard to tackle, and climate change lost its high-level constituency of urgency. A critical chance to grip the problem early was squandered and greenhouse emissions continued unencumbered, even though UN meetings on climate change proceeded every year.

In December 2015, the UN held its annual climate gathering in Paris, where the world's governments convened in a nearly last-ditch attempt to again agree on how to head off the drastic climate change disruptions that science continued to report lay ahead.

This time, 150 heads of state attended. The Paris meeting was COP21, meaning the 21st Conference of the Parties to the Climate Change Convention to take place, or 21 years since the original Framework Convention came into force after being finalized in Rio, give or take a few conferences that took place before numbering of COPs began, plus more COPs since Paris, COP28 in 2023, COP29, 30?—a parade of conferences to refine next steps and try to keep international attention focused.

Since basic recognition of the climate change problem surfaced, and we could choose to start our clock at the remarks of Charles Keeling in 1970, if we total the person-hours of time spent in conferences, debates, panels, workshops, brainstorming sessions, blogs, tweets, podcasts, webinars, research, commentary, analysis, synthesis, speculation, presentation, opining, and exhorting, in person and countless more on Zoom, we could find we have spent perhaps hour for hour more time discussing the climate change problem than creating it, and yet have to face the fact that we are still way behind solving it.

The Paris COP21 conference lit up the Eiffel Tower and captured the global imagination, including the pope's with his *Laudato Si.* Countless interest groups attended, the buzz of hopeful progress in the air as notable as the aroma of French roast coffee at every pop-up café break area. COP21 and all its accouterments reminded the world how well the French can host.

I read and reread the draft texts, my head awash in well-honed formulations and phrases I had read scores of times in earlier UN negotiating texts, struggling to convince myself that the words before my eyes were fresh. At times I felt an algorithm must have searched all the least contentious clauses from the 21 or so prior UN negotiations and cut-and-pasted them into the Paris documents. Still, COP21 called for a steely-eyed belief that positive change is possible despite many undeniable signals to the contrary.

The conference produced the laudable new "Paris Agreement," a pledge among all nations, now including developed and developing countries on the same timeline, establishing national plans, called Nationally Determined Contributions (NDCs), to reduce greenhouse gases. Couched in careful diplomatic language, the agreement specified that the world's nations would seek to delink emissions growth from economic growth by 2030, or as they put it, "aim to reach global peaking of greenhouse gas emissions as soon as possible recognizing that peaking will take longer for developing country parties and to undertake rapid reductions thereafter in accordance with best available science."

The agreement also aimed to hold the "increase in the global average temperature to well below 2°C above preindustrial levels and pursuing efforts to limit the temperature increase to 1.5°C," edified language that could still cause an average person to wonder how a change of one degree or half a degree could be so significant. After all, if we take our body temperature, a degree or so change doesn't send us into a panic.

The major Paris political breakthrough was securing a legally binding general agreement among all that nations that climate change policies should be dictated by science, nearly irrefutable by 2015, implicitly lining up all national and emitter-specific reduction plans with climate science as well. This gave birth to the term "science-based targets," a comprehensible shorthand for the otherwise arcane references in the agreement.

Still, I wondered, is it thinkable that the world could change its consumption habits and ideas about energy use if ads I saw online during the Paris meeting promoted airborne delivery of gift pajamas in time for Christmas anywhere in the world in 24 hours, including "for your dog"? We know in our heart of hearts that, as must come to all childish things at some point, such gambits as flying pajamas will have to be put aside.

Paris was intoxicating, as *toujours*. However, even if the Trump administration had not pulled out of the Paris agreement in 2017, transforming the United States, the world's second-largest emitter of greenhouse gases after China, into an environmental pariah worldwide, and even though the Biden Administration swiftly rejoined and issued sweeping plans to reduce emissions in the United States, the Paris Agreement still fell short of being able to enforce the dramatic reductions needed globally to forestall the worst expected effects of climate change within the authority and decision-making arc of those who signed the agreement. The baton of responsibility endlessly passes on.

Assessing progress in meeting the Paris terms since COP21, the agency that monitors implementation of international climate change agreements, the secretariat of the United Nations Framework Convention on Climate Change (UNFCCC), had stark words in its 2022 Synthesis report. The report declared "an urgent need for either a significant increase in the level of ambition of NDCs between now and 2030 or a significant overachievement of the latest NDCs, or a combination of both . . . If emissions are not reduced by 2030, they will need to be substantially reduced thereafter to compensate for the slow start on the path to net zero emissions."

Discouragingly, it took a virus to accomplish what no national or global climate policy and activism yet had. In 2020, the COVID-19 pandemic and its lockdowns achieved the greatest drop in CO_2 on record, according to United in Science, a consortium of international organizations including the IPCC, United Nations Environment Programme (UNEP), and the World Meteorological Organizations (WMO). This drop may have confirmed the worst fears of heel-draggers that holding down emissions is incompatible with economic activity and economic growth.

Since COVID restrictions have loosened, reported United in Science, "CO_2 emissions have exceeded pre-pandemic levels recorded in early 2019."

Given lack of progress, data from UNEP synthesized by the United in Science consortium concluded, "ambition of new mitigation pledges for 2030 need to be four times higher to limit global warming to 2°C and seven times higher to get on track to limit global warming to 1.5°C." These are heavy demands, and the higher aspirational goal of limiting warming to 1.5°C, sounding slight but being grave, would seem to be neither truly within nor out of reach.

Despite advances and exploding public concern, relative to the actual exigencies of the climate change problem, near and long term, our success remains nearly nil, as does our success in crystallizing and capturing the stealthy economic drag climate change represents in generally accepted economic accounting, planning, and financial cost terms. The global economy, more than 50 years after Keeling's paper, still effectively depends on free atmospheric dirty diaper storage.

The cap-and-trade system, subsumed into the general term "carbon markets," aims to break this chain of dependency. The raison d'être of a cap-and-trade is to price carbon, meaning explicitly pricing each ton of CO_2e emitted to manifest and make financially inescapable the fact that greenhouse gas emissions are not cost-free and must fall.

Maligned as a "right to pollute," cap-and-trade actually rests more on a right to borrow a fraction of priceless "property"—the atmosphere— otherwise treated as free to occupy. Alternatively, through cap-and-trade, the atmosphere acquires the value profile of a very high-rent district, on behalf of the public.

All our routine acts harbor hidden costs of greenhouse gases but the atmosphere never charges us, and we have never charged ourselves or taken carbon atmospheric balance into ongoing economic account until the cap-and-trade system. Cap-and-trade achieves consistent and ongoing environmental improvement when, and likely only when, paired with official regulated "caps," or limits on pollution, set as mandatory by regulatory bodies, and when market rules intend to enforce and tighten that limit.

Cap-and-trade, which can also dovetail with carbon tax regimes that discourage emissions with outright public levies, is the only system that has applied financial acumen to define atmospheric scarcity and reverse the commandeering of the atmosphere as a dumping ground. Carbon markets break this habit by making it increasingly expensive to dump, and increasingly sensible economically not to.

Without a visible carbon price, pollution enjoys a free ride to the sky, an invisible hitchhiker on every ton of fossil fuel burned. The global industrial economy has coasted on the fact that we have paid no financial price for endangering the atmosphere. This means that carbon pollution adds a parasitic uncounted cost of climate change havoc to every product and process that comes into existence through burning fossil fuel—every human need for heating and cooling met, any gas tank filled, any pavement poured, any light switched on. Moreover, without an international system for transparently pricing carbon across borders and all major emitting economic sectors, there is little chance of outrunning the compounding impact of greenhouse gases and atmospheric violation.

Author Jonathan Franzen candidly and succinctly framed the scope of climate change in a pre-COP21 *New Yorker* article in 2015: "The problem here is that it makes no difference to the climate whether any individual, me included, drives to work or rides a bike. The scale of greenhouse-gas emissions is so vast, the mechanisms by which those emissions affect the climate so non-linear, and the effects so widely dispersed in time and space that no specific instance of harm could ever be traced back to my 0.0000001-percent contribution to emissions."

Franzen's dismissal of grassroots activism seemed heretic to many environmental observers, but he was right, especially about the nonlinear nature of the problem. No amount of individual action, well-intentioned but fragmented and personalized, can effectively consolidate to reroute economic activity at the scale required to excise fossil fuel prevalence.

The individual's moral impulse is best channeled and scaled up through national systems and regulatory institutions to both force and entice large entities that pollute most to pay, reduce emissions, and continue reducing. Carbon markets, designed well, can provide the necessary rigor, scope, incentives, and flexibility.

Cap-and-trade aims at sectors that emit millions of tons of CO_2e annually. such as utilities and industrial enterprises, cement, shipping, and aviation. The overall cap, and the sectors it covers, are best set by governments as a matter of environmental regulation. Emitters who run afoul of the law face fines and reputational risk and possibly criminal charges as well, depending on local regulatory variations.

What makes the cost of emitting climb, however, is the clear recognition of that original atmospheric scarcity, and that there is only so much room left for pollution. This dwindling supply in atmospheric real estate, so to speak, has become known as the world's "carbon budget"—how much more occupancy space remains in the atmosphere before the worst effects of climate change run rampantly out of control worldwide forever.

In Paris Agreement terms, staying within the global "carbon budget" looked quite taxing as of the end of 2022, given the targets and ambitions projected in the national commitments. The UNFCCC synthesis report said, assuming a 50% chance of the scenario limiting warming to 1.5°C, "cumulative CO_2 emissions in 2020–2030 based on the latest NDCs would likely use up 86 per cent of the remaining carbon budget." That scenario would leave only about two years of projected carbon budget post-2030. Holding the rise in temperature to 2°C, the report said, "in 2020–2030 based on the latest NDCs would likely use up around 37 per cent of the remaining carbon budget."

Then in March 2033, the IPCC released its latest report, shortening the running room for holding warming to 1.5o to just ten years, the goal becoming increasingly difficult, stating: "Global modelled mitigation pathways that limit warming to 1.5°C (>50%) with no or limited overshoot or limit warming to 2°C (>67%) assuming immediate action imply deep global GHG emissions reductions this decade." Either way, even to dream of staying within any reasonable budget exacts a radical and constant recognition of the value of its remaining space. That critical function cannot be left to private commercial interests. If the atmosphere is a global commons, so is the value of its scarcity.

Therefore, governments, at least nominally the most legitimate representatives of their people, must define the scarcity in the name of those people, the ultimate beneficiaries of a cap-and-trade. Governments gradually ratchet down the "cap," tightening the number of tons sent to the atmosphere, calibrating the national carbon budget as a portion of the global carbon budget.

Emissions below the collective cap are allowable; emissions above the collective cap are not. The regulatory agency overseeing the cap-and-trade system issues "allowances," colloquially known as "credits," to each emitter covered by the reduction requirement, corresponding to the emitter's allotted portion of the allowable emissions pie. Each allowance represents one ton of emitted pollutants, expressed as CO_2e.

Allowances are serialized so that they can be tracked, and each round of allowances issued is limited. Like the opening deal in a card game with only 52 cards in the deck, the only way to add cards is to cheat or counterfeit.

Caps must be set in line with environmental science if they are to generate a tangible ecological benefit. For example, how many tons of emissions need to be reduced by when to harness the climate change problem.

As governments restrict the number of tons permissible, the "supply" of usable space in the atmosphere gets tighter. In theory, as supply tightens, its value rises. So, in theory, if supply—room in the atmosphere—becomes too costly to use, with "storage costs" exceeding costs of alternatives, the default tendency to pollute is negated. Alternatives to fossil fuel use will be substituted more quickly, including investments in energy efficiency to more responsibly use fossil fuel where needed for the time being, or direct switch to renewables like solar or wind that produce little to no direct emissions and so no dirty diapers to store.

Emitters in a cap-and-trade must calculate a baseline of all their emissions covered by the regulation and then reduce emissions from that baseline. As emitters one by one manage their own carbon budget, they contribute to national carbon budgets and goals being met.

Emitters, though, have individualized starting points. Some emit heavily, others less. Some emitters burn fossil fuel directly, known as Scope 1 emissions. Others emit indirectly, by buying electricity, Scope 2 emissions. From the atmosphere's point of view, however, these are the same: my utility's direct fuel burn Scope 1 emissions would be considered my Scope 2, but only one ton of greenhouse gas is actually emitted—by the utility. Who is best positioned to reduce at scale? The utility, obviously, with a baby step of help from me, the consumer, if I press the utility to switch away from fossil fuel, but regulations on the utility have more sway and consumer taste is fickle.

While it is obviously true that household reduction of energy waste also reduces emissions and cost of household energy, household reductions fall far short of the millions of tons of reductions and removals required to meet the climate change crisis. Emissions reductions from the heavily emitting sectors with large emissions baselines are most material to trying to achieve atmospheric safety, given the shriveling carbon budget.

Cap-and-trade uses classic supply-and-demand to get at the need for major emitters to reduce their direct emissions as deeply as possible, as fast as possible, using the most effective technologies. Tightening the cap means progressively reducing the pool of available allowances. As allowance supply shrinks, allowance demand climbs and, in theory, allowance prices climb too.

This sequence gradually makes buying allowances more costly than cutting emissions directly. This stimulates each emitting entity to look for ways to reduce, to keep feeding the transition from high-carbon to low-carbon fuels and processes. Buyers in the market stir demand for the new technologies they need to deploy, as these technologies become cost-effective compared to continuing to buy allowances.

Cap-and-trade sets up a competition among emitters. Emitters who cannot keep their annual emissions below the prescribed cap for whatever reason are "short" in the market, while emitters who exceed their requirement to reduce, also for whatever reason, are "long." Short buyers cannot escape compliance, so regardless of the cost allowances prices, they must buy. The longs make money selling to the shorts, another revenue incentive to move from buyer to seller by constantly reducing emissions. In theory, reduction wins out when the price of buying allowances squeezes more than the cost of reducing emissions.

Some emitters, for whatever reason, can more cost-effectively follow their emissions diet than others. For example, a hypothetical factory can perhaps install cleaner solar power sooner or more cheaply than other emitters because the factory is new, or has ideally sloping roofs. Conversely, an aging electricity plant that must keep providing power even as it is required to reduce emissions faces high retrofit costs. Cutting emissions is likely far cheaper for the factory than the utility. Yet they are both required to reduce emissions under the regulation.

The factory is likely long in the market, the antiquated utility likely short, so they can trade allowances between each other, agreeing on a price. If costs to the utility are $50 a ton to try to retrofit and amortize those improvements, and the allowance market price remains under $50, the utility is better served by buying allowances while it gradually phases out the polluting plant. When allowance prices rise above the cost of retrofitting for the utility, it would likely undertake the retrofit.

This type of flexibility functions a bit like ligaments and tendons that cushion and connect bones. Without the fiber intermediaries, bone would scrape bone and sooner or later crack to bits. Carbon markets similarly lubricate emissions reductions, cushioning reduction schedules with a bit of extra time, as in the case of the antiquated utility. Spreading out costs can make the "bone on bone" regulatory and environmental requirements economically tolerable, while at the same time rewarding emitters who can reduce emissions enough to sell.

Brokers and commodities traders who themselves are not covered by the regulation because they are not industrial emitters buy, sell, hold, and trade allowances as any other commodity, such as soybeans or wheat. Futures and forward markets also evolve the more robust the market becomes.

However, these non-emitting market players, sometimes derisively dismissed as mere "speculators," transact allowances issued from the same shared pool and card deal, so the allowances they trade also represent emissions that remain under the cap. If "short" emitters need to buy from brokers or the market directly, that generally means that long emitters are banking their surplus, either waiting for a higher price or anticipating needing to use them for future compliance. It can also mean that sharp-eyed traders have sopped up available surplus for speculative purposes to sell back to needy buyers as caps are tightened and prices climb, down the road.

While speculation is considered a dirty game by many outside of markets, thoughtful speculation is a bona fide business, and the more participants in a market, the more "liquid." The more liquid, the lower the transactions costs, a critical plus for a carbon market where the goal is not profit per se, but achieving emissions reductions and pricing scarce atmospheric space.

Injecting liquidity to the market is vital, but critically important is to be sure the purpose of the cap-and-trade remains to advance environmental goals, and not trade for trade's sake to maximize fees earned by traders. So in well-regulated capped markets, limits are placed on how many allowances can be held by "speculators" and non-emitting trade parties.

Regardless of who owns the allowance, its price serves the same purpose—to prod emitters to shift from high carbon to low. Total emissions cannot exceed the collective target or cap because only so many allowances are in circulation.

Ideally, because cap-and-trade markets have a public environmental purpose, all trading transactions occur on regulated bona fide public exchanges, like stock exchanges, so that carbon prices are transparent and provide a constant open public market price signal. In this sense, like the atmosphere it protects, a public price on carbon is also a public service. It proclaims the "what the market will bear" price for an allowance (i.e. the minimum cost of occupying the atmosphere). A clear public price signal is essential to public trust, as well as to evaluating claims made by emitters that emissions reductions might be too costly to undertake.

Because the carbon price is a surrogate expression of the cost of actually making a reduction of a ton of greenhouse gases, a public carbon price tells the world, including the general public, what the direct costs of cutting emissions are on a given day. The carbon price also conveys the direct savings an emitter would accrue per metric ton if that ton were not emitted. A public allowance price is the most tangible expression of a "price on carbon" available that can also be credibly financially booked.

Even for emitters who are not regulated or required to comply with an emissions schedule, pricing carbon is not a foreign concept. Given the Paris agreement, all emitters know that it will never become cheaper to emit and that, sooner or later, carbon pricing will find its way to them.

Many companies do assign themselves an "internal price on carbon" or a "shadow price on carbon" to discover and illuminate their potential buy-sell position if regulations were to come into place. Microsoft was the first company in the United States to adopt this technique, in 2012. To motivate managers to reduce emissions, the company charged each department a "carbon fee" of about $7 per ton, increased to $15 in 2019, and higher for certain activities.

To reduce this extra carrying charge on their budgets, managers had to reduce their departmental emissions, pinpointing and eliminating hidden hitchhiking fossil fuel emissions. In early conversations I had with Microsoft on their internal price, I suggested they might call the price the "green cursor."

By 2023, many companies used internal carbon price calculation to preplan carbon market exposure across all their operations, even if they were not required by regulation to make emissions reductions quite yet. Companies charged themselves hypothetical carbon prices ranging from $5 per ton, a gentle exercise, to $80 or more per ton, a price consistent with the high end of European Union Emissions Trading Scheme (EU ETS) allowance prices. Matching actual market prices to hypothetical internal carbon prices is a sign of best practice and a sentinel of compliance costs likely to come.

In an actual carbon cap-and-trade, if allowance prices climb, who suffers? In the first instance, it's the "short" emitters who must buy in order to remain in compliance with reductions requirements. At some point, though, costs of full-scale transition away from fossil fuels and costs of deep emissions reductions will likely land on consumers, and it's naïve to think otherwise—for example, higher energy costs if overall fuel supply is squeezed.

However, the bite on consumers can be lessened by tax credits, exemption for low-income households, or other customized public policy adjustments. Most directly, governments can tax all carbon market–related earnings and divert proceeds from carbon trades to public purpose. Governments can also auction allowances, generating revenue, just as governments auction bandwidth for telecommunications use.

Proceeds from carbon market transactions are substantial worldwide. According to 2022 review data from the Institute for Climate Economics (I4CE), a think tank founded by the French bank Caisse des Dépôts and the French Development Agency, "Carbon revenues were nearly USD 100 billion in 2021. This represents a more than 80% increase year-on-year (USD 53.1 billion in 2020, USD 97.7 billion in 2021). This increase is largely driven by the rise in allowance prices on the European carbon market. . . . For the first time, the majority (70%) of this revenue is provided by emissions trading schemes, rather than taxes (30%)."

In January 2023, New York Governor Kathy Hochul projected new revenue of $1 billion per year from the state's expansion of its cap-and-trade system beyond the power sector only. Terming the program "cap and invest," Hochul announced the state's cap-and-trade would become economy wide, to ensure the state would meet its requirement of 40% emissions reduction by 2030 and at least 85% reduction from 1990 levels by 2050.

Cap-and-trade was invented in the US, developed and implemented in the 1970s by the US Environmental Protection Agency (EPA), in conjunction with the historic Clean Air Act. At the time, heavy smog and acid rain plagued the northeastern states due to gritty sulfur dioxide (SO_2) emissions drifting over from coal-fired power plants in the Midwest. The EPA sought to require SO_2 reductions from the plants.

Still, coal-dependent utilities protested that investment in technologies to "scrub" coal emissions would be too costly, or that the technologies were not yet viable at all, the same "go slow, don't rock our boats" claims made by recalcitrant emitters of greenhouse gases as public policy on climate change attempted to evolve throughout the post-Rio process.

However, as to proof-of-concept, as a result of the SO_2 cap-and-trade system, technologies to reduce SO_2 emissions came to market more quickly because of over-emitters' need for reduction options to comply with the act, and costs of reductions were much lower than projected. Eventually, the acid rain problem disappeared, with considerable health and other upside.

The EPA reported "annual benefits of the program in 2010 at $122 billion and costs for that year at only $3 billion(2,000$)—a 40-to-1 benefit/cost ratio." This included $119 billion in health benefits, in reduced premature deaths, chronic bronchitis, asthma hospitalizations, lost work days, and so forth, plus about $2.6 billion in improvements in overall air quality and vitality of natural resources no longer receiving caustic acid rain.

The relevance of the SO_2 cap-and-trade model to climate change got its first main exposure at the 1992 Earth Summit. I was there, but did not know that economist Dr. Richard L. Sandor, globally recognized for financial innovation, was also there.

The UN had invited him to speak on how the SO_2 program might apply, since he had advised the US EPA on the original SO_2 cap-and-trade design.

Of course, the acid rain program covered only one gas, SO_2. In contrast, greenhouse gases were at least six, each with different global warming potential and therefore different cost for emitting and value for reduction. Still, Sandor believed cap-and-trade might be adaptable to the complexity.

Sandor, known widely as the "father of financial futures" and former chief economist for the Chicago Board of Trade, is an inventor of financial markets. He is also a prominent collector of contemporary photography, which perhaps helps him visualize how markets in intangible goods can take shape. At Rio, the assembled delegates listened to Sandor's views, and the cap-and-trade idea, but went back to their Rio business. A carbon market was still an alien being to climate change policy.

By 1997, at COP3 in Kyoto, Japan, the world was more ready. The United States and other countries painstakingly negotiated the Kyoto Protocol to the original Rio climate change convention, which elevated a role for cap-and-trade systems. Political tea leaves suggested that relatively soon a global network of cap-and-trade systems would take shape, with compulsory requirements to reduce emissions under an eventual global cap. The long haul to officially ratify the Kyoto Protocol nation by nation began.

I had initially met Sandor some years earlier at a workshop convened by UN Secretary-General Boutros-Ghali, to explore ways to finance the Earth Summit's twin ambition of addressing climate change while also advancing economic development in low-income nations. As he had at Rio, Sandor tossed out the idea of trying cap-and-trade for climate change. He explained its workings and reminded attendees, drawn largely from international development banks and agencies, that cap-and-trade systems can stimulate home-grown investment in new technologies as well as various forms of revenue directly to governments, as carbon revenue data has subsequently shown.

"We will only know if we try it," said Sandor passionately. The audience nodded, but no one present picked up the suggestion.

So, in 1999, when I was named president of the Joyce Foundation, a private philanthropic foundation based in Chicago known for piloting innovation, I called Sandor right away. We were on the eve of the millennium, and Sandor's idea seemed to me to have massive intergenerational importance. Climate change was unquestionably intergenerational, and carbon pricing, not yet then much referenced, would be a concept all future generations would need to master.

In 2003, with the support of a design grant from Joyce, Sandor and his team launched the Chicago Climate Exchange (CCX), then and still, as of 2023, the world's first and only cap-and-trade system that covered all six greenhouse gases. CCX created a brand-new tradeable unit to price emissions, namely the Carbon Financial Instrument (CFI), each CFI equivalent to one ton of CO_2e. The CFI functioned as an allowance and carbon-based currency, and was the first financial tool to price carbon in US history.

CCX followed classic cap-and-trade design, a voluntary test bed to adapt it to climate change. Emitting enterprises joined CCX voluntarily but were then subject to legally binding rules. Each emitting CCX member signed a civil contract committing to reduce emissions from all its North American operations on a demanding reduction schedule, the member's individual "carbon diet." Members also agreed to trade CFIs on the CCX platform to implement reduction requirements, and follow the Chicago Accord, the governance rules of the CCX system. The accord laid out the collective "cap" and carbon budget, annual reduction requirements, and market operational guidelines.

In effect, CCX was a for-profit network of early adopters, emitters who wanted to get ahead of likely regulation and learn the ropes of carbon pricing. It was a large-scale and heady market experiment to carve out a bit of the climate change problem and bring it under control using cap-and-trade. At the time, there was no other systematic rules-based plan for greenhouse gas reduction in the United States.

When Sandor designed CCX, he was betting that the Kyoto Protocol would kick in globally and be ratified in the United States, with an eventual mandatory cap-and-trade operated under US government supervision, like the EPA SO_2 program. Sandor's business plan was to corral as many major emitters in CCX as possible, so that when emissions reductions became mandatory, that critical mass of emitters would be familiar with the CCX trading platform and stay on as customers. CCX would then integrate its operations into the mandatory system and function as any other commodities trading platform, focusing on transaction business and development of extended and related products.

Sandor's reputation for farsightedness and his powers of persuasion were such that, by 2003, when CCX actually launched, Sandor and team had convinced leading industrial companies and utilities, like Ford Motor Company, American Electric Power (the largest consumer of coal in the United States), IBM, Honeywell, Baxter Pharmaceuticals, Bayer, Manitoba Hydro, Waste Management, and others, to join CCX as charter members, the original "carbon club." This meant that these emitters chose to act as if regulated and required to reduce emissions.

As in a classic cap-and-trade, members agreed that "short" emitters that failed to meet reduction targets would buy CFIs from "long" members with surplus to sell, no matter the going price, or from liquidity providers and traders that had also joined CCX. Members also included many traders based in Chicago, a city with a long history in US grain and other prairie products commodities markets. Emitting members also submitted their emissions records to tough annual accounting oversight, and paid membership and audit fees as high as US $50,000 per year, depending on the size of the member's emissions baseline.

Why did companies voluntarily take on these obligations, without being forced by law to do so? Why choose to act as if regulated and required to reduce emissions, doable but not effortless? Because, apart from the wish to be environmentally responsible, even then smart corporate leaders understood that climate change posed operational and financial risks, and was likely to draw eventual mandatory government control. Strategic business thinkers foresaw a learning and experience need.

At the time, most companies had little knowledge of their carbon footprints and, overall, CCX offered a de facto emissions management system, unheard of at that time. To tally greenhouse gas emissions from all operations to create a CCX baseline was a useful corporate exercise, since that provided a snapshot of all potential emissions sources where regulation might require compliance. Also, reducing emissions to meet the CCX reduction schedule meant hunting out every shred of energy waste, saving money in the process, and making sure that future operational investments would not undo reduction progress and increase emissions willy-nilly.

By 2005, I had joined CCX to help expand its reach and once visited the power plant of a small college we hoped to recruit. I was given a tour of the school's on-campus energy plant by the manager. He, of course, wanted to keep energy bills as low as possible for the college. As we walked around the plant, he pointed to pipe fittings in the ceiling and said, "See that up there—that's why I can't do any better than I'm doing right now." I looked up, seeing nothing special.

"See those right angles in those corners?" he explained. "If those were curves, I could make the reductions you want." Simple engineering. More ample curves in the power ducts would enable energy to circulate more fluidly and so less fuel injection would be needed. "But we aren't making any investments in upgrades right now," he continued, "so I'm afraid we'd have to be buyers."

In this case, the utility feared the cost of buying allowances as just an added expense. Reducing emissions for the sake of climate change lost out.

That fish got away, but we caught another. An astute plant engineer at a utility in Pittsburgh was planning to upgrade insulation in power transmissions systems to remove SF6. He knew the compound was a highly potent greenhoue gas, so he called us to see about joining CCX.

The utility ran its baseline numbers and we helped calculate their buy-sell position. Findings were that over the whole CCX reduction period, the utility would likely be a net seller.

The utility joined. They had planned to make SF_6 improvements at some point, but they could monetize those improvements by selling CFIs to buyers in the market, and so CCX membership sped them along.

Recruiting industrial companies proved fascinating, because it meant a bit of detective work. We always felt that to recruit a company, we should try to know more about a company's emissions profile than the company itself. That meant digging into their annual reports, product promotion, and other public documents for touchpoints with the climate crisis.

Once, a colleague, Rohan Ma, and I visited a leading US industrial company to woo them into CCX membership. In preparation, Rohan did a full-scale analysis of the company's business line with climate change implications in mind. He made a diagram of all the intersections between the business and greenhouse gas emissions, and where membership in CCX could bring advantage.

We had scored a preliminary meeting with the chief financial officer and heads of leading departments, and our group of about a dozen met in a well-lit conference room and mini-theater. We gave an overview of CCX and then Rohan popped his blueprint on the screen.

With a laser pointer, he led the audience on a journey through their emissions landscape. Landing the light beam on this or that manufacturing location, he said, "Here are your units with major sources of emissions and this is your potential cost if you were charged for these emissions in a carbon market." He gave them a rough number based on his estimates of the company's emissions and averages for the sector, and prevailing EU prices.

Then Rohan put forward the possible business gains, again swirling his laser and pointing out images of the company's products. Highlighting their state-of-the-art smart thermostats, massive industrial filtration systems, energy-efficient heaters, and so forth, he said "These products would likely become much more in demand if there is a US regulation to cap emissions, so you may want to consider promoting them more vigorously." The company stood to become a go-to supplier of emissions reduction equipment for emitters that would seek, or be required, to reduce emissions.

Rohan went on, like a physician giving a grand rounds to other physicians on the condition of a patient. When he was done, the CFO turned to the assembled team and said, "Have we ever done an analysis like that?"

The company joined CCX and became a global advocate of addressing climate change effectively. In fact, addressing climate change became a major theme of their business since nearly all their products aimed at energy reductions of some sort.

And so we worked, company by company, speaking in general terms about reductions and in specific terms about risks and opportunities for the company. To learn to manage emissions, preplan for potential regulatory requirements, and maybe be a seller, cream on the cake, made CCX membership a bargain.

A key message we tried to get across was that carbon emissions reductions did not have to be punitive, and we felt that articulating the advantages of addressing climate change could only accelerate progress. All in all, CCX offered a home for first-mover cognoscenti eager to understand these dynamics, the potential of carbon trading, and the workings of carbon price.

Meanwhile, though, inauspicious political winds blew in the United States. Climate change deniers in the US Congress, the US Chamber of Commerce, and other influential lobbying groups pounded the Kyoto Protocol to the public as unfair to US business because it exempted developing countries, including China, from also reducing emissions. They contended American companies would be disadvantaged if they had to rein in energy use while competitors in other nations did not.

Kyoto Protocol opponents blanketed the airwaves with television ads featuring actors opening up a map of the world riddled with holes for missing developing countries, calling the Kyoto Protocol "Swiss cheese."

The Clinton-Gore administration blinked, despite being elected on environmental credentials and promises to address climate change. The administration sat on the Kyoto Protocol and never advanced it to the US Senate for ratification, fearing overall political implosion of their electoral mandate.

This left the European Union (EU) to implement cap-and-trade, even though the United States had invented the system and was its natural leader with more know-how. The EU did begin designing the European Union Emissions Trading Scheme (EU ETS), which remained the world's flagship mandatory system as of 2023.

In the United States, cap-and-trade went into eclipse until 2009, when the US House of Representatives narrowly passed the historic American Clean Energy and Security Act, known as the Waxman-Markey bill. This legislation established a national cap-and-trade system, the first time the US Congress had come anywhere near a national plan for climate change mitigation, let alone carbon pricing. However, political resistance again scuttled progress, as ominous warnings about lights going off all around America and the US economy stagnating dominated public debate. The hard-won Waxman-Markey bill languished, the Obama administration did not champion it, sufficient support in the US Senate was not cultivated, and the bill never saw the light of day in that chamber.

With Waxman-Markey stillborn, cap-and-trade, mandatory reductions, and the prospect of a national carbon price in the United States entered oblivion. Scores of market practitioners and traders left the carbon market field, erasing a decade of institutional memory, experience, and enthusiasm that climate change could be tackled.

Greenhouse gas buildup percolated along anyway. Despite national legislative failure in the US Congress, California and a consortium of northeastern US states set up local cap-and-trade systems to keep the concept alive and assert state-based control of emissions given that the federal government was making no effort. These state systems, though, suffered from lack of size, liquidity, and international connections and so, as of 2023, did not serve as stepping-stones to integrated global carbon pricing.

As for CCX, it operated throughout the political ups and downs, and strongly supported the Waxman-Markey bill. CCX grew to roughly 450 members, including high-profile companies, cities, and universities across the United States. At its peak, the capped CCX baseline of emissions was about one-third the size of the whole EU ETS, demonstrating significant appetite among a large cohort of America's emitters for climate change action, based on the prospects that, sooner or later, the United States would have to take on climate change with a coherent national approach. However, the failure of Waxman-Markey extinguished the early adopter advantage. CCX members had learned what they'd set out to, and mandatory national climate change action was no longer remotely on the horizon.

CCX completed its Phase II reduction schedule in 2008 and gradually wound down operations. In 2010, its remaining international business assets, including the European Climate Exchange (ECX), the largest futures exchange in the EU ETS, were purchased by the Intercontinental Exchange, the largest commodities exchange in the world and a major player in the EU ETS. CCX ceased to exist and no similar model ever emerged.

Still, we had laid down a critical marker. By the time of COP21 in Paris in 2015, according to a report by the International Emissions Trading Association (IETA), 90 of the national reduction plans filed heading into the conference cited a carbon market as key to achieving the given nation's overall climate change goals, nearly half.

The demise of the Kyoto Protocol in the United States was perhaps a fatal tragedy in the battle to overcome climate change, because it broke global momentum. More importantly, the political vagaries of the Clinton-Gore era were pablum compared to subsequent distressing circumstances, including the sweep of the COVID-19 virus, the Trump era's poisoned partisanship, and the 2022 invasion of the Ukraine by Russia.

Whether the freshly elected Clinton-Gore team could or should have pulled out all political stops to overcome opposition to the Kyoto Protocol remains a matter of hindsight. Regardless, the march to address climate change and price carbon in the United States was likely irretrievably set back at that point.

Not to say that cap-and-trade is the perfect system. It tantalizes with potential, but its basic operating premise—that some emitters can over-emit while others do not—riles and irks critics, who argue that the buy option lets emitters off the hook, enabling them to spend their way out of taking direct action.

Yes, of course, some polluters work harder than others to cut and avoid emissions but, if the cap is tight enough and the rigor serious, no emitter can escape the system or buy a way out forever. Also, by pricing carbon, cap-and-trade encourages the least costly emissions reductions to occur first, as sellers demonstrate the benefits of best practice, speeding its uptake, gradually herding in the rest of the emitters under the cap. As caps are tightened, laggards have nowhere to hide, as it were.

Sooner or later, the cost of making actual reductions becomes financially irresistible compared to buying allowances. Cap-and-trade does allow emitters to buy time, but not indefinitely.

Since emitters by definition have diverse emissions scope and profile, cap-and-trade offers refuge from a "one size fits all" approach, but with teeth. Considering that our suffering atmosphere is blind to which emitter spends more, which reduction technology is used, or who is driven by ethical zeal or profit motive, all that matters in a cap-and-trade is that emissions growth stops and begins to fall.

The price for allowances can fluctuate just like corn, silk, wheat, or any other commodity. In this case, the commodity is the right to deposit a limited and diminishing amount of pollution in the atmosphere, for a price.

Also, cap-and-trade design needs ongoing monitoring. Much can go wrong, and has. In its days of growing pains in 2005, the EU ETS let allowances expire from its first design phase to the next, causing prices of these allowances to plummet due to administrative shortsightedness, in turn destroying buyer assurance in long-term value of allowances.

Also in its early days, the EU ETS overissued allowances, flooding its own market, so to speak, setting caps too high so emitters barely had to cut emissions to stay below. This weak first phase achieved no meaningful emissions reductions and the overissued allowances were ridiculed as "hot air."

However, the EU ETS learned from its errors, tightened its caps, kept expanding its reach, and in 2021 covered 36% of all greenhouse gas emissions in the EU. In 2021, according to the annual Refinitiv Carbon Market report, and prior to the cut-off of fuel to Europe by Russia that disrupted energy prices, carbon trading in the EUT ETS was valued at €683 billion, 90% of the global carbon market value of €760 billion ($851 billion), a stunning proxy for the value of that year's atmospheric scarcity. For perspective, the US Department of Agriculture estimated the value of the US corn crop in 2021 at $86 billion.

On the carbon pricing front, allowance prices reached a high of €98 in August 2022, breaking through the US $100 mark for the first time in EU ETS history. This milestone is important because $100 per ton is considered a price high enough to trigger investments in costly long-term technologies needed to grapple with climate change.

On the emissions reduction front, according to the EU ETS, prior to the 2022 disruptions, through the EU ETS, emissions from stationary sources in the covered area decreased by 43% roughly since 2005, including drops due to the COVID-19 business shutdown.

In December 2022, after intensive deliberations stretching nearly through New Year's Eve, EU negotiators agreed to significantly increase the emissions reduction requirements for the EU ETS, adding coverage and refining design, setting a target of 62% below 2005 levels by 2030.

So why permit any greenhouse gas emissions at all and why not a straightforward ban on fossil fuels and guaranteed phase-out by a date certain? Because, as Jonathan Franzen wrote just before the Paris Agreement, the problem of climate change is as encompassing and complex as the global economy. Simple bans on burning fossil fuels are likely untenable in the scheme of near-term world energy use needs, and the pace that alternatives to fossil fuels can become widespread and reliable for all uses, especially heat, even given quickening pace and falling costs.

Meanwhile, as climate change tosses out weather shocks, so can unexpected politics of energy, so nefariously apparent in 2022 when Vladimir Putin punished Europe for supporting sanctions against Russia by stopping natural gas supplies. The interruption caused fossil-fuel producing countries, like Norway, an affirmed advocate of addressing climate change, to release more natural gas from its system to Europe, exposing the hard-to-shake contradictions involved in meeting the climate change crisis.

In a world in flux, progress on climate change fluxes too, and fossil fuel contingency backup systems seem unavoidable. In fact, fossil fuel backup could become even more economically valuable than fossil fuel burned, perhaps, if the world continues to use energy for political blackmail.

As our grab bag of climate policies meets a grab bag of real-world events, we try to make and accelerate change on climate issues as best as we can. A global cap-and-trade could provide a needed regular touchtone and constant global reference point through policy and political thick and thin. Still, what has undermined the essential uptake of a coherent global cap-and-trade has in some ways been its own seeming complexity, and pushback from the suspicious, righteous, and ill-informed.

Most controversial, though, relative to carbon markets is the offset component. Offsets—another reasonable idea—have been pummeled with suspicion for decades, including the comparison with the unscrupulous sale of papal indulgences, as if any action other than flat-out shutting down a fossil fuel source at the stack must be fraudulent or morally inferior abracadabra.

For one thing, offsets have laudable goals and generate financial value only if they credibly remove, avoid, or reduce emissions. If we picture direct emissions from fossil fuel burning going up and down all over the earth, like pistons in an engine, an offset in one location can logically neutralize emissions in another as long as, globally, all emissions remain within the dwindling carbon budget. The earth's atmosphere encompasses all, in a single system.

Offset projects, included in what are known as "nature-based solutions," maximize earth's natural processes to trap or neutralize greenhouse gases. Reforestation offers a classic example in that many trees by their very existence take in carbon dioxide in the normal photosynthesis cycle. In this sequestration process, a given tree of a given species can enjoin carbon dioxide emitted to the atmosphere far from that tree.

We translate emissions tonnage offset by such projects into project "credits" used like allowances, each "credit" measured as one metric ton of CO_2e. Offset credits can also be sold into carbon markets and applied by emitters to reduction goals, including a mandatory cap, at least in theory. Offset prices reflect the carbon pricing dynamic, and the market price for an offset credit should generally track with allowance prices, give or take.

Since offset projects by definition derive from natural processes, they are also a financial expression of the "going market value" of atmospherically beneficial ecosystem services, ton by ton, and perhaps the only indicator of the value of those "ecosystems services" that is not an estimate and can be reflected in actual markets daily.

The science of measuring sequestration, actual and potential, is well developed worldwide, blisteringly complex, and subject to constant undermining by vagaries. For example, a single conventionally intense storm, let alone a climate-change induced super-storm, can fell trees in a flash that had been expected to remain standing and presumed to be able to sequester carbon for years.

However, these exigencies can be anticipated and addressed in project design and contracts. The financial risks of a failed offset project or unpredictable events are the project owner's to bear, or insure against.

Verifying environmental benefits from offset projects involves scientists, accountants, field supervisors, and countless others. Numerous protocols stipulate project design and tight controls, on paper at the very least, to avoid false offset results.

Still, though, offsets suffer opprobrium such that at least two bodies appointed and self-appointed to oversee offset supply and demand felt obliged to include the word "integrity" in their names: the Integrity Council for Voluntary Carbon Markets (ICVCM) and the Voluntary Carbon Markets Integrity Initiative (VCMI). Beyond the integrity question, overblown for sure, as if offset project developers were motivated to cheat, offsets live under the scornful view that they offer an easy way out for emitters.

However, dismissive and purist arguments are also easy ways out, demoting the need to value atmospheric functions and price their demise. Reducing emissions reaching the atmosphere is such a universal task that all measures must be considered.

Offsets value the work nature has timelessly done for free, by commanding a price in the carbon market structure for that work. Put simply, as the early study of ecosystem services in Myanmar and others since show, a tree left standing can be more economically valuable than a tree cut down, if carbon prices truly value atmospheric health.

Take a typical carbon market day. An emitter may find an offset "credit" to be less expensive than an allowance reduction credit, so an emitter might win some wiggle room in its overall reduction plan buying an offset toward compliance. However, in a well-regulated cap-and-trade, emitters can turn to offsets to meet their reduction obligations only on a limited basis, keeping the pressure on achieving direct reduction emissions.

Buying offsets, too, keeps demand for diverse offset projects flowing, such as reforestation or capturing methane, one of the nastiest greenhouse gases. Because offsets are per-ton representations of ecosystem services, the financial value of nature's services mounts.

Offsets also have practical consumer appeal. For example, airlines offer passengers an option to purchase offset credits equivalent to the emissions per capita of the flight in question, establishing a "carbon neutral" account for that passenger. While these individual actions offset a minuscule number of tons per capita, they do serve to illustrate the idea of a global carbon budget.

Meanwhile, offset providers and project developers earn revenue from selling project credits into carbon markets, making project development viable, provided the given offset generates an environmental benefit that can be verified by accepted environmental and market standards.

Secondary beneficiaries of an offset market are governments that can collect tax on credit earnings. Governments can also enhance the offset pool, by offering incentives to farmers to replenish stands of trees or farmers sequestering carbon in soil by using no-till practices that do not release carbon from soil.

For example, CCX worked with hundreds of midwestern farmers and foresters from Iowa to Michigan to develop and apply protocols to account for emissions benefits from no-till agriculture and reforestation. CCX also encouraged cities to develop projects to capture methane from landfills, and reduce electricity consumption in municipal buildings and operations.

CCX was even developing a protocol to help guide the capture of methane emissions in coal mines. This type of offset would have generated tax or transaction income in coal-mining states and simultaneously helped make mining safer for coal miners since methane buildup in mines is explosive.

Methane capture offsets should have appealed to coal-mining companies and policymakers in US states such as West Virginia. However, at the time, their opposition to any form of climate change action that might invite negative blowback or cast aspersions on coal mining was absolute.

Still, even allowing for the complexities of carbon trading and despite the recognized importance of international and credible carbon pricing, the major impediment to expedient global implementation of cap-and-trade has been the too-many-cooks and perfect-is-the-enemy-of-the-good syndromes.

Despite good intentions, post–Paris and COP21 efforts among governments, nongovernmental environmental organizations, and market practitioners to establish an international global cap-and-trade have proceeded excruciatingly slowly. Progress has been impeded by fear of "leakage," emissions escaping legal control between one country and another. Common too is the taint of "non-additionality," meaning a reduction action that might have been undertaken anyway without the stick of compliance to regulations (i.e. a gold star for merely business-as-usual).

Many complaints about weakness in the carbon market system are credible, but most are overwrought relative to the climate change problem at hand. The result is that each step forward on carbon pricing has had to meet the consensus check of being environmentally sacrosanct, an impossible hurdle in the imperfect world of climate change science, atmospheric changes, political upheaval, and leadership scramble.

In the meantime, as of 2023, 30 national and subnational mandatory and compliance-based carbon markets or cap-and-trade systems were operating, covering nearly one-fifth of global greenhouse gases. But these were not linked, like individual musicians playing near but never with the orchestra. Isolated markets trap carbon pricing within national borders, and so allowances are not fungible among emitting nations even though emissions know no frontiers. Emission reduction systems confined to national boundaries are inconsistent with the global atmospheric supply-and-demand dynamic, and artificially limit allowance prices to the price tolerance of a given local market or political context. Ultimately, isolated markets dilute the value of atmospheric scarcity globally.

The absence of an integrated and reliable global cap approach also squelches investment in new long-range expensive reduction technologies such as capturing "dirty diaper" emissions before they enter the atmosphere and injecting them back into the ground, called carbon capture and storage (CCS); or sucking back emissions already situated in the atmosphere, called direct air capture (DAC). "Green hydrogen," which uses non-fossil sources to generate hydrogen, a fossil-free fuel, also requires hefty long-term investment, as do ultra-efficient nuclear plants that can recycle their radioactive waste as fuel, eliminating the dilemma of where and how to manage waste disposal. While nuclear energy carries its own set of worries, notably fear of nuclear accident, relative to fossil fuels, nuclear energy is zero emissions. Ramping up waste-free nuclear energy may become essential to containing climate change.

Demand for untried or unproven technologies remains spotty without clear price signals tied to the permanent and unrelenting pace of required greenhouse gas reductions. Emitters need to know that, over time, they will definitely be required to hold emissions in check and reduce by all available means. Carbon pricing is a key to gauging break-even points for each technology choice or option.

Global regulatory certainty would create a global need and customer base for innovations, sparking investment and driving technology costs down.

Breakthrough thinking on costs of technologies to mitigate climate change came as early as 2007, when McKinsey and Company published its famous abatement cost curve. Using various reduction schedule scenarios and climate science recommendations, McKinsey established that most emissions reductions technologies based on energy efficiency were cost-effective already at that time even with a zero carbon price, but not yet in sufficient demand. The report further concluded that many technologies would become cost-effective with a carbon price of under $50 per metric ton, and that the most far-reaching and effective reduction technologies, such as CCS, would be cost-effective at just above $100 per metric ton.

At the time, such a carbon price seemed fantasy—the EU ETS was still struggling with its early design flaws. But in August 2022, that $100 price bell did ring, only to drop again with the energy price havoc that accompanied tightening fuel supplies in the face of Russian's pipeline closures. Faced with that circumstance, Europe had insufficient energy backup. Heading into the northern winter of 2023 with fuel supplies uncertain, carbon prices as tools for mitigating climate change ranked low in public concern. Energy costs dominated.

Another double-edged confusion has been the growth of the voluntary carbon market outside a coherent globally linked system. Voluntary markets operate mostly on offset transactions, without mandatory or consistent emissions reduction rules. CCX was a voluntary system, but it required a binding emissions reductions schedule enforced through a civil contract.

Contemporary voluntary markets have no common binding obligations or reduction goals, and they exist primarily to enable one-off transactions. In a voluntary market, an emitter volunteers to set its carbon diet and reduction plan to meet that goal. The volunteer may buy offsets or not, make direct reductions or not, keep the goal one year but not the next, advance or withdraw. In a strictly voluntary market, while a specific transaction may exude integrity, no standard diet applies year to year, difficult to meet or not, with no enforceable common diet or "cap."

In 2023, though numerous emitters and companies pledged to voluntarily reach "net zero" emissions or carbon neutrality by 2030, 2040, or 2050, there was no official oversight of these goals. Without such controls, even allowing for maximum goodwill, the contribution of voluntary actions to solving the climate change problem can be in the eye of the beholder and may start and stop without scrutiny.

In 2023, the urgent task may be setting up a demonstration platform across borders to integrate voluntary and mandatory carbon markets. Such a pilot would allow kinks to be worked out transparently and globally so that voluntary actions feed and advance broader national plans and maximize efficiencies among all market participants. The whole atmosphere represents global "supply" and we, flawed and mixed-motivated as we may be, represent the global "demand."

Carbon markets, including cap-and-trade—imperfect, controversial, but exciting—are likely the only system that can help implement, rather than merely conceive, a coherent approach to addressing climate change in financial and pricing terms, both carrot and stick.

By clearly pricing carbon, markets express the value of atmospheric services so that taking up scarce atmospheric space in explicit financial terms is no longer external to an emitter's balance sheet. A carbon price functions like an online daily newsfeed on the cost of storing pollution that is otherwise above and out of sight. Buyers and sellers of allowances in a cap-and-trade must show carbon costs and earnings in their budgets and financial reports. In the process, atmospheric health is translated into the precise terms of money.

Through cap-and-trade, accounting systems "learn to speak in carbon," a universal global language represented by a new currency, the metric ton. Consequently, allowances or carbon credits could trade globally, adjusted for local and current variables just as any other currency trades across borders and fluctuates daily. Letting carbon allowances trade like other monies would mean the value of atmospheric "ecosystem services" was being specified and made financially visible for the first time in human history.

Of course, we must avoid emitting by radically improving our energy efficiency in the first place and moving faster to non–fossil fuel energy sources, self-evident givens. Yet no matter what, a certain amount of fossil fuel will be unavoidable for some time ahead, especially in poor countries that did not contribute to the original atmospheric buildup. China and India, first and third in world emitters, plead this same equity case, along with other countries where per capita greenhouse gas emissions are de minimis compared to the industrial world: for example, Egypt, barely 3 tons, or Croatia, just about 4, while 15 at the least in the United States or Canada.

Countries with low per capita greenhouse gas emissions suffer from other air quality problems regardless, and richer countries have failed to meet pledges decade after decade to invest sufficiently in renewable energy to enable poor countries to leapfrog the "carbon pollution" phase for most of their needs. While grit and SO_2, the chief components of run-of-the-mill air pollution, can be relatively easily scrubbed out of fossil fuel combustion, greenhouse gases cannot. They are indivisible from burning—diabolical freeloaders, unless we nip them in the bud.

Enter the controversy, though, and the morality question. To express in economic value terms the atmospheric scarcity with which we have been so cavalier, carbon markets do have to rely on a sense of the atmosphere as a form of possession, though owned by no one. It is true, therefore, that each ton of carbon pollution permitted does convey a discordant "right to pollute" seen as even more distasteful because these rights can be bought and sold like other commodities, with carbon marketeers making money on the trades and transaction fees.

That such rights could exist, carving up the atmosphere into user permits or rentable lots subject to financial wheeling and dealing like any other worldly product, does not sit well. Carbon markets may always draw derision like the pope's condemnation in *Laudato Si* as offering only the "guise" of action and the consignment of the common home of earth to crass commercial terms.

The alternative, though, is what we have experienced—lamentable abuse and inexcusable delay. Eliminating carbon pollution just out of moral imperative has proven far easier said than done. In dismissing or slow-walking carbon markets because they tinge us with philosophical discomfort, we suffer oversimplification derived from a fear of mistake, a naïve insistence that greenhouse gases are renegade pirates, even perhaps a paralysis of esteem for nature that can insulate us from a sense of complicity.

We are the polluters—all of us—because greenhouse gases are not extraordinary or aberrant but banal, as tied to us as our shadows, inextricable from everything we normally do. Yes, we have begun to end our economic addiction to fossil fuel. Theoretically, we can further alter our habits, as we substitute fossil-free energy sources, and eliminate cars and trucks powered by gasoline, drive less, and improve energy efficiency. Costs for solar and wind energies have fallen sharply, making them increasingly attractive economic alternatives to scouring and blasting to unearth reserves of oil and gas.

On the other hand, climate change undoes even best-laid plans. Concerning wind energy, for example, temperature extremes are suspected of lowering wind speeds, causing a once unheard of "wind drought" at times, threatening an even more unfathomable condition called "global stilling." A globally stilled world, obviously, could not count on wind energy, much as we may wish.

Climate change boxes us in, surrounds us with nagging trade-offs. Progress to meet the problem does proceed worldwide, but unevenly and insufficiently. Each nation faces unique energy and social needs, each new technology its limitation, and varied cost—each answer, its question. So we dither even as we try hard.

It may well take several generations to make a complete transition out of current fossil fuel–based economic norms, if we ever can, especially given the paralysis that grips the world on this and virtually every other topic of global importance.

Despite constant prescient warnings from scientists that there would likely be dangerous side effects of continued fossil fuel dependence, greenhouse gases steadily entered the atmospheric penthouse, where they lingered, to be dutifully counted and monitored. International experts issued regular evidence of increasing concentrations of greenhouse gases in the atmosphere, but still climate change became a turf of debate and denial. Ideology played a crucial role in maintaining that ignorant resistance, and rabid fossil fuel lobbyists worked hard against coherent greenhouse gas emissions regulations.

Resistance to addressing climate change also got a strong toehold because, by definition, the scientific method of proving cause and effect is slow and out of sync with electoral cycles, not to mention financial cycles where investors make decisions on where and how to invest capital annually, quarterly, and, with digital markets, even in nanoseconds at lightning speed. Scientific evidence rolls along on one track, while money moves on another path altogether, parallel and largely indifferent.

To honestly give teeth and power to climate science, these tracks need to merge, and finance needs to join forces to meet the urgency, complexity, and scope of the climate change problem. The language of science needs to be credibly and equitably reflected in the language of money, and carbon markets and carbon pricing are imperative dialects.

Environmental progress needs a jolt, perhaps akin to the breaking power of interference colors in the color palette that skip and roil among the wavelengths to frazzle familiar reds, blues, and yellows, achieving new and unexpected vibrance. Interference colors are not pigments themselves, but flecks of mica that refract and play with light. When mixed with familiar colors, interference colors add and diffuse sheen, disrupting known color patterns.

Perhaps carbon markets are a form of interference green to refresh the optic and admit the serious valuing of scarcity. The ultimate role of a cap-and-trade system is to price use of the infinitesimal sliver of outer space that keeps our planet alive, and to indirectly transfer financial value to that sublime wisp, to slow down our dangerous and indifferent use. Without that price at work, our only way out of full-blown climate change is to invent an entirely new atmosphere, defying all known limits of physics, ecology, planetary science, and human endeavor.

Given that we have lost so much vital time in addressing climate change, all presumptions warrant regular critique and review, and the ideal solution is no longer attainable, leaving perhaps only the "less pleasant and rational" corrective measures that Charles Keeling predicted in 1970.

Are we destined to circumstances where all we can do is let climate change settle in as the normalization of extremes?

The dichotomies are vivid, certainly, but as mad as it may seem, maybe it is the cold-blooded nature of pricing that can—if properly designed, administered, and overseen—bring warm-blooded outcomes to rescue livability on our fragile planet, the ultimate one-of-a-kind.

7

Dare to Surmount: China Joins the Marathon

When you want to learn something, go to China, said an ambitious young banker from Nigeria as we bobbled along in a rusty bus headed to Yan'an, the original stronghold of Mao Tse-tung himself. Her imam back home had offered this sturdy counsel. Some years later, in my pursuit of carbon markets in China, that advice poured back into the new swirl of China's opening to finance and market experimentation.

The prize was the gold, an original adventure, the chance to negotiate a landmark deal that would set up China's first pilot carbon market and cap-and-trade system, bringing carbon pricing to China and catapulting carbon pricing worldwide. By 2007, founder and CEO of the Chicago Climate Exchange (CCX), Richard Sandor, and I, then executive vice president for recruitment at CCX, had attended various drawn-out discussions about next steps in carbon pricing since CCX opened in 2003. We felt success in China could speed progress and maybe save the world a decade on gripping the climate change problem.

Ever thinking ahead, Sandor envisioned a CCX in China as the vital stepping stone to a global cap-and-trade. China's national greenhouse gas emissions were roughly 5 billion tons and poised to surpass US emissions. In the United States, carbon markets were still politically alive, and the EU ETS perked along. If China entered the family, we believed its sheer size would significantly advance the crafting of a tight global carbon budget and the trading of emissions credits as seamlessly as currencies, with emissions reductions occurring nation by nation each year.

Environmental issues were cresting within China too. China's leaders seemed on the cusp of admitting to their country's environmental problems, as if they were not already undeniable to the Chinese people and the rest of the world. A "clean air day" made national news.

At the time, China was running at full tilt, posting a nearly 12% projected economic growth rate in 2007–8. Still, the air in China was more like smoke, including in Beijing at the center of national power, an incontestable advertisement for the stark need for improvement. Smog was so constant and dense, especially in winter, that when I licked my lips I tasted metallic car exhaust.

Big projects drove decisions, though, as China invested massively in infrastructure such as high-speed trains, national highway networks, sprawling industrial cities in far-flung provinces, and gargantuan slate and marble office and apartment buildings driving the real estate sector.

On the other hand, Chinese manufacturing was reeling from headlines exposing contamination of exports, such as poison paint on toys and toxic drywall. A leadership step on climate change could help neutralize the impression that China's industrial environmental, safety, and regulatory standards fell below international norms. Favorable too was China's newly intent glance at developing its financial services sector, with capital markets fledgling and commodities markets nonexistent, to align with international systems.

Carbon markets would be an oblique entry into deeper market-based experience, a further experiment with capitalism itself, but run on a track outside the momentum of the main economy, so no harm done if it failed.

Through the introduction of a colleague in China, Jeff Huang, we had found a vein of avant-garde thinking in an unlikely setting—PetroChina, the largest company in China at the time by market cap, through its subsidiary China National Petroleum Corporation (CNPC). These giant fossil fuel operations were thinking ahead and, like CCX members in the United States, wanted to learn the ropes of carbon trading, which they believed had to come one day.

They invited us to visit China to begin discussions, and at the first meeting, a key official said, "In China now there is more emphasis on environmental protection . . . conditions are conducive for us to discuss details of possible cooperation with you." That we might move such leviathans down the path of environmental leadership, let alone interest them in helping set up CCX-China, the first market joint venture of its kind there, was irresistible.

We began our CNPC collaboration, and our partners set up one road show after another, to build allies and lay track for the industrial, cultural, commercial, and, above all, political approval we would need. We became ubiquitous in China, eventually known everywhere we went as "Dr. Sandor" and "Miss Paula."

I got caught in the crazy wheels of working in China. China was always on, answering calls day or night, seeming never to take a break or cut any slack. In the *China Daily,* the "go-to" paper for English-speakers in China, I once spotted an ad placed by a firm recruiting for an executive secretary who had fluent written and spoken English and was also "willing to skip meals without complaining." That felt familiar. Pre-smart phones, yet so busy with calls, I had two flip phones, one in each pocket. One day I was so frazzled and crazed with tasks, I actually called myself, one pocket to the other.

Though our plan for a CCX in China was a flight into the unknown, and the climate change problem vast, we bit off our piece and headed out. Our mantra was "just get started."

Go to China to learn something, indeed. As much as I had been impressed on my first visit to China in 1999 by the crackling momentum of the country, I still felt it would take China a while to catch up to the West. After all, I thought, how fast can a country develop if so many people still handle sales with an abacus?

What innocence.

"Dare to Surmount" read a billboard at the Beijing airport just outside the parking lot when I arrived for CCX to take up our China carbon market quest in earnest. Every day after that, I lived that sign, working through the labyrinth of Chinese business mysteries and lazy Susan meals.

China took over. I felt China and I were two distinct circles spinning along, at times interlocking harmoniously, then off spinning separately again. I had no control over when the Chinese circle took over mine, nor could I enter the China circle when I felt like it. China managed both circles.

On one trip, I stayed so long in China to try to make the most of my every minute that I had to fly around the world to arrive on time for another unrelated but long-planned meeting in Minneapolis to try to recruit a major company to CCX. I calculated which direction away from China would gain me the time I needed to get me to the meeting on the right day, like Jules Verne's Phineas Fogg in the classic *Around the World in 80 Days*. I flew east to catch the dateline gain, 5,000 miles in 10 hours, a night gone to make two Sundays. For me that year it was December 9 for what felt like 48 hours.

I did not think anything of it. Eventually, I always flew through Finland—the shortest route from Europe to Asia said Finnair, which was also pioneering lowest-emission routes and fuels. It seemed so elegantly efficient to slip over the dome of the planet from the today of America to the tomorrow of China.

Once regular coming and going to Asia enters your life, the globe feels the size of the palm of your hand.

Ultimately, we did open that first pilot in 2008 in the coastal city of Tianjin. The Tianjin Climate Exchange (TCX) and China later set up six other pilot markets around the country to study and dissect. In 2021, China took to the world carbon market stage. In July of that year, China launched the national cap-and-trade system it had been germinating since our first forays there.

Dreamers the whole way, we had the rough idea at the outset to adapt the CCX model on a semi-voluntary basis in China, recruiting foreign and national members, while also weaving within, and concurrently trying to divine, China's volatile national policies and moods. Various large corporate CCX members, such as DuPont, operated in China. They would have to comply with China's evolving climate change directives, and we believed would want to be part of the learn-by-doing example of China's first carbon market, as they did.

The CCX experience offered reasons for hope. CCX had grown emitter by emitter, pitch meeting by pitch meeting, and its first phase was humming along. Before we could recruit members in China, though, we needed a viable business structure. A true joint venture would be in itself path-breaking since, to that date, no US-based entity held shares in a Chinese financial services company, which a carbon market would be.

The deal division of labor we reached was that CCX would provide carbon market expertise, CNPC cash plus staff, and the city of Tianjin, eager to situate itself as a financial hub, would provide a home office for TCX and its electronic trading platform systems.

However, from the start, though we were all three willing and congenial partners, that CCX was a foreign entity shadowed our dealings, especially since our market design role and responsibility meant we would acquire information such as Chinese emissions data, considered the equivalent of state secrets at the time. The fact that we were not Chinese elicited chronic suspicion among the more conservative political officials who, despite our influential Chinese partners, remained mixed minded about forays into capitalism and Western ways, let alone unprecedented environmental markets.

The legal dimensions of deal-making in China then were dazzlingly demanding. For months, we and our attorneys marched through the joint venture documents, point by point, page by page. At our seats at the shining mahogany conference table in the CNPC boardroom, lovely blue-and-white lidded porcelain cups always waited, and an ever-present hostess silently slipped in and out to keep the cups brimming with green tea. She came up right to my elbow anytime I took a sip, ready to refill.

We broke punctually for lunch, but I soon realized that mealtimes were subtly cordial extensions of the negotiations where we could recover whatever good karma had been drained away at the hard-edged long table. Lunch could be more important than the formal sessions by far.

Meals revealed a lot about your person and how tough or wily a negotiator you really were. Could you:

- Make pleasant small talk?
- Amuse the others?
- Handle chopsticks with aplomb?
- Not drop grains of rice onto the tablecloth?
- Enlighten with any useful gossip or information about the outside world?
- Spin the lazy Susan serving dish at just the right time but not too fast, or when someone else was about to pitch into a dish?
- Propose eloquently artful toasts?
- Clink your glass below the rim of your toastee out of due deference?
- Stand up and begin to toast the underling table, but not before toasting the superiors?
- Hold your alcohol?
- Be back sharp as a tack for the afternoon session and pick up the same points exactly where they had been left off, remembering to incorporate the sidebar points made at lunch? ("Miss Paula, I know you feel strongly about shifting the vote ratios for board decisions, but here is why it has to be our way.")

When do you give in, hold firm, or walk out?

I tried to respond to complexity with simplicity. So had US President Richard Nixon when he dramatically broke the Cold War freeze and visited China, reestablishing US-China relations after decades of enmity and Chinese isolation. I had read that when the tense negotiations overwhelmed Nixon, he retired to his suite with a legal yellow pad on his lap to write up the day's ins and outs on one page, divided into three sections: "What we want; what they want; what we both want." I adopted this boiled-down rubric, which worked to calm me for a time.

Each day was an eye-opener. One day we received an invitation to meet with a research group of China's Development Research Center (DRC), the academic and intellectual advisory body on strategic issues reporting directly to China's State Council and Communist Party. All we were told was that the group wanted to meet with Richard. In fact, nearly daily, an unexpected meeting landed on our agenda, either because our topic was so fluid and fascinating or to keep us a bit off balance—I never knew which.

At the DRC, we expected to provide a carbon markets 101 session, and enumerate what the advantages to China would be. A poker-faced usher guided us to a large seminar room where at least 50 officials were assembled, coiled up with scrutiny, ready to let go. Seated in the middle of the dais, a woman struck the pose both of student and professor and acted as emcee. She was an economist and vice president of the DRC, also well armed with inquiry.

For an hour or so, Richard held forth as if at a tennis match, one question lobbed after another about environmental markets, their prime function, our thoughts about why China would be a worthwhile setting. They especially grilled Richard about derivatives trading and his work on interest rates from his Chicago Board of Trade days, about which they all seemed fully briefed.

We later learned that the DRC had been studying carbon markets for more than a decade as an academic construct, and that our appearance on the scene caught the eye of the State Council as an actual working example. We would also learn, of course, that we would never have gotten a toehold with TCX if the State Council had not signed off on the try. PetroChina was, after all, state-owned. In fact, as part of our TCX proposition, we had tossed out the idea of PetroChina also recruiting an international consortium of other state-owned oil companies around the world who would agree to cap and reduce emissions and trade on

TCX. No such idea could have advanced an inch without State Council sign-off and in fact this extra layer of action we proposed never did.

At the DRC we felt we were in a seminar at any significant US university where seasoned faculty interrogated a new faculty member's research hypothesis. Gradually, we saw carbon markets in China were not virgin theoretical territory at all, but definitely in need of a practical spark. It became clear that we were to serve that purpose.

The same holding-forth format applied when we were invited to meet the heads of the China Securities Regulatory Commission (CSRC), the government ministry of China's State Council that oversees China's securities industry, then fairly undeveloped, and the China Banking Regulatory Commission (CBRC), authorized by the State Council to oversee China's banking sector.

At each meeting, the CEOs of these paramount government entities were gracious and in no rush, again probing Richard about US securities law, market development, the evolution of derivatives, and other financial instruments. They knew their files and many details of Richard's Board of Trade history.

Gradually I began to get the drift—at each meeting our Chinese hosts inspected us, kicking our tires, at the same time as we provided information and experience in informal settings. We were climbing the ladder to our deal to which rungs were always being added and none of which we could skip.

On with the road shows, back and forth from the United States to China. On one trip, we also had several sessions at the China Quality Certification Center (CQCC), whose mandate was to monitor and help develop international industrial performance standards and feed them into China's manufacturing plans. On this sprawling campus, the CQCC was training roughly 1,000 staff in the basics of carbon accounting. Measuring and tracking greenhouse gas emissions would be a critical skill not only for cap-and-trade where emissions baselines and reduction measurements were basic, but also to calculate the emissions savings from low-energy industrial products that China planned to manufacture and export, such as more efficient toasters, computers, light bulbs, electric vehicles, solar panels, wind turbines, and so forth.

At the time, we did not fully understand we were a relatively minor thread in the vast tableau that was China's conviction to lead the low-carbon economy in the 21st century. We were not the only advisors on carbon markets. Consultations were ongoing between the EU ETS and various Chinese officials, and nonprofit organizations, including the US-based Environmental Defense Fund (EDF), offered opinions as China made its carbon market plans.

Still, we were the only entity trying to set up a business and an actual emissions reduction trading system.

I stopped counting the number of meetings and meals we attended with ministries and official agencies, plus presentations at universities where hundreds of students were often in the audience, all posing complex, well-researched queries. It was obvious that after a few graduating classes, an expertly versed inspired generation could take any carbon market system China sought to established to maturity and world-class stature.

We found the preparation phase fascinating, a truly inside look at China's climate change thinking, and we stuck patiently with negotiations even as they dragged out. Then, on one critical negotiating trip when I thought our agreement was close to being finalized, I hit a wall. I had to head home empty-handed earlier than planned because our joint venture discussions broke down on a critical contractual point, a serious impasse.

I had learned something in China about saving face, and I knew I would lose face by lingering. I announced that in view of the lack of compromise, I would be leaving China the next day. The Chinese did not melt. On the contrary, my counterpart gladly offered me a car to take me to the airport.

Though I knew and had confirmed with Richard by phone that we could not give in on the point, I still woke with the awful feeling of failure. As I waited in my hotel lobby to depart, I gazed at the magnificent miniature ivory carving of the "10,000 Miles of the Great Wall" I had mostly just walked past each day. I must have exuded sadness because the dawn-duty receptionist came out from behind her desk to admire the object with me, as if she knew intuitively that I was going home without what I had come for. Perhaps she knew from other sources, too—I always wondered if the walls had ears and how much privacy I actually had.

Our deal went dormant, followed by a few months of silence. Then, out of the blue, in midsummer 2008, my negotiating counterpart called from China to tell me that the impasse had dissolved, and the partners were ready to sign the contracts. The joint venture was suddenly, amazingly, formed. We had indeed created a three-way bargain between CNPC, CCX, and the city of Tianjin, giving birth to the Tianjin Climate

Exchange (TCX), China's first emissions trading market, and we would be the first US enterprise to own equity in a Chinese financial institution, experimental though it was.

Months of angst had dissolved in an instant of "yes," and things sped up. Now legal documents flew across the digital universe overnight. In Chicago, Richard signed 26 electronic copies of the contract. Some weeks later, he was also asked to sign 26 hard copies, the Chinese loving tangible paper backup.

After the cyber-flurry, our partners still wanted to seal things with a personal touch, and they summoned me to China for a formal contract signing ceremony. "Please come, Miss Paula," said the entreaty.

I'd have to get in and out of China before the mass influx of athletes, tourists, and dignitaries arrived for the summer 2008 Olympics, and the timing meant a four-day round-trip into the hellish heat of Beijing. But how could I refuse, when finally the deal seemed done?

Red and gold banners fluttered at the ceremonial venue in Tianjin, a sprawling marble and brass-trimmed hotel and international center. Outside, hostesses pinned everyone with a red carnation boutonniere, and inside the ambiance floated between intoxicating success and strict protocol.

When the CNPC brass arrived, together we were ushered into the main VIP room, where we made small talk and drank tea. Then a group of handlers gently guided us into the main hall, where we joined local and national officials standing ramrod straight in three rows on a stage, including me in the first row with our TCX counterparts. As the VIPs spoke in Mandarin, Jeff Huang discreetly whispered the translation into my ear. When my turn came to speak, I offered profuse thanks and high-minded comments about the historic nature of the undertaking.

A hundred or so honored guests attended the celebratory lunch, and waiters weaved efficiently among the crowded archipelago of tables. Then, just as the final course was being cleared, gong! An abrupt brass chime end to lunch.

I was driven back to Beijing through the endless molasses of pre-Olympics traffic, the high-speed train back to Beijing double and triple booked that day. Because of the Olympics love-fest, hotel rooms had been hard to come by at late notice, so I had to book a hotel far in the northwestern corner of Beijing, a building so new it was still partly under construction.

I was spent from the heat and post-ceremony tension release, but couldn't help but get into the upbeat mood of the Olympics when the hard-working bellman said to me in his prideful English, before taking another incessant call about a defect in an unfinished room, "Excuse me, my cell phone is *singing*."

I arrived back in Helsinki the next day just in time to watch the Olympic opening ceremony live from Beijing on TV. Pixels were fuzzy, but when I pecked around for better reception, I landed instead on the real-time invasion by Russian troops of South Ossetia in the former Soviet state of Georgia—a practice run perhaps for Russia's march into the Ukraine in 2022. On the screen, armed tanks rolled across a national border while only one TV channel notch away, the world was in thrall to Lang-Lang on the piano in Beijing and dozens of performers clad all in black dancing as if notes of calligraphy across a square mile of pure white silk.

I slept the sleep of the dead that night.

The August contract-signing ceremony was nothing compared to the day when TCX actually opened its doors that fall. That was practically an affair of state. Richard Sandor attended this event, of course, and we were both agog at the effort to which our partners had gone.

They commandeered the roadways, arranging for giant posters on all highways giving directions to the new TCX office in downtown Tianjin so that visitors would not get lost in the maze of Tianjin's roads. Such were the feats that the well-connected and powerful in China then could pull off.

The TCX office in the heart of Tianjin's brand-new financial center was festooned with swaths of red silk ribbons, China's good luck color, and packed with giant bouquets and congratulatory gifts of all kinds. A squad of young women called "shiny girls" lined up to host and greet, all wearing red. The ceremony was ultra-formal, with speeches by key figures and standing-room-only visitors, though I suspect some had been paid or ordered to attend. The VIPs stood shoulder to shoulder in protocol order along the curtain line of the stage.

After obligatory congratulations, the CNPC principals grouped together for yet another photo around the shiny bronze "here's to the birth of TCX" plaque. Then, to top it off, they lit the fuse of a mini-cannon that shot a rain of glittering red and gold confetti. That evening we had an elaborate partners dinner with cascading toasts and festive pronouncements. When the mayor of Tianjin circled the table to tip his glass to me, he said he had been impressed with my spirit and energy "from the beginning." When I pointed out that I had saved up the

Mandarin-style silk jacket I was wearing for just this occasion, he replied politely, "Well then it belongs in a museum."

The official embrace of carbon markets by China not only signaled the importance of China's environmental leadership ambition but also furthered acceptance of international market norms, such as accounting rigor, reliable price discovery, and transparency of information.

TCX began limited operations, but despite our ownership and role as expertise provider, local staff soon took off on their own decision-making, conducting "trades" as if they were just straight-up barters among local companies. The original idea of designing a compliance structure was put on hold, pending a more explicit and clearer national policy signal. Suddenly, political ambivalence on a greenhouse gas cap-and-trade seemed to be lurking and filtering down. Still, an electronic platform was set up, and TCX went into business of sorts, including handling sulfur dioxide "permits" on a somewhat rudimentary basis.

The circle of China spun as it would, and we devolved into hopeful observers. Though the CCX team spent much time in Tianjin advising and training the staff, the CCX model was never implemented.

In the end, though, we had broken joint venture ground and TCX, backed so publicly by a state-owned enterprise, firmly legitimized the cap-and-trade concept. Within a year or so, other pilot programs in Shanghai, Hubei, Shenzhen, and Beijing had opened offices, too. Then, however, the yin of China's momentum met the yang of US inertia.

When the Waxman-Markey bill died in the US Congress at the end of the 2010 Congressional session, so did any realistic hope for a national cap-and-trade in the United States, and the linchpin for a credible global cap-and-trade. This legislative demise also meant CCX too came to an end and the vision of CCX in China was not to be.

At the end of the year, when ICE bought the assets of CCX and its parent company, Climate Exchange PLC, it acquired TCX as well. Having its own business in China already, ICE sold its TCX shares back to CNPC.

Though the first Obama administration had failed to fully get behind Waxman-Markey, in 2015, the second Obama administration tried to get the United States back on the leadership track to address climate change. This included forging a strong bilateral partnership with China, especially as China had continued to dominate key related industries such as renewable energies, low-carbon materials, solar panels, electric vehicles, and others.

Heading into COP21 in Paris, the world needed a breakthrough. Francois Hollande, president of France, and colleagues in the French government with long-standing experience in the ways of the UN on climate change, such as Foreign Minister Laurent Fabius and Special Ambassador Laurence Tubiana, took COP21 as an event of personal honor. Christiana Figueres, who led UNFCCC, applied her powerhouse energy to racking up national pledges one after the other, hoping they would knit together to become well more than the sum of the parts. She was right, and the much vaunted "Paris Agreement" emerged.

However, by far, the world looked to the United States and China to set irreversible international momentum, and, for a shining moment, they did.

By COP21, China had stored up its accumulated knowledge of cap-and-trade like a geyser, preparing for a national approach. The Obama administration, recognizing that the US Congress would not act to establish a national reduction requirement, tapped into executive branch powers to design the Clean Power Plan, which proposed emissions standards, at least for US power plants. For months the Obama White House, notably the president's chief of staff, John Podesta, worked closely with the government of China to bring American and Chinese efforts into sync and ready for Paris unveiling.

In Paris, the Obama administration did officially announce its Clean Power Plan, and China officially announced its intention to put a national cap-and-trade in place. China's Minister of Environment, Xie Zhenhua, walked around the Paris conference with the proud look of a new father. I had met Xie in China several times and tailed him to say congratulations and thanks. He also served as vice chair of the key policy authority, China's National Development and Reform Commission, and had been among the many officials to green-light the TCX experiment.

The world glowed with optimism that China and the United States, the world's two biggest emitters, had at last committed to meaningful synergistic actions. The announcement of a national cap-and-trade in China was indeed a great leap forward considering that China had no other commodities markets in place at the time. Still, from our experience with the opening of TCX, we knew pieces could be lined up feverishly once the political signal illuminated.

Then a death blow: Donald Trump's election to the US presidency in 2016.

Unfortunately, despite the success and fresh will and verve the Paris agreement exuded, Trump's election cut it all off in the United States, including the sense of new US–China collaboration. Trump instigated a round of trade wars with China and a stream of anti-China rhetoric, canceled Obama's Clean Power Plan, and used a scornful Rose Garden speech to abandon the Paris consensus. Then China, more or less in a "so there" response, tacitly postponed the launch of its cap-and-trade, further highlighting how environmental issues become geopolitical levers and surrogate issues for other swirling tensions.

Finally, however, after the election of Joe Biden to the presidency in 2020, and the return of the United States to the Paris Agreement, China's national cap-and-trade opened for operations in July 2021. A mandatory system, at first it would cover only the power sector, including coal plants, CO_2 only, but a whopping 4 billion tons of emissions plus 2,000 companies with small baselines of at least 26,000 tons of CO_2 emissions per year. In the first year, China's system transacted nearly 194 million tons of China emission allowances (CEAs), the Chinese tradeable unit.

Gradually, China's market would require compliance and reductions from all industrial sectors in China, an unprecedented scope and size globally with extraordinary potential to rein in China's greenhouse gas emissions and influence global carbon market activities. A cap-and-trade system covering all of China's industrial economy would be the largest commodities market, as it were, in the history of the world.

Prices in China, however, were not free-floating and tracked close to the low end of global voluntary market prices.

In the first year of emissions trading in China, the CEA price fluctuated between €6 and €9, climbing 20% in the first year since opening day. For comparison, in 2021 in the EU ETS, the first year after reform of the system to tighten allowance supply, average cash spot price for EUAs was just under €40.

The EU ETS and China's system is far from apples to apples. Chinese market regulators can establish price ceilings and limit trading days, so the market remained a well-controlled experiment with heavy government oversight, involvement, and, some might say, manipulation.

The China cap-and-trade can also seem like a bit of a sweetened pot, in that it does not require emissions reductions in absolute terms (i.e. reductions of physical tons purely) but instead reductions measured in reduced "carbon intensity" (i.e. reduction in physical tons emitted per economic unit of output). This means a first emphasis on fossil fuel efficiency rather than fossil fuel elimination outright.

For example, we can take one refrigerator as an economic unit and suppose that half an absolute ton of carbon dioxide is emitted from start to finish to manufacture that fridge, including mining of ore for steel, transport, production of steel, and fabrication of the refrigerator. If the manufacturer reduces emissions in the production chain so that two refrigerators can be manufactured but still only half a ton is emitted, a 100% reduction in carbon intensity has occurred. Half a ton still hits the atmosphere, but now that half ton of emissions has supported double the economic work, two fridges for the emissions of one. Double earnings on the same emissions level means that an increase in economic output has occurred without emissions growth.

Such decoupling of emissions growth from economic growth is a nirvana of climate change mitigation because it splits economic nor-mal economic activity, including jobs creation and the prosperity people hope for, from continued reliance on fossil fuel. If reasonable economic growth can be maintained without increasing emissions, and as emis-sions fall, an economy-climate steady state could be reached, the true incarnation of net zero emissions, likely elusive but surely a carbon emis-sions ideal.

All in all, China began its market trading intensity tonnage units rather than absolute tonnage units, perhaps to express its autonomy and to stand out from all other carbon markets. Ultimately, however, a trove of emissions management knowledge can be yielded by the intensity approach.

As power plants and manufacturers in China are forced in a cap-and-trade to cap and reduce carbon intensity, but also expected to keep up productivity, they will have to be quite inventive in using less carbon, and perhaps adopt best-in-class procedures quickly.

Driving down carbon intensity product by product, yuan by yuan, could also in theory catalyze potential commercial benefits for prod-ucts made in China under intensity reduction rules, perhaps earning them a sales advantage if they can be marketed as less carbon intensive than competitors. Many manufacturers worldwide calculate the carbon intensity of given products so they can understand the product's whole "carbon footprint," but only China is attempting a carbon market cap-and-trade using intensity as the tradeable unit.

In this sense, an intensity cap-and-trade can work to decarbon-ize economic activity both at the process and product level and push Chinese products to the forefront.

The intensity metric is not fungible with markets based on absolute tonnage reductions, a disconnect that could isolate China's market, even as other markets press toward global integration. Still, recognizing this, as China moves its market eventually to scale, China could keep and publish carbon accounts in both intensity and absolute terms. In fact, to determine carbon intensity, absolute tonnage must first be calculated—it is the denominator. So, not to wildly oversimplify, it is just one calculation to translate intensity back to absolute metric tons so that China's market could eventually engage in global transactions. Harmonization, in other words, is not mission impossible.

Plus, sooner or later, in the real life of the atmosphere, over time, reduction in absolute tons has to occur as a result of reductions in intensity. At some point the reduction trend lines have to both head down, or China's entire cap-and-trade exercise will have been for climatological nothing.

China has been leaning toward trading intensity reductions units rather than absolute tonnage for at least since the first TCX days. In fact, a leading Chinese policy expert involved in designing what would become China's national market asked CCX for advice on this as early as 2008, and a CCX principal, Michael Walsh, who is expert at market design, responded with suggestions.

For sure, intensity reductions can seem less onerous than absolute reductions, a kind of have-your-cake-and-eat-it-too situation, but in terms of valuing atmospheric scarcity and gauging comparative impact of one economic activity over another, China's intensity approach may prove highly educational for the rest of the world. Through the Paris agreement at the least, all nations will face choices on which economic activities to continue or phase out, relative to climate change and emissions impacts.

In the end, how do we balance the negative environmental impact of an economic activity against the profit it generates, the need it meets, or pleasure it brings, and to whom? Such choices are not coming maybe tomorrow—they are well arrived.

In early 2023, for example, France introduced a plan to eliminate all flights between cities already linked by train journeys of less than two and a half hours because the carbon intensity of aviation surpasses train travel significantly. Plenty of protest ensued, from airline companies and the general public, but does the plan not make environmental sense?

China's public reduction targets are to reduce carbon emissions per unit of GDP by 18% by 2025, compared to 2020 levels, then to peak CO_2 emissions before 2030, while lowering CO_2 emissions per unit of GDP by over 65% from 2005 levels. These goals are very ambitious and mean cutting out significant fossil fuel use. They are tricky to calculate and even trickier to monitor, and China is regularly criticized for inadequate verification of reduction claims made by companies covered in the national market, a potentially lethal vulnerability to the market's environmental benefit and credible trading within or beyond China. If reductions, whether intensity or absolute, cannot be verified as having occurred, likely they did not—carbon accounting is relatively well developed and physical measurements can also be taken.

Devices known as continuous emissions monitors (CEMs), installed literally on smokestacks tracking actual emissions in real time, can easily verify CO_2 output accurately. CEMs have been installed on US power plants at least since the original acid rain program under the US EPA. In China, CEMs have been much discussed, including in discussions with the US EPA, but were not widely installed, though they would greatly help resolve what is known as the "monitoring and verification" (MRV) problem that haunts China's carbon market as observers remain skeptical of China's compliance rigor.

Charges of poor MRV have not escaped China's highest political levels. In fact, in October 2022, President Xi Jinping, in his report to the 20th National Congress of China's Communist party entitled "Hold High the Great Banner of Socialism with Chinese Characteristics and Strive in Unity to Build a Modern Socialist Country in All Respects," said crisply, "We will improve the statistics and accounting system and the cap-and-trade system for carbon emissions." This could likely include the installation of CEMs, made in China.

Beyond MRV details, though, Xi laid out China's overall approach to its climate change commitments: "Reaching peak carbon emissions and achieving carbon neutrality will mean a broad and profound systemic socio-economic transformation . . . we will advance initiatives to reach peak carbon emissions in a well-planned and phased way in line with the principle of building the new before discarding the old." Xi added that China would "transition gradually toward controlling both the amount and intensity of carbon emissions."

These are tall orders. China's cap-and-trade may be imperfect and stand-alone, but still its raison d'être is to safeguard the invaluable atmosphere above that cannot indefinitely absorb greenhouse gases emitted from economic activities below.

For the foreseeable future, China's carbon market will likely serve to smooth out past and future energy use practices, as Xi said, to build the new "before discarding the old" while also driving toward economic growth targets.

When we were introducing TCX to potential users, including high-emitting companies, I vividly remember a meeting with five gentlemen who came to our hotel in Beijing. They all wore heavy clothing and boots as if just coming in from rugged terrain, clipboards in hand. They were the CEOs of China's five largest coal companies who were spooked by what they had heard about cap-and-trade. They wanted to better understand how they could keep burning coal and still follow what they expected would be a governmental order to get involved with the carbon market.

"How can we stay in business with this system," they asked, sharply, "and how do we keep making money?"

Despite the "great banner of socialism," the profit motive is baked into China's economic planning and business management, and industrial leaders will feel the pressure to keep up. They could resist emissions reductions plans or reject them outright in a more behind-the-scenes version of the protests that engulfed China in 2023 over the COVID-19 zero-tolerance measures.

Other signs, however, point to a possible categorical shift in economic thinking in China, namely President Xi's branding and associating himself with what he described as "better growth" in August 2021, according to Xinhua, China's official news agency. He said, "As socialism with Chinese characteristics has entered a new era, China's economic development has also embarked on a new phase. . . . Recognizing that 'our solutions are in Nature,' we could strive to find development opportunities while preserving Nature, and achieve win–win in both ecological conservation and high-quality development."

Xi reiterated this view in his October 2022 remarks to the Communist Party Congress, where he stated, "green water and lush mountains are golden mountains and silver mountains." In Bali at the G20 meeting in November 2022, Xi and President Biden also reaffirmed the need for close collaboration between their nations on climate change.

Credible carbon trading to put a value on reducing greenhouse gases and price the cost of failing to reduce is integral to the high-quality growth notion, along with shifting accounting systems to recognize the financial and economic value of intangible natural assets. China has also embarked on developing a system of national environmental accounts to do that.

As of 2023, the Shanghai Energy and Emissions Exchange, one of the pilots, conducted most of the national trades while the other pilot markets focused mostly on related products, including offsets. Ant Financial

Services, the financial services arm of China's megalith Alibaba, bought shares in TCX in 2018, and has explored various ways to link the Alipay system with carbon markets, potentially enabling individuals to participate in the national carbon market.

As we learned with TCX, China's timeline is its own. Still, the issue is not time ahead of us, but time already elapsed and how to try urgently to recover it.

From 1992, when the idea of using cap-and-trade for climate change was first invoked as possible at the Earth Summit in Rio de Janeiro, to the opening of TCX in 2008, 16 years passed, plus another 7 to the Paris agreement in 2015, plus another 15 to 2030, the year that many estimate as the last best chance to grip the climate change problem.

For certain the climate change crisis will boil over without credible and systemic leadership from China, but superpower geopolitics could turn climate change into a mere cat-and-mouse game.

Carbon markets may gradually prove to be a stabilizing and encouraging force for progress, given the ebb and flow of political priorities, and perhaps the more integrated carbon markets internationally, the more immune to national distractions climate change action can be.

In China, we could not have worked harder to set up TCX. We had the shelter of being in the vanguard with influential patrons, and I would like to believe ignition on carbon pricing in China hit sooner than might have occurred without us.

However, even with China's entry, worldwide carbon pricing proceeded erratically, and more consistency is vital. Despite controversies and technical debates, pricing the scarce space of the atmosphere needs a global architecture that must come together in time. We have a known due date: today.

The through line to success will never be without interruptions. We must all dare to surmount.

8

Wall Street to the Rescue? Nauru May Answer

The opening bell rings each day at the New York Stock Exchange on Wall Street as always, but few are there to hear it. Instead of the raucous shouting crowd of brokers and traders racing off at the bell to elbow each other to buy or sell and keep up with trade tips, media commentators use the trading floor as a theater set. Stock trading went instant and mostly silent as of the giant global stock market downslide of 2007, as the IT and digital revolutions moved trading information and traders to tap at screens or pace around on mobile phones to zip capital across the world. The venerated New York Stock Exchange floor gradually became a backdrop or cocktail party venue, because the fountainhead of capital flows no longer needed a physical home and investments could move invisibly at app speed.

The rise in environmental, social, and governance (ESG) investment coincided a bit with the eclipse of real-life hot news trading, and so for a time the ESG phenomenon was less visible. However, its rolling narrative recast the face of capitalism in the 21st century and will likely determine our environmental destiny for decades.

Dubbed "The New Differentiator" by S&P Global, the touchstone financial information and ratings provider founded in 1860, ESG investment demonstrates that the Wall Streets of the world have awakened to the power of forces beyond numbers and themselves.

ESG refers to a suite of environmental, social, and governance factors that investors—including private asset managers, institutional investors, and the personally wealthy—may consider when deciding where to place capital or how to allocate portfolio assets. ESG criteria are increasingly wide-ranging, reflecting society's concerns and sensitive spots—such as a company's performance on helping avoid or prepare for climate change, racial diversity, and gender parity among executive leadership of a company and corporate boards. Increasingly, ESG investment is the litmus test on whether expressions of objective capital can capture subjective hopes and judgments.

Bloomberg Intelligence projected global ESG-infused assets to exceed $54 trillion by 2025, or roughly one-third global assets under management, and ESG factors cut across all active and passive capital investment strategies to include indices, mutual funds, bonds, and stock funds. Some use exclusion, such as screening out weapons contractors or "sin" stocks like alcohol or tobacco or divesting entirely from fossil fuels. Some use the opposite, screening in companies that specialize in renewable energy or new technologies aimed at resolving climate change or other environmental problems. Thematics can be quite specifically sliced and diced.

In its report "Investing in Times of Climate Change 2022," Morningstar states, "The climate funds universe represents a wide range of approaches, which we subdivide into five mutually exclusive categories: Low Carbon, Climate Conscious, Green Bond, Climate Solutions and Clean/Energy/Tech."

Morningstar describes, for example, the Northern Trust World Sustainable Select SDG Index Fund, covering US $3.5 billion in assets as seeking to "achieve at least 50% carbon footprint reduction relative to the parent benchmark by excluding companies with the highest carbon emissions intensity and the largest owners of fossil fuel reserves." The AXA World Funds-ACT US High Yield Bonds Low Carbon targets 20% reduced average carbon intensity and water intensity relative to its reference benchmark.

Money managers tend to closely guard their secret sauce of techniques for evaluating why and where to inject capital, and investment firms vary in how explicitly they publicize their recipes. Still, a random sample of well-known investment firms, as described in the extensive Funds Directory compiled by Sustainable Investing, a research and advisory service, illuminates common threads.

Ariel Funds

"The funds do not invest in companies whose primary source of revenue is derived from the production or sale of tobacco products or the manufacture of handguns. Ariel believes these industries may be more likely to face shrinking growth prospects, litigation costs and legal liability that cannot be quantified."

Calvert Socially Responsible Fund

"The portfolio seeks to invest in companies that:

- Take positive steps to improve environmental management and performance, advance sustainable development, or provide innovative and effective solutions to environmental problems through their products and services. . . .

The portfolio seeks to avoid investing in companies that:

- Demonstrate poor environmental performance or compliance records, or contribute significantly to local or global environmental problems; or own or operate nuclear power plants or have substantial contracts to supply key components in the nuclear power process."

BlackRock Impact Investing Funds

"The fund will select corporate bonds of companies to seek to generate alpha (i.e., returns on an investment as measured against a benchmark) and positive aggregate societal impact outcomes. . . .

Among the principal societal impact outcomes that are currently measured are the following, although they may change at any time:

- Corporate citizenship—'Corporate citizenship' focuses on companies whose employees have a high level of satisfaction working for their employers.
- High impact disease research—Companies that work on 'high impact disease research' are companies that are researching treatments for diseases with the highest potential for global impact, measured by the number of lives affected due to potential reduction in early mortality and disability.
- Greenhouse gas emissions—Companies that report lower levels of carbon emissions."

BNY Mellon Funds

"To pursue its goal, the fund normally invests at least 80% of its net assets, plus any borrowings for investment purposes, in equity securities (or derivative instruments with similar economic characteristics) of US companies that demonstrate attractive investment attributes and sustainable business practices and have no material unresolvable ESG issues.

A company is considered to engage in 'sustainable business practices' if the company engages in such practices in an economic sense (i.e., the durability of the company's strategy, operations and finances), and takes appropriate account of material externalities caused by or affecting its business."

BNP Paribas

"In all its investments, BNPP AM includes ESG-based exclusions based on the 10 principles of the United Nations Global Compact. . . . These sector-based policies cover, for example, palm oil, paper and pulp, coal-fired power plants, nuclear energy, mining and asbestos, agrochemicals and water, food safety and tobacco. . . . Industries such as controversial weapons (antipersonnel mines, cluster bombs, nuclear arms and uranium-based arms) are ineligible for investment."

Federated Hermes

"As part of the investment strategy assessment of quality and its approach to risk management, risks associated with a company's approach to ESG issues are actively assessed. Data on Hermes' proprietary ESG Dashboard, which contains a wide range of ESG factors and ranks companies on their behaviors versus peers is considered. . . .

No sector or industry is excluded from the initial analysis. The ESG score favors companies with lower ESG risks than companies who are actively improving their focus on ESG issues."

Glenmede Funds

"Glenmede uses a screening process to identify, at the time of investment, companies that satisfy its ESG criteria. Typically, environmental assessment categories include climate change, natural resource use, waste management and environmental opportunities. Social evaluation categories include human capital, product safety and social opportunities. Governance assessment categories include corporate governance, business ethics and government and public policy. . . . Using quantitative analysis, under normal market circumstances, the fund invests at least 80% of the value of its net assets (including borrowings for investment purposes) in equity securities, such as common stocks, of US large cap companies that are demonstrating commitment to advancing women through gender diversity on their boards or in management."

Lazard Funds

"The investment manager considers . . . a company whose financial productivity is likely to be supported or enhanced in the future as a result of the move toward a more sustainable world and how the company counters potential risks arising as a result of environmental and social concerns that may be material to the particular companies or the industries or sectors in which they operate. A proprietary sustainability analysis methodology is used to assess . . .

Human capital: the extent to which the company follows best practices in managing its workforce in a responsible manner, such as health and safety considerations and diversity and inclusion policies . . .

Natural capital: the extent to which the company, and its supply chains, are reliant on using resources that generate significant environmental impact and actively seek to reduce the impact they have on the environment.

Corporate governance: the extent to which the company's board composition and policies, executive management composition and compensation, and the exercise of shareholder rights and voting powers are in line with current best practices."

Matthews Asia Funds

"In addition to traditional financial data, the stock selection process takes into consideration ESG factors that the portfolio managers believe help identify companies with superior business models. There are no universally agreed upon objective standards for assessing ESG factors for companies. Rather, these factors tend to have many subjective characteristics, can be difficult to analyze, and frequently involve a balancing of a company's business plans, objectives, actual conduct and other factors.

. . . Examples of environmental factors that may be considered include . . . low environmental footprint, pollution alleviation, and resource management. . . . Businesses that meet one or more of the fund's ESG standards are generally businesses that currently engage in practices that have the effect of, or in the opinion of Matthews, have the potential of, making human or business activity less destructive to the environment or businesses that promote positive social and economic developments."

Matterhorn Group, William Blair
"Matterhorn manages two actively managed, proprietary strategies for investors seeking both financial and social returns: Gender Parity Strategy (a gender lens equity model) and the Matterhorn/Refinitiv Diversity & Inclusion Strategy. Matterhorn further oversees complete client-values-oriented portfolios: one based on ESG investments, one taking aim to bring about racial justice."

Neuberger Berman
"Portfolio managers may integrate governance factors into the investment process. They seek to invest in companies that have effective and independent boards. . . . They look for companies where management and shareholder interests are aligned (often through high ownership of the company by management), with long-term incentive plans and CEO and management compensation and succession plans in place."

Schroders
". . . [T]he adviser considers certain environmental, social and/or governance factors when assessing investment opportunities that otherwise meet the adviser's investment criteria. These factors may include, but are not limited to, business strategy, performance, financing and capital allocation, management, acquisitions and disposals, internal controls, risk management, the membership and composition of governing bodies/boards and committees, sustainability, governance, remuneration, climate change, environmental and social performance."

UBS Funds
"The advisor will employ both a positive and negative screening process with regard to securities selection for the fund. The negative screening process will exclude securities with more than 5% of sales in alcohol, tobacco, defense, nuclear, GMO (genetically modified organisms), gambling and pornography from the fund's portfolio. . . . The advisor aims to identify the best investment ideas . . . within the eligible investment universe (the impact universe) . . . comprised of companies whose products and services can create measurable, verifiable impact within specific impact categories (such as climate change, air pollution, clean water and water scarcity, treatment of disease and food security and others)."

Trillium Mutual Funds

"Trillium seeks stocks with high-quality characteristics and strong ESG records. . . .

These companies may have strong board diversity, such as two or more women on the board. . . . The adviser believes that the best long-term investments are found in companies with above-average financial characteristics and growth potential that also excel at managing environmental risks and opportunities and societal impact. . . . The adviser considers a company's position on various factors, such as ecological limits, environmental stewardship, environmental strategies, stance on human rights and equality, societal impact as well as its corporate governance practices."

TIAA Funds/Nuveen Funds

"The fund's investments in fixed-income securities issued by corporate entities or certain foreign governments are subject to certain ESG criteria. . . . How well companies adhere to international norms and principles and involvement in major ESG controversies . . . (examples of which may relate to the environment, customers, human rights and community, labor rights and supply chain, and governance) are other considerations.

The fund will not generally invest in companies significantly involved in certain business activities, including but not limited to, the production of alcohol, tobacco, military weapons, firearms, nuclear power and gambling products and services."

Pax World Funds Summary

"Pax World Funds pursue a sustainable investing approach—investing in forward thinking companies with more sustainable business models. . . . The Global Environmental Markets Fund, in addition to applying Pax World's customary sustainability or ESG criteria, has a particular focus on environmental markets—investing in companies whose businesses and technologies focus on environmental markets, including alternative energy and energy efficiency; water infrastructure technologies and pollution control; environmental support services and waste management technologies, and sustainable food, agriculture and forestry. The fund also strives to be fossil fuel-free."

Regardless of investment style or decision-making acumen, the core purpose of the ESG lens is to align the priorities, values, and attitudes of the owner of the capital involved with the deployment of that capital, while gaining financial return, the expectation and rate of which varies significantly among the owners and their managers.

ESG investment attempts to walk the walk, as it is said, to link the use of money with professed appreciation of value beyond money. One of the most cited proofs of ESG prominence is the annual letter to corporate CEOs from Larry Fink, CEO of Blackrock, the world's largest asset manager, which hit $10 trillion in assets under management in 2022. In his letter that year to the leaders of companies in which Blackrock owns shares, "The Power of Capitalism," Fink wrote about climate change, for example:

> Most stakeholders—from shareholders, to employees, to customers, to communities, and regulators—now expect companies to play a role in decarbonizing the global economy. Few things will impact capital allocation decisions—and thereby the long-term value of your company—more than how effectively you navigate the global energy transition in the years ahead. It's been two years since I wrote that climate risk is investment risk. And in that short period, we have seen a tectonic shift of capital. . . . This is just the beginning—the tectonic shift towards sustainable investing is still accelerating. Whether it is capital being deployed into new ventures focused on energy innovation, or capital transferring from traditional indexes into more customized portfolios and products, we will see more money in motion.

Challenging CEOs on the sweeping need to reduce greenhouse gas emissions, Fink predicted, "Every company and every industry will be transformed by the transition to a net zero world. The question is, will you lead, or will you be led?"

Such crisp ESG declarations evolved slowly. Mainstream investors trailed behind environmental science by at least a decade, only gradually awakening to the financial risks it portended. Larry Fink's 2012 CEO letter was a few paragraphs long and mentioned neither ESG nor the word "environment."

The voice of global finance was not present in 1992 at the Rio conference, where the bedrock UN Frameworks on Climate Change and Biological Diversity came into being. Agenda 21, the key recommendations that Rio's political assembly laid out, spoke only in passing of the need for more "venture capital" to address environmental and social concerns, adding a generic suggestion that governments work more closely with the private sector.

Maurice Strong, the secretary-general of the Rio conference, did draw in Swiss billionaire Stephan Schmidheiny, and together they formed the World Business Council for Sustainable Development to, as Schmidheiny put it, "bring the voice of business to the Rio process."

They hoped to open the eyes of industrial corporate leaders to environmental protection as a moneymaker to meet the likely increased demand for innovative products and processes that would reduce waste of energy, water, and other natural resources.

For the most part, though, highlighting business advantages at Rio did not look behind the companies to their shareholders and the influence investors wielded on near-term business priorities and direction.

Yet the UN did become the wellspring of contemporary ESG, not at first directly but through the philosophical inquiry of how to advance broad human progress, once the climate change problem and its predicted ensuing upheavals had been recognized by the governments of the world at Rio, poor and rich.

The brilliant, stately, and at times officious Boutros Boutros-Ghali, secretary-general of the UN at the time, tried to convey the stakes in relatively simple terms: How to leverage prosperity to alleviate poverty? How much government leadership, how much hands off? How much capitalism was too much?

As he put it in his landmark "Agenda for Development" in 1997, a plan the UN General Assembly requested to chart the future relevance of the UN, Boutros-Ghali envisioned a worldwide "culture of development," distilling this one-for-all, all-for-one vision to five timeless principles that read many years later as if fresh ink:

– without peace human resources cannot be used effectively;
– without economic growth (as the "engine to development"), there cannot be any sustainable, broad-based improvement to material welfare;
– without environmental protection, the basic needs of human survival are eroded;
– without social justice, growing imbalance threatens society; and
– without free political participation, development remains fragile and permanently endangered.

Boutros-Ghali did not shrink from declaring "whether this vision is fulfilled or not will be measured by what this living generation of the world's peoples and their leaders make or fail to make of the United Nations."

Nor did Boutros-Ghali shrink from the hoofbeats of the free market economy, speaking radically of a "social market economy" instead, and laying out the economic navigation required: "Finding the right blend of government direction of the economy and encouragement of private initiative is perhaps the most pressing challenge of economic development. This is not only a problem for developing or transitional economies. In the search for the difficult path which lies between dirigisme and laissez-faire, all countries are involved. Major market economies, with recurrent recession and persistent high rates of unemployment, are also facing this challenge."

Meanwhile, in the large economies he referenced, scrutiny of capital markets bubbled up in the form of socially responsible investing (SRI) and sustainable investing (SI), mostly idiosyncratic undertakings by a handful of activists who launched investment vehicles skewed toward environmental or social priorities.

In the United States, SRI often took root in liberal religious or anti-war views, exemplified in investment vehicles like the Pax World Fund, much cited as America's first SRI fund, inspired in 1971 by pastors of the United Methodist Church who did not want church financial holdings to support the US presence and war in Vietnam. In the mid-1970s, companies and investors gradually pulled capital and operations out of South Africa, using boycotts to pressure the government there to abolish apartheid. Even then, as Blackrock's Fink said in 2022, money was "in motion," though largely external to conventional financial flows.

Uptown in New York City on Riverside Drive, almost as far as possible to be from Wall Street and still be in Manhattan, an office building became known as "The God Box" because it housed the Interfaith Center on Corporate Responsibility (ICCR). This association of religious and other advocacy groups specialized in pricking staid corporate annual shareholder meetings with agenda resolutions on environmental and social issues.

A heroine of the God Box was Dominican nun Patricia Daly, known as Sister Pat. She leveraged her canonical order's small pension portfolio and investment preferences to influence corporate priorities. Eventually Daly's reputation grew to the extent that she could access leading CEOs such as William Ford Jr. of Ford Motor Company who, when Daly died in 2022, referenced her influence as important to his thinking and success.

Another key concept to emerge was the "blended value proposition" credited to financial advisor Jed Emerson, which confronted persistent either/or investment habits.

In a groundbreaking paper titled "The Nature of Returns" published in 2000 by the Harvard Business School, Emerson wrote:

> It is true that there are social costs and economic costs, and that each should be tracked. However, it must also be understood that the interaction and trade-off between the two do not take place in a smooth line, one operating in directly inverse relationship to the other. *The issue isn't wealth creation or social change—it is the creation of value, applying resources to the creation of the greatest value possible and the simultaneous pursuit of both economic and social good for investors and investees, as well as the greater community.*

Still, though, these provocative views remained marginal to the era's financial structures, and the inherited language of straight profit-and-loss hung on.

Securities regulators worldwide required disclosure of basic operational information, but not on whether corporate leaders or board members recognized long-term environmental risk or prioritized new eco-efficient business opportunities. The mission of securities regulation was to scrutinize and make public the fiduciary basics of how companies managed capital entrusted to them by shareholders. That environmental or social factors might erode the capital value or interject vulnerability fell outside securities market oversight.

A breakthrough came in 1999, through the energies of four young visionaries and optimistic thinkers based in the UK: Paul Dickinson, an entrepreneur and co-author of the book *Beautiful Corporations*; Jeremy Smith and Paul Simpson, investment advisors; and Tessa Tennant, the Scottish galvanizer of the group who would go on to be named by the *Economist* as "a giant of green finance" when she died in 2018.

Tennant had seen the future and co-founded the Merlin Ecology Fund in 1988, the UK's first sustainable investment fund, and worked earnestly to expand similar thinking worldwide. Always witty and calm, Tennant was nevertheless tireless in her efforts to reinvent the use of capital. When we spoke at the Paris climate conference in 2015, she could barely stop for a coffee, because she was in so much demand as a reference point for the large crop of ESG investors she had inspired by then.

Tennant and her original London colleagues understood that the interrelationship between financial performance and environmental issues, especially climate change, could only crystallize if annual corporate disclosure to shareholders illuminated it. That, they believed, would happen only if securities regulators required so-called "nonfinancial" information, such as updates on corporate environmental strategies, including alertness to risks of potential shortages of raw materials or increased flooding, drought, or other untoward environmentally related events.

To put this nonfinancial and financial information on the same footing, working from a small London basement apartment, Tennant, Simpson, Dickinson, and Smith launched their disruption. Since no mandatory environmental disclosure system existed anywhere, they created their own, a wholly new structure, the voluntary Carbon Disclosure Project (CDP), giving birth to the practice and principle of environmental disclosure that steadily became a norm.

The founding CDP premise held that corporations and investors had an obligation to pay attention to climate change risks and opportunities, as inherent to the fundamental obligation to prudently steward shareholder assets. Ignoring environmental risks, they felt, was imprudent, and their objective of introducing environmental dimensions to the marching orders of the "prudent investor" and capital stewardship had no precedent.

Building on the basic fiduciary principle that if shareholders pose questions, corporate management has to answer, the founding CDP quartet drew up a one-page questionnaire, recruited 35 like-minded investor and financial services firms in the UK to sign on as "CDP signatories," and mailed this "investor information request" to as many CEOs of public companies in the UK as they could afford with their limited postage budget. About 80 companies responded and CDP collated and published the results in 2003, the world's first coordinated presentation of the environmental performance of public companies expressly put before investors and the general public.

Without consistent, comparable, and transparent fiduciary disclosure of how a company responded to environmental factors, investors had no window on how those factors might influence the success or stability of a company, certainly not prior to modern AI and data scraping possibilities. Without environmental disclosure ESG could not take off, and environmental uncertainties could not be priced into market behavior.

Alas, in the meantime, mainstream investment capital continued to flow to familiar and lucrative extractive use of natural resources, especially fossil fuels, at the expense of advancing alternatives, such as renewable energy technologies. The comfortable view prevailed that corporate executives and their boards of directors were responsible only for generating and disclosing financially sound performance.

Environmental disclosure upended that notion and helped accelerate ESG expansion by providing a central source of environmental information not otherwise readily available, as recognition of the climate change problem heightened across society at large.

Other momentum built. In August 2000, Bloomberg LLP added its first proprietary ESG scores to the offerings of its ubiquitous business data terminals, covering 252 companies from the oil and gas sector and board composition scores for roughly 4,300 companies.

Bloomberg's announcement for the new product said, "ESG scores provide a data-driven measure of corporate environmental and social performance that investors can use to quickly evaluate performance across a range of financially material, business-relevant and industry-specific key issues, such as climate change and health and safety, and assess company activities relative to industry peers."

The mainstream ESG candle was finally lit, however, in 2004, when Kofi Annan, Boutros-Ghali's successor as secretary-general of the UN, issued a centralized UN-sanctioned call to investors to categorically revamp the essence of financial practice. Annan invited 55 CEOs from the financial services sector to join an initiative "to develop guidelines and recommendations on how to better integrate environmental, social and corporate governance issues in asset management, securities brokerage services and associated research functions," according to the report "Who Cares Wins" that resulted.

Apparently unafraid to associate themselves with the subjective concept of "care," 25 leading financial firms, with $6 trillion in assets collectively under management, from AXA to Westpac and World Bank Group, including Goldman Sachs, HSBC, BNP Paribas, and others, took up Annan's invitation and came together to brainstorm.

"Who Cares Wins" synthesized the purpose, rationale, and hopes for ESG investment, a rubric that has changed little, and the importance of recognizing ESG issues broadly:

> The institutions endorsing this report are convinced that . . . companies that perform better with regard to these issues can increase shareholder value by, for example, properly managing risks, anticipating regulatory action or accessing new markets, while at the same time contributing to the sustainable development of the societies in which they operate. Moreover, these issues can have a strong impact on reputation and brands, an increasingly important part of company value.

The report put aside prior terms such as SRI and SI, instead enumerating specific environmental, social, and governance elements, such as climate change, control of other pollutants, labor rights, board structure and accountability, anti-corruption controls, and executive compensation, subsumed into the abbreviation ESG that came to dominate the discourse. Perhaps the most radical component of "Who Cares Wins" was its demand for longer-term thinking that also transcended quantitative matters:

> This report focuses on issues which have or could have a material impact on investment value. It uses a broader definition of materiality than commonly used—one that includes longer time horizons (10 years and beyond) and intangible aspects impacting company value.

ESG leadership became a contest between 10 years of responsibility and broad accountability versus quarterly investor relations calls on numbers only.

Pushing expectations of return and risk well out beyond the familiar financial rat-tat-tat relieved pressure on both companies and investors—integration of ESG to portfolios by definition could not be an immediate gratification affair.

The ESG field only continued to grow. By 2023, Bloomberg's ESG scores and other data analyses covered 14,000 global companies, 474,000 active ESG securities, and 88% of global market across 100 countries.

According to the Morningstar report on climate change investment, at the end of 2022, "Europe remains the largest and most diverse climate funds market, accounting for more than three-fourths of global assets. . . . For the first time, China overtook the United States as the second largest climate funds market, more than doubling in size to USD 47 billion."

The ESG approach expressed itself across all continents. Research by the Official Monetary and Financial Institutions Forum, a think tank serving central banks worldwide, and ABSA, a major financial services group in South Africa, reported, "Africa has been a key source of progress on these fronts in 2022. For instance, South Africa introduced a green taxonomy; Botswana and Eswatini completed guidelines on ESG reporting for listed companies; and Tanzania saw the first social bond insurance in sub-Saharan Africa. In total 17 of the 26 countries . . . now have sustainability focused financial policies, five more than in 2021."

In Saudi Arabia, the Saudi Exchange, one of the world's largest stock markets, issued ESG disclosure guidelines, along with more than 100 other stock exchanges around the world incorporating ESG guidelines to their listing rules, indicating that ESG recognition had become significant in the competitive hunt to attracting and retaining listings.

By 2022–23, the ESG field had become mature enough to have cheaters, chastised as "greenwashers," triggering a cleansing of the field.

Until then, ESG uptake seemed to be only strengthening. According to the Sustainable Investment Forum (SIF), a US-based nonprofit that tracks ESG application and trends, in 2012, 1 in 9 dollars invested in the United States was screened for an ESG impact; in 2016, 1 in 5 dollars; in 2018, 1 in 4 dollars; and in 2021, 1 in 3 dollars.

However, in December 2022, SIF shocked the ESG world when its 14th biannual report showed a marked decline in ESG application. SIF reported that ESG investment assets in the United States were $8.4 trillion, down from $17.1 in 2020, representing 12.6% of the roughly $67 trillion in assets under professional management, or 1 in 8 dollars invested.

These drops, SIF explained, were attributable to more granular data-gathering, and redrawing of sample boundaries to include only investment firms that offered specific ESG products, rather than firms that generally claimed "firmwide" ESG awareness. SIF also noted that in 2022 the US SEC had "released two proposals that focused on preventing misleading or deceptive fund names" and so investment firms might have modified their offerings and fallen out of the SIF sample.

Reporting SIF's 2022 findings, Barron's headlined "US Sustainable Investments Plunge 51% from 2020," a misleading emphasis, perhaps, but accurate.

Despite flux in the agreed parameters of ESG, Verdantix, a major research and advisory firm, forecast a 17% annual growth in the ESG consulting market to reach $16 billion in 2027, a projection likely also based on anticipated corporate need to self-interrogate regarding ESG confusion and greenwashing, outright or accidental.

The ESG field also matured enough to provoke political backlash, especially in the highly polarized dynamics of the United States, as if ESG were a devilish elixir and environmental imperatives false.

In August 2022, the state of Florida passed a resolution to ban consideration of ESG factors by the investment board of the state's Retirement System Defined Benefit Pension Plan, which covers more than 1 million of the state's public sector workers, retirees, and survivors. Taking straight aim at the breadth of ESG considerations and turning the clock back at least two decades on the relationship between financial and nonfinancial information, the Florida resolution instructed that in-vestment decisions must be based on only "pecuniary factors," defined as those that "the board prudently determines is expected to have a mate-rial effect on the risk and return of an investment based on appropriate investment horizons . . . [and] do not include the consideration of the furtherance of social, political, or ideological interests."

In a press release lauding the resolution, Florida Governor Ron DeSantis, a trustee of the pension fund, said, "Corporate power has increasingly been utilized to impose an ideological agenda on the American people through the perversion of financial investment pri-orities under the euphemistic banners of environmental, social, and corporate governance and diversity, inclusion, and equity. . . . We are prioritizing the financial security of the people of Florida over whimsi-cal notions of a utopian tomorrow."

In October 2022, Louisiana announced it would be pulling $794 million of state funds away from Blackrock's management within the year. Louisiana State Treasurer John Schroder, wrote Larry Fink, Blackrock CEO, whose annual letters now brought him talismanic pro-file, alleging that Fink's "blatantly anti-fossil fuel policies would destroy Louisiana's economy. . . . I'm convinced that ESG investing is more than bad business; it's a threat to our founding principles: democracy, economic freedom, and individual liberty." Layering on, Schroder said that ESG:

> threatens our democracy, bypasses the ballot box and allows large investment firms to push political agendas. It threatens our economic freedom because these firms use their massive shareholdings to compel CEOs to put political motivations above a company's profits and investors' returns. Finally, it threatens our personal liberty because these firms are using our money to push their agendas contrary to the best interests of the people whose money they are using! There is a difference between offering an ESG investment option for those investors so inclined and using other peoples' non-ESG investments to promote ESG shareholder initiatives.

In December 2022, Florida also pulled $2 billion from management by Blackrock, and the state's CFO, Jimmy Patronis, said that in uncertain financial times, "I need partners within the financial services industry who are as committed to the bottom line as we are—and I don't trust BlackRock's ability to deliver."

Patronis also declared, "BlackRock CEO Larry Fink is on a campaign to change the world . . . he's championed 'stakeholder capitalism' and believes that 'capitalism has the power to shape society.' To meet this end, the asset management company has leaned heavily into Environmental, Social, and Governance standards—known as ESG—to help police who should, and who should not gain access to capital. . . . Using our cash, however, to fund BlackRock's social-engineering project isn't something Florida ever signed up for."

Florida's divestment from Blackrock, implicitly rejecting climate change concerns inherent in the ESG approach, came as the state also mandated that all Florida homeowners buy flood insurance in the aftermath of the catastrophic costs of Hurricane Ian that had hit the state just that September, dropping torrential rains. Verging on Category 5 status, Ian's wild winds approached 150 miles per hour, tearing structures apart, and whipping up storm surges and widespread flooding. The superstorm reduced many towns and homes to shambles, and, at the time, only roughly half the state's homeowners had coverage against flooding.

As of October 2022, estimates of uninsured flood losses to homeowners in Florida from Ian ranged from $10 billion to $17 billion, according to CoreLogic, a research firm specializing in the real estate industry, in addition to $30–$48 billion in insured losses. Karen Clark and Company, an international advisory service that pioneered catastrophe modeling for economic and insurance purposes, projected total insured losses in the United States from Ian, mostly in Florida, at $63 billion, excluding uninsured homeowner losses.

Also, by the time Florida and Louisiana and some other US states sought to secede from ESG influence, CDP disclosure rates perhaps provided evidence that, on the contrary, far from inciting radical social engineering, ESG inquiry had become de rigueur among investors and public companies. In 2023, CDP reported it had approximately 600 signatory investors, representing well over $100 trillion in assets under management, with nearly 20,000 companies and suppliers worldwide disclosing to CDP's various programs.

Additionally, securities regulators worldwide were developing mandatory environmental disclosure regulations, especially concerning climate change risks, spearheaded by the European Union. In the United States, the SEC issued its draft proposal for mandatory disclosure in March 2022, which drew sharp accusations of overreach from opponents in the

US Congress. At hearings of the Senate Banking Committee, Committee Chairman Pat Toomey (R-PA) charged in his opening remarks:

> . . . the climate disclosure rule isn't about an informed investment decision. It's about equipping climate activists with data to run political pressure campaigns against companies, often to the detriment of shareholders. . . . The endgame is to discourage capital investment in oil, natural gas, and other traditional energy industries. . . . The SEC is wading into controversial public policy debates that are far outside its mission and its expertise. . . . In doing so, the SEC risks politicizing the agency, slowing economic growth, increasing inflation, and even undermining national security.

However, even with political headwinds, and the continuing war in Ukraine, ESG remained prominent to investment advisors. According to a 2022 ESG survey of 1,130 global investors by Capital Group, a global investment firm that reported $2.6 trillion in assets under management, "as with 2021, more than a quarter of global investors say ESG is central to their investment approach. . . . [T]he increasing ESG momentum is being fueled by client demand and external pressures." The report also found that, as compared to 2021, fewer investors said that "academic evidence showing a positive relationship between ESG and performance would prompt them to raise their ESG focus. . . . This suggests investors are less concerned about sacrificing returns, linking with the . . . finding that more are now adopting ESG specifically to improve performance."

A survey by EY in 2022 of 1,040 corporate financial leaders and 320 senior investors found that 78% of investors surveyed "think companies should make investments that address ESG issues relevant to their business even if it reduces profits in the long term." On the other hand, only "55% of companies surveyed are prepared to take that stance. . . . Just over half of large companies surveyed say they 'face short-term earnings pressure from investors which impedes our longer term investments in sustainability.'"

As expansive as ESG considerations had become, EY also highlighted a persistent gap between what investors and corporations claim to want:

> While companies are investing more time resources and leadership effort into sustainability there is still a significant disconnect between the respective expectations and goals of companies and their investors when it comes to corporate and sustainability performance. . . . Investors are showing a degree of skepticism about companies sustainability

commitments and ESG disclosures. . . . Some companies feel their long-term investments and sustainability are not always recognized and 'rewarded' by the investment community also long term plays can be difficult when investors are quick to react on short term dips in financial performance.

As to whether ESG vehicles financially outperform benchmarks and other investment forms, studies proliferate. A literature review by the Rock Center for Corporate Governance and Stanford University School of Business in 2022 found "The financial benefits of ESG are not clearly established. . . . Various studies find that ESG increases, decreases or has no discernable impact on corporate performance or stock-price returns. In aggregate they provide no clear direction to inform institutional investor voting."

The quirks of stock prices took on a vivid hue in late 2022 when Tesla, a corporation whose central business mission is to decarbonize automobile and other vehicular transportation and green the world's electricity grid overall, lost 70% of its value in one year. The reasons had nothing to do with Tesla's contribution to ESG goals, and only to do with the acquisition of Twitter by the volatile Tesla founder, Elon Musk.

As to appetite for risk and reward among individual investors, in November 2022, the Rock Center and the Stanford Business School also published results of its survey of 2,470 individual investors distributed by geography, age, wealth, race, and gender. Seventy percent of young investors, defined as those between 18 and 41, were "very concerned" about environmental issues, while only 35% of older investors said the same. On social issues, 65% of young investors expressed concern about links to social issues, compared with only 30% of older investors. Sixty-four percent of younger voters and only 28% of older voters said they were concerned about governance.

Less than half of older voters said it was extremely or very important to them to influence environmental practices of companies, compared with 79% of younger investors. According to this research, "Older investors are overwhelmingly opposed to the idea of forfeiting investment return to advance ESG objectives."

For example, "86% of older investors do not want to forfeit any of their retirement savings or only a trivial amount to have the companies they are invested in change from industry standard carbon emissions levels to 'net zero' by 2050, while 64% of young investors said they would pay moderate or large amounts." The survey found that "across all issues and wealth levels . . . older investors would be willing to give up only around 2% of their wealth to support ESG."

On average, the survey found that younger investors with large levels of wealth reported they would give up about 14% of their wealth to advance ESG issues, concluding "this underscores that young investors, in particular young wealthy investors, are the primary drivers of ESG." The research speculated that "aside from ideological preferences" these views among the younger demographic could be "due to the fact that they have accumulated large investment balances early in their lives or recognition that they are the most exposed to the long-term cost of environmental or social failure. It may also be driven by unrealistic expectations of future market returns."

At the time of the COVID-19 pandemic in 2020, ESG funds were cited as more resilient to the catastrophic economic pressures of the COVID-19 economic downturn. In February 2021, the Morgan Stanley Institute for Sustainable Investing said, "An analysis of more than 3,000 U.S. mutual funds and exchange-traded funds (ETFs) shows that sustainable equity funds outperformed their traditional peer funds by a median total return of 4.3 percentage points in 2020." S&P Global issued similar findings.

Perhaps the outperform issue is overblown, subjecting ESG to an unrealistic summit. Perhaps the greater news, after three decades of evolution, is that ESG screens do not erode earnings, and are constructive, not disruptive, to prudent asset management.

Perhaps, for example, more notable is that in 2023 and for at least a decade earlier, the S&P Carbon Efficient Index, which overweights companies with low carbon emissions–revenue ratios, tracks almost perfectly with the conventional S&P 500, illustrating that companies reducing carbon dependence do not lose economic standing.

The expansion of ESG was bound to push against attitudinal and political walls, and may demand rock-solid perseverance and perhaps a constant self-reflection among even its most ardent practitioners.

Still, new products are developed regularly, all striving to capture some intangible ESG element in a tangible measurement—a mix of measurement and morality, so to speak, not a natural match unless we lean on common sense, a belief in purpose, and a willingness to rethink the meaning of cost and benefit.

The age of environmental imperatives is likely inflexible unless we intelligently gamble.

Bill Gates, founder of Microsoft and a chief investor in clean energy technologies, wrote in a 2022 year-end note of the unyielding need to hollow out fossil fuel use to truly face climate change. He said, "I can sum up the challenge in two sentences. Getting to zero will be the hardest thing humans have ever done. We need to revolutionize the entire physical economy—how we make things, move around, produce electricity, grow food and stay warm and cool—in less than three decades."

Straightforward, for sure. However, we have already spent just about three decades describing, analyzing, and commenting on the problem.

As to accountability for progress, the UN's "Who Cares Wins" 10-year risk-reward horizon falls well outside the average job tenure of most CEOs and board members. When they move on to other roles, who then owns the moral obligations they proclaimed? How widely can that blanket of morality be cast?

Who will be responsible for delivering on emission reductions or gender parity goals set for delivery in 2050, decades after the pledges by investors or companies, or even interim milestones for that matter?

Perhaps the "governance" in ESG could evolve to expect that all new CEOs hired be contractually required to implement Paris agreement objectives, or be contractually bound to environmental promises made by predecessors? Or boards of directors could be explicitly chartered to keep the firm on a decarbonization path?

Debates over how far responsibility extends on whose watch mean that personal values teeter on the razor edge of legal fine points and fear of liability prosecution.

In 2022, ESG was deemed so fluid and sweeping, investors and regulators clamored for a definitive framework of ESG "standards," infallible definitions that would serve as a playbook to remove uncertainty from choice and protect investors from accusations that their products do not warrant an ESG blessing.

However, are we not always dealing with the moral compass of investors, well beyond regulations and distinct codifications? In attempting to capture the value of intangibles will we not always be drawing on criteria set by the heart and mind and the sense of purpose, rather than pride in the Midas touch?

Of course, ESG definitions and rigor cannot be reinvented each day, but it also may be naïve to think that official regulatory guidelines, that must, after all, serve a common denominator and level playing field, will extend the vanguard.

On the other hand, is the ESG approach destined to be a process of trying to force round pegs into square holes, over and over again? Have we created a new investment model merely to complicate the old, or to actually transform the old? Time will tell. Perhaps, too, the definitive sign of maturation of ESG is that it can please no one and no purpose fully.

Perhaps an acid test of ESG will arrive as the global investment community evaluates the financial viability and desirability of deep-sea mining in the remote Pacific Ocean, notably around the island of Nauru.

Nauru is only eight square miles in area, a nearly perfect circle shaped like an upside-down dinner plate, several thousand miles from any major landmass. Alone in the sea, Nauru is bereft of natural resources long since lost to extraction for short-term cash and nearly out of economic options to support its worried population of 10,000. As global climate change increasingly melds environmental and social concerns, Nauru radiates and revives its warning.

Nauruans are a Pacific people, with their own language and culture. In 1798, the first whaling ship arrived on the island, opening up Western commerce. In 1896, Henry Denson, an office manager for the Pacific Islands Company, an enterprise through which Britain managed its colonial holdings in the region, picked up a rock on Nauru and used it as a doorstop in his office in Sydney, taking it for a curio fossil.

The discovery in 1899 that it was actually a phosphate rock dictated the course of human, natural, and economic events across three continents. In the fashion of privateers, buccaneers, and racketeers too, came the phosphateers, business scouts with explorer's bent who embarked on an insatiable search for phosphate. The phosphate rock of Nauru was exceptionally high quality and became the key ingredient of superphosphate fertilizers, gradually applied worldwide to make agriculture possible where soil was otherwise too poor, especially in Australia.

However, to unearth the phosphate riches locked below ground, exploiting companies and nations first had to strip every single tree from what is known as "topside," the flat plateau area of Nauru. Coral pinnacles make up Nauru's basic underlying geological structure; over millennia, the sea had left minerals and other deposits between the coral fingers, gradually forming the highly prized phosphate rocks.

Once the trees were out of the way, diggers and bulldozers scraped out the phosphate, leaving behind only the stark white pointy coral towers. Most of Nauru's phosphate rocks are gone, and what is left of topside looks like an army of hooded Ku Klux Klansmen on the march, baking hot.

When I visited Nauru in 1989, the spectacle underwater was nearly as horrendous. Far from anywhere, still the sea too had become a dump. Not just common garbage but typewriters, bicycles, drywall insulation and padding, and countless rubber flipflops all made up a bizarre and dispiriting fauna and flora, some debris escaping from Nauru itself, some washing in from oceans worldwide. Much of Nauru's coral was also caked with fungus as siltation from phosphate mining smothered healthy reefs.

Nauru sits near the equator and its reefs were also dying of the heat, as ocean temperatures were by then well on their way up, unabated since. According to research by a consortium of scientists published in "Advances in Atmospheric Sciences," the world's oceans in 2022 "were again the hottest in the historical record and exceeded the previous 2021 record maximum."

Nauru had earned significantly from trade in phosphate for decades, and for a while Nauru had a higher per capita income than oil-rich Kuwait. Nauru also received financial infusions from international legal settlements intended to compensate for the ravaging of Nauru's landmass. But Nauruans soon experienced the limits of money alone, and since nothing could grow anymore on Nauru itself—even eggs were flown in on a jet from Australia when I was there—soon expensive imported junk food overcame the local diet. This in turn led to the highest rates of obesity and diabetes in the world. Nauruans had no work to do, and so literacy and other social indicators began to fall.

In the meantime, various governments of Nauru and its foreign advisors squandered phosphate revenue in dubious investments, and Nauru gradually became a haven for petty crime, money laundering, and many other diabolical services that faraway places can provide the unsavories of the world. It has been alleged that some of the money used to engineer the 9/11 attacks on the World Trade Center in New York in 2001 was cleansed and transferred through Nauru.

Around the same period, Australia began leasing Nauru as a holding pen for refugees it had intercepted on the high seas bobbing around the Pacific in leaky boats, to prevent them from reaching Australia. Australia paid the limited government of Nauru to manage the Refugee Processing Center, establish camps, and later distribute refugees around the tiny island.

In August 2016, Amnesty International snuck an observer onto Nauru and reported that refugees, including families and children, from as far away as Iraq and Syria, including Rohingya from Myanmar and

Bangladesh, were being subjected to abuse and debased conditions in the crowded camp. Australia denied the charges, and the refugee center closed, though Australian government retained the right to revive it. Remaining refugees were said to be living among the Nauruan community.

Remote, out of sight, and used up by outsiders, Nauru and Nauruans have long suffered environmental exhaustion, and so the refugee debacle was just one more link in the chain of demise. But we would be foolish to think the story ends there. Is Nauru legacy, or precursor?

Nauruans want to stay on Nauru, so they resort to whatever they can to keep a semblance of an economy alive—fish farming, cultivating giant clams, installing a solar energy plant to wean off imported diesel oil. However, many projects went dormant due to COVID-19 restrictions and all in the face of lasting drought, water shortage, and encroaching sea level.

In Nauru, the livable edge of its dinner plate shape grows ever narrower. The pastime of "going around" when Nauruans take to their cars to drive the island's single circle highway grew increasingly nerve-racking as the sea nibbled the road.

In fact, standing knee-deep in the ocean for effect, the foreign minister of Tuvalu, Simon Kofe, sent a video message to the COP26 UN climate conference in Glasgow in 2021, pleading with developed economies on behalf of small Pacific islands, including Nauru, to act urgently to forestall climate change.

The Nauruan government's post-2020 economic plan, called "Desperate Imagination," put Nauru at the world's service again, once again for natural assets. This time, though, the treasure is beneath the sea—manganese nodules, ancient conglomerates of rare and important minerals and metals essential to batteries, like cobalt, nickel, zinc, and iron oxides, strewn on the remotely deep ocean floor. The compact nodules offer one-stop shopping and so were seductively dubbed "batteries in a rock" by one of the first companies poised to go after the polymetallic bonanza.

Nauru's president, Lionel Aingimea, was a leader in the finalization of the draft regulations on exploitation of seabed minerals at the International Seabed Authority (ISA), created by the United Nations to administer the Convention on the Law of the Sea, including rules to govern seabed mining, an activity long envisioned but never undertaken until trials started in 2023.

Negotiations on how to monitor seabed mining slow-cooked for decades, and Nauru had been a sponsoring state of the discussions, simultaneously creating its own commercial enterprise, Nauru Oceans Resources Incorporated (NORI), to exploit the enticing deep-sea rocks.

According to the September 2021 Nauru Bulletin, the government's newsletter, "the decision aligns with this government's vision of 'desperate imagination' in finding new economic opportunities for Nauru as we continue to work through challenging times we are in—the COVID pandemic and climate crisis. Accessing these polymetallic nodule resources will be vital to building a clean energy transition for large economies like the US and the European Union."

Thank you, Nauru?

The deep-sea nodules are unique on the planet, their special virtue that each nodule contains at least four key metals central to battery strength, a quadruplex of immense cash value scoopable with little waste compared to digging for scattered land-based ores.

The ruin of Nauru's topside after phosphate mining was there for all to see, as was the Refugee Center and the refugees themselves. There would be few eyes, though, on undersea mining of the nodules. The first ship that planned to scour the seabed in 2023 near Nauru was even called *Hidden Gem*.

The Metals Company (TMC), which is outfitting the ship and owns at least three seabed mining contracts issued by ISA, said it will be "the world's first ship classed as a subsea mining vessel by the American Bureau of Shipping" with projected first commercial operations at the end of 2023. More than a dozen other companies from around the world also hold contracts.

Outside of any national jurisdiction, the coveted zone of action is Clarion Clipperton (CCZ), a 1.7 million-square-mile area of deep ocean between Hawaii and Mexico, a stretch of sea that would cover the continental United States and according to TMC, "the world's largest known source of battery metals."

That the polymetallic nodules existed has been known since the late 19th century and according to ISA, "Nodule growth is one of the slowest of all geological phenomena—in the order of a centimeter over several million years. The age of Pacific Ocean nodules is therefore 2 to 3 million years."

So the phosphate script declares that nodules formed over time immeasurable in human terms can be exploited, likely exhausted, in a few human decades, including, we can assume, cost to oceanic biodiversity.

Exploitation of deep-sea minerals remained dormant for lack of commercial viability, but the projected insatiable demand for batteries hastened the seabed mining idea. NORI and TMC planned to move ahead with their plan, invoking a two-year notice provision that allows parties to announce their intention to mine to ISA, which in turn commits to review any given proposal, even if no environmental protection regime yet exists.

But how, realistically, to monitor seabed mining with what might be claimed as environmentally responsible procedures, if environmental caution or remediation is even possible so deep undersea? To mine seabed nodules means scraping the seafloor, drilling, and sucking up seawater and sediment to ships above, where separation of seawater and rocks takes place, after which the residue sediment is shot back into the sea in a plume of return we can hardly envision as healthy.

Or as a group of marine scientists put it in technical terms in a note to the US National Academy of Sciences, "Given the risk of ecological harm, the need to consider the potential adverse effects from seabed mining to midwater ecosystems and services, and our state of knowledge in evaluating these risks, is critical." To be explicit, NAS explained, "a single polymetallic-nodule mining operation is estimated to discharge 50,000 meters-cubed of sediment, broken mineral fines, and seawater per day (~8 kilograms per meter-cubed solids) and a hydrothermal vent operation could discharge 22,000 to 38,000 meters-cubed per day."

The NAS further highlighted that "these discharges could run continuously for up to 30 years, producing 500,000,000 meters-cubed of discharge over the lifetime of one operation. Very fine clay sediments could stay in suspension for several years, and along with dissolved metals they could be carried by ocean currents for hundreds of kilometers dispersing far beyond the mining zone in concentrations that are still to be determined."

Yet the rationale remains. According to TMC, "The NORI area alone contains enough metal to potentially supply battery metals for 140 million electric vehicles. Our studies estimate that the number of polymetallic nodules within our three exploration areas is enough to electrify a quarter of the world's passenger vehicle fleet (approx. 280 million EVs)."

So we enter yet another high-stakes environmental trade-off, but who will arbitrate, and for whose benefit? After all, we do need those batteries to power electric vehicles, smart phones, data centers, headphones, the Internet of Things, and consumer electronics of all kinds, and to meet countless other demands for noncarbon power, right? But at what price? Is the atmosphere more priceless than the deep sea, or the contrary?

The ocean is as visible as our atmospheric ring is not, the stunning azure-blue surface covering most of our planet as it hangs in the black velvet backdrop of the universe. Sadly, just as we've released greenhouse gas emissions mindlessly into the atmosphere, however innocently at first, we've used our oceans as dumping grounds for virtually every single land-based mess—from sewage to plastics, toxic chemicals to household trash to obsolete railroad cars that need to be disposed of somewhere, but we have no other place, we think.

Like the atmosphere, our oceans have lent themselves to us for free, their endless pricelessness uncounted in the costs or benefits of our seafaring and sea using, their health not even figured in. Just as we have not priced the cost of climate change disruptions into our economic models, we have not priced the cost of ocean disruption into the idea of deep-sea mining.

I once sailed on a very large tanker headed to the Panama Canal from New Jersey, and some crew members were painting a section of deck when we were a day or two out in the Atlantic en route. Once finished, they neatly collected their brushes and packed them into the empty paint cans, lining up the cans like troops. Then one of them made a hurler's show of tossing the cans, one by one, each jammed tight with brushes and slick with globs of unused paint, as far out in the sea as he could. Giant backswing of the arm, raise, throw. Each can flew high into an arc and held for a second like a kite, then splashdown. On to the next until none were left—only the gleaming deck and the warning signs "Wet paint." Deed done.

The hurler looked proud of his cleanup and how far out he'd launched the cans. True that those cans and paints may not have done much damage in the grand scheme of the sea, but that is the point—the gigantic nature of the sea has been its cloak of protection and our refuge from guilt.

Like the atmosphere, out of sight, out of mind. So shall be deep-sea mining?

Like the atmosphere, the oceans have coped to a point with our onslaught, subsidizing our habits with their vastness, swallowing our excesses and swirling our solids and liquid trash around in the mesmerizing pattern of ocean currents that help stabilize our weather, but also pull the flotsam of our surplus far from the coast, often literally sinking the evidence. Yes, we've legislated against ocean dumping and for coastal protection. We do protect the seas.

But offshore mining of the type proposed off Nauru is unprecedented and might as well be on the moon for the ease of keeping watch.

Just as we need a global price on carbon, to tag the costs of free rides on natural resources, should we not consider a "price on oceans" if deep-sea mining goes forward? After all, some ocean cost will be inherent when the batteries fed with deep-sea minerals light up a screen, whether for life-saving telemedicine, quantum computing, Mars landings, video games, drone war tools, mobile phones the size of fingernails, or any other of the likely countless battery-based inventions that will theoretically displace dependency on electric grids and their concomitant dependency on fossil fuels.

Pricing the pricelessness of the ocean would say, at the very least, that the ocean is no longer just another usable disposable of the paradise that is earth. If we claim that deep-sea mining is essential to our addressing of climate change, should we not first do absolutely all we can to stem climate change from our home base on land?

In a vision of earth as Eden, we would reverse taking to giving, and certainly we would not embark on an extensive mining operation to scrape the ocean floor and remove its riches, even for the nobility of batteries, without more stringent dedication to energy efficiency and reduction of energy waste as the keystone to coherently addressing climate change, nor without an all-out assault on carbon intensity in all existing products and processes. And certainly not without an integrated transparent global carbon price to speed decarbonization across all economic sectors, or a valuation structure for natural capital assets to compare against possible ocean-based biodiversity loss.

Nor perhaps without an obligation of the seabed mining companies to contribute significantly to a fund to indemnify future generations for what we will have expended in theory in their name, in theory to hold off the worst climate change impacts we can envision but have failed utterly to prevent so far with the means we've had at hand?

As we continue to wrestle with the challenges so well known to us—climate change, water scarcity, deforestation—the whole litany of disturbance that we know by heart, Nauru is not the distant head of a pin. Nauru can trade itself off for batteries, then maybe back to refugees again. What is a small island to do?

As of 2023, no credible international rules existed to oversee seabed mining, and the nodules seemed to be thought of as lying around in the oceanic abyss primed for the taking, the ocean itself on the way to being treated as dismissively as the atmosphere, its ecosystem services grossly underpriced. Like the fossil fuels, the nodules presumably would help displace, exploitation of the batteries in a rock will likely proceed with little concern for long-term consequences, either for the deep ocean itself and ocean creatures, or for the squandering of inexpressible value of the geological forging the nodules represent.

Uncontrolled and out-of-sight mining of manganese nodules in the reaches of the world's ocean, especially the far Pacific, seemed poised to become the next rapacious and unjustifiable act in the drama of climate change. As ESG investing embraces the idea that environmental and social issues are increasingly inseparable from financial decisions, so Nauru reminds us that neither can opportunity be separated from responsibility.

How will capital address the deep-sea trade-off, especially given the pledges made in the waning days of 2022 in Montreal, when national delegations updated the UN Convention on Biological Diversity, a global agreement also launched at the Earth Summit in Rio de Janeiro in 1992. Montreal was that convention's 15th Conference of the Parties, COP15, and delegates agreed to definitively protect 30% of our planet's land and oceans by 2030. Hailed as just as transformational as the Paris Agreement on climate change, the agreement was nicknamed "30x30," but can a Paris for the oceans be compatible with ocean mining intentions?

At the end of December 2022, TMC had raised about $300 million from private and public investors, including Glencore, Macquarie Capital, and Maersk, and its Q3 2022 earnings release stated cash on hand as $67 million, which TMC said, "will be sufficient to fund operations for at least the next 12 months."

In Norway, Norsea, a major logistics supplier supporting North Sea oil platforms and other oceanic energy operations, and others had invested in potential deep-sea mining for minerals off the Norwegian continental shift. Meanwhile the more traditional on-land search for the same rare-earth battery minerals proceeded unabated across all continents where minerals were known, especially in Brazil, south Asia, and Africa.

The undersea metals vision is seductive. As TMC put it:

> Imagine if 100 years from now our great grand-children could use the exact same metal atoms inside our phones, cars and homes. These metal atoms could continue to serve humankind through countless cycles of technological ingenuity. We're building a carefully managed metal commons that will be used, recovered, and reused again and again—for millennia. No more metal taken from the planet. No more metal lost to landfills. No more damage to the planet and the people on it. A society built with a metal metabolism, similar to how many biological systems have evolved over time.

Getting there will be tricky. The world is embarking on a massive, multi-decade project of decarbonizing global energy and transport. These carbon-free systems will take billions of tons of metal to build. And as the world's population continues to grow, urbanize and develop, this will require billions of tons of metal, too. So how do we build up our metal commons with the lightest possible touch? This is the global challenge we've made our own.

As with ESG itself, time will tell. Nauru may be an island off by itself, but so, alas, is planet earth.

9

Never Another Drop:
The Flow of Water
Markets

Pick up a honeycomb and likely your finger is sticky. Rub the finger in water just a bit and gone is the stickiness. Water is nearly a universal solvent, in addition to being our ubiquitous global cleanser, refresher, irrigator, quencher, bather, mixer, transporter, moisturizer, eroder, corroder, carver, connector, babbler, purifier, sanitizer, distributor, extinguisher, trickler, transporter, mesmerizer, and mystifier—gentle, forceful, and indispensable. Tangibly wondrous as it runs through our fingers and intangibly too, invoked in poems, chants, paintings, music, photography—a theme, force, setting, and reference all can recognize.

For example, the song of the yellow-tailed oropendola bird found in Central and South America was described in a guidebook as sounding like a flute being played through water, and so it does, a slightly shrill glug. I listened for the oropendola once in the Colombia rainforest, hoping the bird was close, never sure I was hearing it but always imagining I could. An oropendola's body weight is actually about 60% water, roughly the same average for all mammals and multicellular creatures, including humans, give or take some variation among human organs. For example, our hearts and brains are about 60% water, as inter- or extracellular fluid, compared to about 10% for our teeth.

These and any other startling facts about water infuse the indisputable essence—water is unique and there is no life without it. For that matter, no agriculture, nor industry, nor economy either, and yet there is so irreducibly little.

All the freshwater that has ever been or ever will be on earth owes its presence to the natural distillation engine of our magnificent oceans. Constantly, wind and heat cause seawater to evaporate and rise into the atmosphere, leaving salt and other sea minerals behind. The vapor condenses around airborne particles into clouds and then, after an average of nine days cloud-borne, falls to earth as rain, mostly back to the ocean to start the cycle again.

However, about 10% of that condensed water vapor falls on land, where it feeds streams, lakes, rivers, grass, forests, cisterns, buckets, and puddles, finding its way into countless earth-bound purposes, freezing up as ice here or there, or getting captured in a tank or plumbing system or seeping underground in a radiating plume. Eventually, though, following the slow-motion time clock of geology and gravity, every drop of water that fell as rain on land will creep its way back to the sea.

We can seed clouds with particles to speed up the condensation process and try to push out more rain where it is needed, but cloud seeding can create no new drops. HSBC, formerly known as the Hong Kong Shanghai Bank, capitalized on this basic water truth in a major marketing campaign, with ads plastered on jetways and airports worldwide, juxtaposing on sublime natural landscapes the tagline "Water. The most precious currency of all."

Our water cycle is a marvel, but it is an unremittingly closed system and there will never be another drop of freshwater on earth that is not already here or pending arrival from the moving clouds above.

Unlike our atmosphere, water does not go by entirely free. Water taxes and charges are common, and so water is to an extent priced. Still, given its ultra-scarcity, and its ubiquitous necessity, water has thus far defied an economic structure or approach commensurate with its value.

From a commonsense point of view, however, if one falls back on GDP as a gauge of valuable economic activity, if the annual global GDP in 2022 was reckoned by the International Monetary Fund to be roughly $100 trillion, is that not a reasonable surrogate for the value of earth's water? Why would the value of water be divisible from the value of the economic activity it uniquely underpins, directly and indirectly?

In *The Wealth of Nations,* Adam Smith crisply summarized the dilemma of valuing water differentiating "value in use" and "value in exchange": "Nothing is more useful than water, but it will purchase scarce anything; scarce anything can be had in exchange for it. A diamond, on the contrary, has scarce any value in use; but a very great quantity of other goods may frequently be had in exchange for it."

In his precursor *Lectures on Jurisprudence,* Smith also wrote, "Cheapness is in fact the same thing with plenty. It is only on account of the plenty of water that it is so cheap as to be got for the lifting, and on account of the scarcity of diamonds (for their real use seems not yet to be discovered) that they are so dear."

Diamonds do have practical uses—their obdurate strength is ideal for drill tips and similar industrial uses—but the "plenty" of water began eroding since the day Smith wrote the words. Natural water scarcity grows worse due to deteriorating water quality and growing demand, in turn limiting the "value in use" since water usability is also increasingly constrained by water contamination of all sorts. The idea of water "got for the lifting" is tragically long gone, even if it were still as cheap as Smith believed.

If the global water system were a checkbook, it would be overdrawn throughout the world, likely now permanently, with, as Smith might say, "scarce any" way to work off the debt to supply.

Research by McKinsey in 2020, "Water: A human and business priority," summed it up this way:

> The majority of the world's fresh water is divided among 410 named basins, which are areas of land where all water that falls or flows through that region ultimately ends at a single source. These include the Huang He, Nile, Colorado River, Indus, and many others. Of these 410 named basins, almost a quarter (90) are considered 'high stressed' (meaning that their ratio of total annual withdrawals to total available annual supply exceeds 40 percent). These 90 highly stressed basins account for just 13 percent of the total area of named water basins but account for 51 percent of withdrawals. About half are located in three countries with enormous water needs and high economic activity: China, India, and the United States.

In general human terms, disturbing statistics multiply. According to the World Health Organization (WHO) in 2022:

- Over 2 billion people live in water-stressed countries, which is expected to be exacerbated in some regions as result of climate change and population growth.

- Globally, at least 2 billion people use a drinking water source contaminated with feces. Microbial contamination of drinking-water as a result of contamination with feces poses the greatest risk to drinking-water safety.
- While the most important chemical risks in drinking water arise from arsenic, fluoride or nitrate, emerging contaminants such as pharmaceuticals, pesticides, per- and polyfluoroalkyl substances (PFASs) and microplastics generate public concern.

Among ideas to price water to spur more efficient use, privatization of public assets came into favor in the 1990s in policy circles, to rid public budgets of maintenance and operational carrying costs. In theory, private capital would pick up the slack and make money investing in meeting public needs. In 1998, however, the corrupt and clumsy privatization of water services in the Cochabamba Valley of Bolivia came to symbolize how deeply and unfairly, even violently, the privatization idea could fail.

Bending to demand from the World Bank and the International Monetary Fund to privatize water assets and remove water subsidies in return for further international financial aid, Bolivia's government auctioned rights to the public water system, such as it was, in the city of Cochabamba. The deal included rights to water in the city's environs supplied by wells, channels, and pipes mostly built by local people at their own expense and not connected to the municipal system on offer.

The sole bidder, Aguas del Tunari, an international consortium that included a subsidiary of the US infrastructure giant Bechtel, won the contract for $2.5 billion, taking over the Cochabamba system with a 40-year concession. Under the agreement, some service improvements occurred, upgrading what had been a poor service baseline. However, Aguas de Tunari significantly raised water charges, doubling and tripling water fees, including introducing charges to users of the autonomous groundwater systems that had never been part of the public network.

Most Bolivians lived in grinding poverty at the time, an average of "around 63 percent," according to research by the IMF and the Bolivian government in 1997, specifically, "38 percent in conditions of extreme poverty . . . 80 percent of the population in the countryside live on income below the poverty line, with 58 percent receiving incomes below the value of a food basket."

Against this dismaying backdrop, increased water charges imposed significant financial pain. Protesting the privatization deal as thievery of public water, city and country dwellers came together and demonstrations snowballed, paralyzing Cochabamba and its surroundings.

Bolivia's national government cracked down with troops, riot gear, and violence. The protests intensified, however, and finally the government rescinded the legislation that had authorized the Aguas del Tunari takeover. Bechtel sued, then withdrew the action in 2005 when the Bolivian government agreed to issue a statement that the concession had been terminated due to civil unrest, and not malfeasance by Aguas del Tunari or Bechtel.

The events became known worldwide as the Cochabamba Water War and the privatizing of water synonymous with trampling of the human right to water, even if it was true that water distribution in Cochabamba was exceedingly uneven prior to the privatization. Bechtel contended that 60% of the water was being lost to leakage or pilferage—and subsidies of the system benefited mostly the affluent, who had most access to the public plumbing system, while the truly poor fended for themselves for water.

In the United States, a similar signature water global infamy occurred about 15 years later in Flint, Michigan, a city once bustling with American manufacturing, but where gradual industrial abandonment left the city financially stressed. Underequipped town officials faced constant budget shortfalls.

The state of Michigan took over Flint's financial management in 2011, in a fiscal emergency similar to that which would soon hit Detroit in 2013 and lead to the crisis over the DIA art collection and the Art in a Box compromise (see Chapter 4).

Detroit, nearby and itself financially stretched, did figure indirectly in Flint's water crisis. Detroit had been selling Lake Huron water to Flint for roughly 50 years. However, in 2013, officials in Flint decided the time had come to instead draw water directly from the Flint River to meet Flint's needs, to cut costs and reportedly save $5 million in water fees.

Prescient and alarmed water engineers and residents pushed back on the switch immediately—the low quality of Flint River water was notorious.

Meanwhile, critically, Flint officials failed to include in the switchover plan treatment of Flint River water with anti-corrosives to avoid lead leaching from antiquated plumbing, a service the Detroit system had provided as a matter of course.

The switchover proceeded anyway, as of April 2014. Within weeks, complaints rolled in from households and businesses about the foul smell, taste, and color of the water. In October 2014, General Motors announced its Flint engine plant would no longer use Flint municipal water because the water corroded its pipes.

Flint water officials changed nothing, but Flint residents received increasingly frequent boil water notices due to alarming levels of bacteria in the drinking water, and in 2014 an outbreak of Legionnaire's Disease struck the city, eventually killing 12 people. Fecal coliform counts rose; boil water notices kept coming. But boiling water concentrates lead, and lead levels in Flint water skyrocketed, as did lead levels in the blood of Flint residents, especially children. Over time, full-blown public alarm sounded in Flint. Finally, in October 2015, Flint reconnected to the Detroit water system.

Flint's fast-moving water crisis had been national nightly news, and what had been propelled by the expectation of cost savings in 2013 ended up in 2021 in a roughly $600 million civil suit settlement won against the state of Michigan by Flint residents who had suffered disease and hardship. Additional criminal charges were filed against numerous city and state officials, including the then-governor, citing negligence. In between, in 2016, President Barack Obama had declared a federal emergency in Flint, triggering an immediate infusion of $5 million in federal funds, with additional $100 million eventually appropriated to meet Flint's needs for water testing, bottled water, and the basic replacement of pipes. Flint's name became infamously associated with water catastrophe.

In 2018, the world watched an anguished Cape Town in South Africa cope with severe drought and water shortage, facing down day zero when the city would have literally run out of water and all municipal taps would be turned off. Strict water quotas of 13 gallons per person per day were imposed on all of Cape Town's agricultural, business, and domestic uses, on the honor system with spot checks, and high fines for exceeding the quota. Many people without plumbing at home waited hours in line to collect the day's allowance.

Thanks to the discipline of Cape Town's people in cutting back on water use, including the poorest whose access to public water systems had been already limited, and a break in the weather, Cape Town did not hit day zero. As the 2020 McKinsey water report put it, "The government also got lucky: rain replenished its basin just in time. All in all, the drought drove at least 5.9 billion rand (approximately $400 million) in economic losses across the Western Cape."

The global water overdraw may well be beyond paying back or restoring, compounded by climate change causing more extended and frequent droughts as well as more tempestuous rain that falls too much where there is little need and too little where need is great. Likely, without coherent forward-looking and fair-minded water planning and pricing, much of the world might eventually have to face the kind of stringent water use oversight endured by Cape Town, water scarcity engendering a specter of potential water police.

Basic to water planning, of course, is the premise of sharing, a quintessential expression of which can be found in Bali, Indonesia, in the subak rice terrace system, where the foundational guidance is that no farmer on high ground may withhold or deter water from a farmer on lower ground. Following the Balinese belief system of Tri Hita Karana, meaning harmony of spirit, people, and nature and known for at least 1,000 years, the subak offers both a spiritual and practical reverential recognition of scarcity and, by extension, value.

From a distance, each subak terrace shelf radiates healthy emerald green moisture, impeccably shaped and cleaved clean. Water from lakes and other collection points on high ground is released to lower lands, maximizing gravity so water flows to all below, and no one has a water advantage.

Farmers tend to water as if it were a liquid ribbon, capturing and directing it through pipes or hand-made sluices this way and that across the rice fields. A complex system of customs and rituals known as *awig-awig* regulates subak operations. In 2012, UNESCO declared Bali's subaks to be World Heritage cultural landscape sites.

Subaks used to be Bali's unmistakable landscape signature. However, industrial expansion, hotels, and homestays gobbled up agricultural land, including subaks, while interest in rice farming as a livelihood declined among Bali's large next generation. As of 2022, about 30% of Indonesia's population was under 24, according to the United Nations Family Planning Agency.

Subaks were split up or made smaller, eroding the viability and efficiencies of the extended network. Some subaks become tourist attractions, and honeymooners and other foreign tourists climb to the uppermost terraces, where farmers seeking extra cash set up swings so visitors can fly out and back looking out over the weaving and rhythmic sculptured hills.

Still, the subak beautifully manifests the fundamental truth of water—it is miraculous and cannot be horded without detriment to others. Water realities are humbling, no matter where.

Some years ago, in Haiti, where general destitution has reigned for centuries due to colonial and national despotism, chronic impoverishment, disease, corruption, and above all exhaustion of natural resources, I watched a heartbreaking and poignant scene, paralyzed.

In a village near the capital, Port-au-Prince, young girls gathered at a public spigot, waiting for it to sputter on. Each child cradled an armful of tiny plastic bottles rinsed of luxury shampoo and body creams, discards from nearby hotels blithely situated in the midst of Haiti's unfathomable poverty. Charged by their families with water duty, the girls held each little bottle one by one to the sputtering spigot, forced to elbow each other to get as many filled as possible before, with no warning, the water stopped dead.

Haiti is practically denuded of trees, its forests decimated for firewood and charcoal. Trees hold land and land holds water, so Haiti no longer has much hope of natural water retention.

Naïve I may be but, for example, given the catastrophic freshwater shortage in Haiti and elsewhere worldwide, while increasingly rain falls in torrents and turns into horrible floods, could it be possible to focus a major concerted effort in Haiti on the goal of establishing at least one reliable source of potable water there, say by 2030? A gleaming public fountain fed by rainfall, purified by existing technology using ultraviolet light, delivered by gravity?

Needed: rain, sun, pipe, pumps, plumbers—available all, and a gigantic jobs program the enterprising and survivalist Haitians could implement in a snap. Rainfall has the advantages of being relatively clean when it lands, unlike most of the surface water in Haiti's lakes and streams, pools and puddles, all pretty filthy with trash and excrement and very tough to clean and render usable, let alone drinkable.

I spoke once about the rainwater harvest possibility to the chairman of a leading French water company that was active in Haiti after the 2009 earthquake. He was intrigued by the rainwater idea, but rather than engage about how to engineer it, he switched the talk over to his business line—cleaning surface water and selling bottled water.

Rainfall, of course, is free, but cleaning up dirty water is expensive and someone must pay. So water companies secured contracts from international aid agencies and relief programs to clean and sell water that very few Haitians could afford to buy, and another decade of disaster plagued Haiti.

In early 2023, Haiti languished just above political collapse as urban gangs took over most of the capital, Port-au-Prince. Valiant teams from

Doctors without Borders and Partners in Health, both nonprofit public health providers working with the beleaguered Haitian Ministry of Health, tried to stem outbreaks of cholera and other health misery that haunted the long-suffering Haitian people, while Haiti remained without any significant public water system in place, rainwater or otherwise.

Rain, of course, is the sole source of recharge of underground water aquifers. To capture rainfall scrupulously would seem an undeniable stipulation of the value of water and its own form of pricing. I first heard about the potential of rainwater harvest in 2013 from Bunker Roy, founder of the Barefoot College in Tilonia, India, who spoke lovingly of rain at the Clinton Global Initiative. The college trained local people in the best techniques of renewable energy and water purification.

According to the World Bank in 2022, "India is the largest user of groundwater globally, extracting more than the United States and China put together. Today, groundwater is the only source of water for most of India's people, providing the bulk of water for farming and domestic use. . . . Already, almost two-thirds—63 percent—of India's districts are threatened by falling groundwater levels."

In an insidious cycle, the overdraw of aquifers and lowering of the water table also concentrates pollutants and saline ratios, so the more groundwater is used, the less usable it can become. Since rainfall recharge is vital to groundwater supply, preventing rain from seeping into the earth can be counterproductive. The genius of Barefoot College, however, is a coordinated approach, both capturing rain to hold and use surface water and letting it fall naturally on land.

As of 2022, according to Barefoot College International, its water management program "has constructed 1,600 rainwater harvesting tanks in government schools & community buildings, benefitting more than 2 million people. Of these, 500 tanks were constructed under a project by Minister of Water Resources, including 220 village ponds which benefit more than 0.12 million people, 15 anicuts [water holding areas set in streams] benefitting more than 0.15 million, 45 dug wells recharging more than 130 million liters of rainwater and 4 small dams benefitting around 48,000 people reaching poorest of the poor communities across 18 states."

Also, according to a May 2022 World Bank report on groundwater in India, in the most water stressed states, "over 2,200 villages have drawn up water budgets that show how much groundwater is available, how much is estimated to be recharged, and how much can be set aside for agriculture, by far the largest user of this resource."

The village water budget process is central to India's Atal Bhujal Yojana program, begun in 2019, which tries to help water-stressed villages in India manage groundwater supply, in seven of the most water-stressed states. A main incentive of water budgeting is to increase farmer and village income even as water use decreases. Since no new water can be created, the goal is to aim for the highest possible efficiencies.

Groundwater settles and percolates invisibly underground, making its management all the harder. To try to illuminate the actual quantity of water at any given day or time of year, village women, men, and children learn—both in classes and in the field—the basics of hydrology and how water travels. All available techniques come into play, ranging from satellite rainfall data dappling as apps across mobile phone screens to the hands-and-knees real-life task of dropping a measuring tape down a tube well to gauge how much water is actually at the bottom.

Farmers consider how to switch away from water-intensive crops like cotton and wheat to pomegranates and cumin that can, according to the World Bank, command higher prices. Irrigation methods are tightened up and monitored locally. Public water facilities and use are also more scrutinized, notably by women, whose opinions on how to save water command extra respect because, worldwide, it is mostly women who have carried the water, literally. Villagers also learn water-quality testing, to keep track of pH and possible contaminants.

Local governments receive the needed equipment and training, with the result that each village manages the groundwater it depends upon like a water checkbook—what goes out must go back in somehow; efficiency is the only new water source. So, in the face of frightening scarcity, water accounting comes to thousands of relatively poor people who still have no control over rainfall.

On the urban level, rainfall capture and natural hydrology define the designs of globally recognized Chinese landscape architect Yu Kongjian and his large firm Turenscape. China has set a goal that 100 cities with more than 1 million people will capture 70% of rainfall by 2030, and Yu's concepts have significantly heightened global attention to managing water through water-focused design.

As in the subaks of Indonesia, Yu's projects are based on the central belief that water flows are allies, not enemies. Yu's projects aim to secure maximum benefit from the natural behavior of water, seeking to understand and design water systems harmonious with how rainfall would flow if no structures were in its way at all. So that water can flow as freely as possible, Yu's designs feature ribbon grasses, wetlands, trees, and all manner of plantings to catch water and give it room to meander and seep into the soil. Even in floods, water is captured, saved, and stored for use for another day, the reduction of water waste at the least cost a key objective.

Yu is a pioneer of the concept of "sponge cities," much favored in China, with President Xi Jinping himself as a devotee, which calls for minimizing the use of hard impermeable materials, like cement, favoring more absorbent and porous materials, especially plantings and absorbent piping, so that water is not clashing constantly with the surfaces it meets. A true sponge city is composed of networks of ponds and parks that capture rainfall and stormwater, filtering and cleansing run-off as much as possible with natural wetland processes, a quintessential "ecosystem service."

Yu's firm is involved in hundreds of projects in China and other countries, as reckoning with flooding, torrential rainbursts, and water shortage becomes more demanding and necessary. Informed and light-touch water management has long been integral to landscape architecture, a field increasingly joining the climate change fray, with no end of innovative and idealized solutions to water management.

Still, even the most enlightened blueprints hit practical impediments of the day-to-day and many communities cannot afford professional design services.

I had my own experience with the practical difficulties of managing water and best-laid plans when I volunteered at a home in Thailand for displaced children from Myanmar's civil wars. Located in a bucolic tropical setting near the Myanmar border, the home sheltered, fed, and took care of about 100 children whose parents were either dead or not in a position to care for their children, and single mothers. The home was hygienically fastidious, but water shortage was chronic even though plenty of rain fell during the rainy season. Municipal water services were sometimes on, sometimes off, and often water pressure was so weak, it could not be pumped up to the second floor. Nor was the municipal water safe to drink.

A French development agency had agreed to install a rainwater capture system at the home, but the project had been mired in red tape. I spoke a bit of French, and the enterprising woman who had founded and run the children's home for more than two decades asked me, "Can you unstick this?"

I phoned the agency and we cleared the paperwork. Within a few months, a French engineering and installation crew arrived, as well as shipments of pipe, gutters, and large plastic cisterns. Hammering and welding, the crew set up a rainwater capture system and transformed the home's water reality. Drinking water still had to be purchased from private suppliers, but the rainwater network largely met house cleaning and bathing needs. The day the taps burst on for the first time with plenty of water, the children cheered.

Priceless joy outside of financial price. But joy dissipates, while the demand to treasure water does not, worldwide.

One obvious expression that clearly stipulates the value of water is to require its recycling, a technique honed to near perfection in Singapore, where equatorial cloudbursts seem to occur 12 months of the year even though there is nominally a dry season. Before Singapore separated from Malaysia in 1965, the island depended on Malaysia for municipal water, politically and economically untenable for the newly sovereign Singaporean state.

Gradually, as integral to its rapid push for economic growth and global leadership profile, Singapore invested heavily in water engineering, building reservoirs to hold rainwater and an intricate system of circulation drains. Singapore also became expert in recycling science and technology. According to the Singapore's Public Utilities Board (PUB), the national water agency, the nation went from chronic water shortage in the 1970s to meeting 40% of its public water demand as of 2022 with recycled water even as population and industrialization increased.

Singapore maintains lavish gardens and plantings to retain rain and recharge its aquifers, and also employs desalinization, itself energy intensive, in the ongoing quest for additional future freshwater. Eventually, though, even with all technologies at maximum, reducing water use is essential, and the PUB constantly promotes efficiencies, including rebates on water fees in return for water savings, and even holding water rationing exercises in schools.

Of course, water rationing feels draconian but is likely inevitable in one form or other, including that pricing itself is a form of rationing.

In the United States, the Colorado River, which travels through seven states and Mexico, epitomizes America's widening water problems. If you stand at the edge of the South Rim of the Grand Canyon and look down the 7,000 feet to the Colorado, you can expect to perceive the river only as a trickle. However, the Colorado became a trickle at eye level too.

In August 2022, sobering news came from the US Department of Interior: "the Department of the Interior today announced urgent action to improve and protect the long-term sustainability of the Colorado River System. . . . Prolonged drought and low runoff conditions accelerated by climate change have led to historically low water levels in Lakes Powell and Mead. Over the last two decades, Department leaders have engaged with Colorado River Basin partners on various drought response operations. However, given that water levels continue to decline, additional action is needed to protect the System."

Amplifying the urgency of cutbacks in use, the Department's Assistant Secretary for Water and Science, Tanya Trujillo, said, "In order to avoid a catastrophic collapse of the Colorado River System and a future of uncertainty and conflict, water use in the basin must be reduced."

WestWater, an economic research firm for the water industry, translated those worried words into facts and figures in a late 2022 report titled "What Large Scale Conservation Looks Like," laying out what economic costs are at stake, given that current uses of water in the Colorado Basin were about 11 million acre feet (MAF), and best estimates were that cuts in basin use need to be to 2 to 4 MAF!

WestWater stated: "The Colorado River Basin has been out of balance for the past two decades. In the Upper Basin, the snowpack has not been able to keep up with requirements to pass water down to the Lower Basin states . . . the river flows received from the Upper Basin have not been sufficient to meet all established uses, a situation often referred to as 'structural deficit.'"

The report added that the current 11 MAF usage figure "already accounts for system conservation efforts in recent years. The rough math tells us that conservation efforts need to reduce basin–wide water use by at least 20% and perhaps up to 40% relative to current use. That is a humbling estimate. To put 20% reduction in perspective, it means eliminating the total municipal and industrial use for 2 out of every 3 people in the basin, or alternatively cutting out roughly a third of all irrigated farms and ranches across the basin . . . these estimates represent a scale of conservation and demand reduction never before attempted."

Moreover, calculated WestWater, "Achieving a 20% reduction in water use comes at an estimated annual cost of at least $1.3 billion." Furthermore, "It is important to understand that the conservation required in the Colorado River Basin is not just a series of annual cutbacks to get through a drought. The science is clear that the basin requires permanent demand reduction to achieve sustainability. The present value of $1.3 billion in future annual conservation costs is roughly $81 billion based on US Treasury Bond real interest rates." Citing the

$4 billion appropriated to improved Colorado Basin management from the Inflation Reduction Act the US Congress passed in 2022, WestWater says, "funding from the IRA buys just three years of needed conservation—it is only a down payment."

Yet even the most frightening estimate of high cost cannot create more water. Only more efficiency and new technologies can address growing scarcity, with a boost from water pricing, not to unduly burden households with unaffordable water costs but to fairly value water as it is consumed relative to supply.

Pricing scarcity is the chief vocation of water markets, already in operation here and there around the world. Water markets are perhaps the last best hope of balancing the principles of sharing with the realities of scarcity to help avoid seemingly inevitable increasingly stringent limits on use, as in Cape Town, or untenably high water fees that could explode into civil unrest, à la Cochabamba, a not outlandish fear.

Like carbon markets, water markets stipulate an overall cap on use, then distribute maximum rights to use. In general, rights holders who use less can sell to rights holders who use more. Price for the rights varies with how much water is actually physically available or projected, and caps warrant regular review.

In the Colorado River Basin, the Colorado River Compact of 1922 governs water allocations among the user states and Native American tribes, known as the Law of the River. This framework established basic rights for water use and has been the subject of lawsuits and amendments since its first days on the books.

Interstate water trading up and down the whole 1,450-mile length of the river is obviously physically undoable, but even conceptually it never came into existence due to complications of interstate jurisdictions, vestigial disputes, and difficulty of measuring and monitoring water use across such great distances. However, intrastate trading does exist, notably in Arizona and California.

The Mojave Desert, the driest in North America, nevertheless overlies California's largest aquifer. As a result, the Mojave Desert groundwater market in California is highly active, with transactions managed by regional water agencies to enable transfer of rights to pump groundwater from one use to another between individual users and municipalities.

The market was established in 1996, after much adjudication and debate on how to further protect the local water table, which had fallen 30 feet between 1964 and 1990 due to historically unfettered access to groundwater pumping for water-intensive agriculture. Crops such as almonds, for example, are highly water demanding. According to the California Water Footprint Network, as of 2022, almond production used up to 17% of total agricultural water in California and 13% of the total developed water supply.

In July 2021, an analysis published in the *Journal of Political Economy* on the Mojave water market concluded that land values where the groundwater market applied were 220% higher than where open access to pumping was still permitted. It also found that aggregate economic benefits to agricultural and municipal users alike was nearly $500 million. Here, the market crystallized priceless benefits of water management, and the higher value that attaches to land where water use can reasonably continue. Higher land values also clearly demonstrate the longer-term value of improved water table levels when more control is exerted on where water was pumped for what.

The Mojave market established a water budget that covers both surface and groundwater. As in carbon markets, described in a 2022 report on "Designing Groundwater Markets in Practice," the purpose of capping the aggregate amount of water to be extracted is "constraining extraction to match the sustainability goals of the basin."

As to the definition of those goals, who's to say?

Generally, integral to managing scarcity, transparent price signals can also shift the use to which water is put, encouraging sale of rights by those who do not need them to those who do, and will meet the price. Water trading can draw as much contention as carbon trading. The presumption of private ownership of rights to use a natural resource that has common public benefit prompts disdain, along with the fact that buying and selling those rights generates profit.

Controversy flared in January 2021 when the *New York Times* published "Wall Street Eyes Billions in the Colorado's Water." The article focused on an outright sale of water rights from the small rural town of Cibola, Arizona, to the more heavily populated Phoenix suburb of Queen Creek, 175 miles away. According to the *Times,* a private investment firm, Greenstone, "quietly bought the rights to most of Cibola's water," then sold the rights to Queen Creek. In practice, the reported $21 million purchase meant water would be physically diverted from country to city, and agricultural land would be taken out of production since the water rights to irrigate had been sold.

Greenstone's business is to buy and aggregate water entitlements that may be going unused. In Cibola, Greenstone bought a portion of the agricultural entitlement from a group of farmers who planned to irrigate only 400 acres. It was reported that the rest of the land would become a private ranch.

Controversy swirled around the Greenstone sale and, in December 2022, several counties in Arizona announced they were considering filing a legal action against the US Federal Bureau of Reclamation for having approved the transaction.

Meanwhile, as legal action simmered, the actual water awaited its zigzag journey, due to get moving as of February 2023. The coveted water, originating in Lake Mead behind the Hoover Dam, instead of heading south to Cibola, would "take a left hand turn at Lake Havasu" as Paul Gardner, director of public utilities in Queen Creek, put it to the *Mesa Times*.

From there, the water would head east to Queen Creek via the Central Arizona Project canal, an elaborate engineering system that runs like a vein for 336 miles across the state. Using gravity, pumps, tunnels, and dams to channel water from the Colorado River, the canal system brings water to 80% of the population of Arizona, making that state's contemporary water-demanding life possible.

In view of recommended severe restrictions of withdrawals from the Colorado River, water rights transfers such as Greenstone's may also face restrictions if the Mojave market entitlements are revamped.

In the end, scarcity reverberates in nearly impossible decisions. Who shall determine whether rights to use water can be transferred from farms to suburbs, or whether almonds should be grown at the expense of other crops, or cotton versus maize or maize versus ethanol? Are the trade-offs and discussion points too complex for our decision-making systems and, invariably, do the rights of some conflict with the rights of others to the point of defying reconciliation? Can a market ever adjudicate fairly and equitably, given the excruciating scarcity of water, the omnipresence of demand for it, and its constantly changing physical location and condition? These open questions are in dire need of response.

The most advanced water market in the world operates in southeastern Australia's Murray–Darling Basin, covering the catchment areas of the two major rivers, plus a network of smaller rivers and tributaries. The basin encompasses a million square kilometers, 14% of the nation's land area, providing water to roughly 2.5 million people and thousands of farms.

In parched Australia, only irrigation could beget agriculture. The Murray–Darling Basin produces wool, cotton, wheat, sheep, cattle, dairy produce, rice, oilseed, wine, fruit, and vegetables for both domestic and overseas markets, plus supporting drinking water in major cities, including Australia's capital, Canberra. The basin also hosts unique biodiversity and wildlife, from the Darling Lily to the platypus, Murray cod, and the red kangaroo, as well as a cultural sustenance of place to the First Nations Aboriginal people who have lived in the basin area for 40,000 years.

Once British settlement took over Australia in the 19th century, British land law also held sway, and water rights were legally regarded as tied into land rights for owners adjacent to water sources. Water availability drove settlement patterns, where water rights were inherent to land.

From 1895 to 1902, severe drought gripped the Murray–Darling river system. Still, as Australian agriculture expanded, water use grew and, over decades, compounded by further drought and other natural vagaries, water demand in the Murray–Darling, as in the Colorado, began to outstrip supply.

Over the next decades, various management plans were tried, mostly managed by each state separately. Finally, in 2007, the national Australian government passed the Water Act, culminating in the interstate Murray–Darling Basin Plan that governs the amount of water that can be taken each year by all users for any purpose. Aboriginal people are entitled to what are known as "cultural flows" of water in the basin, inherent in ancestral rights, but notably yet to be formally arranged, as of 2022.

As Murray–Darling water policy evolved, landowners with water rights traded those rights among themselves, as need for water on a given farm varied. Over time, these informal arrangements coalesced into the organized regulated markets of the Murray–Darling Basin, The markets are overseen by the Murray–Darling Basin Authority, and include commercial market players.

About 11% of Australian water rights are held by foreign enterprises in Canada, the UK, the United States, and China, according to a report on the Murray–Darling water markets by the Australian Competition and Consumer Commission (ACCC) "roughly comparable with foreign ownership in our agricultural sector generally." As in Arizona, water actually moves physically through a complex network of dams, weirs, and channels, with the overall goal of getting water where it is needed and ideally where its use is the most economically and environmentally efficient. This can include transfer of water from agricultural land to wildlife preservation habitats and wetlands.

Trades can be either entitlements to what is known as "permanent water," where a rights holder sells rights permanently, or allocations, "temporary water," where a rights holder stipulates a limited sale term and the traded rights can move back and forth.

Entitlements and allocations go mostly to towns, farmers, and industrial enterprises, and are overseen and prioritized at the state level, with the overall water budget managed by the interstate basin authority. Accurate measurement and metering are key, literally tracking water flow constantly.

The water market supports much of Australia's irrigated agriculture, which, according to the ACCC, in 2017–2018, was valued at $5.7 billion in the Southern Basin and in the Northern Basin about $1.6 billion in real terms.

Tradeable water rights are also now a significant long-term asset for many farmers. According to the ACCC, "the value of water entitlements on issue across Australia in 2019–20, held by active and retired farmers and others, including environmental water holders, is estimated at $26.3 billion." The value of water entitlements can dwarf the value of industries they support, and are critical financial assets for the holders.

Water markets, like carbon markets, frequently meet calls for reform. The same ACCC report, anticipating more participation and reliance on markets, recommends tightening up governance and improved communication with the public. If not, the report says, "misconceptions can interfere with public debates. For example, water markets are sometimes confused with water privatization."

Despite their long history, water trading and water markets in the Murray–Darling can attract heated debate, as summarized in a 2022 paper by Professor Sarah Wheeler, an expert on global water markets, entitled "Debunking Murray–Darling Basin water trade myths." Wheeler writes:

> Concerns center around the idea that water is too unique and important to trade; that trade disadvantages many farms (especially smaller farms); and that water markets create an environment for unethical behavior and the development of water barons. . . . Critics argue that because water—as a basic human need—is fundamentally different to other tradeable commodities, allowing water markets is fundamentally wrong and immoral. Within Australia in particular— despite the decades of success of water markets in reallocating water in times of scarcity—there is still a view by some that water markets are an experiment that has turned into a "casino" and a "catastrophic error."

Wheeler points to various reasons for confusion: "Although some previous water trades have been unethical and immoral . . . commentators who over-exaggerate, cherry-pick faults, conduct a few biased interviews, and ignore peer-reviewed evidence represents poor research practice."

Fully cognizant of complicated social, cultural, and environmental interplays, Wheeler says, "The biggest advantage of water markets lies in their adaptation benefits; allowing irrigators to a) cope with weather uncertainties and share water in times of both scarcity and excess; and b) retire or exit their farms with more dignity and ease when needed." Still, balancing flaws and benefits, Wheeler concludes, "Instead of blaming water markets as 'the problem,' it is possible that they can be part of 'the solution.' Smart design and integration of social and cultural aspects into water trade governance is possible."

No infallible answers exist.

The most salient feature of the Murray–Darling water market is the dichotomy inherent in any environmental market—defining and securing recognition of the scarcity of an environmental asset, in turn translating the value of that asset into some form of financial expression, nevertheless destined to be inadequate.

Perfecting water markets may be long since out of reach, as increasing water scarcity may push water even beyond pricelessness, especially as climate change foretells increasingly dangerous droughts and rainfall pattern disruption, from the Murray–Darling to the Colorado and across other stressed basins worldwide.

Water markets are in operational, planning, or midway design around the world, from the River Po in Italy to West Bengal, India, the Lower Mekong, Mozambique, Nepal, France, Chile, China, and beyond—all with the same general objective and same general flaws.

Meanwhile, an unglamorous villain haunts the water pricing stage—leakage. Not only can we not create new water, but we have also been wasting water at incomprehensible rates, wasting millions of dollars too in the process.

Non-revenue water (NRW) is water lost to water utilities either through obsolete water networks, crumbling plumbing, or poor maintenance. Further commercial losses also occur through faulty metering and usage tracking, undercharging, or illegal water connections where one consumer taps into another. Non-revenue water also includes public purpose water provided as unbilled or least-cost from the start, such as water used for fighting fires.

Recovering non-revenue water doesn't necessarily mean that every flow should be squeezed for maximum revenue or that only high water fees can hold down consumption or recover commercial losses. Rather,

NRW speaks to the generally avoidable level of water wastage in reasonably sophisticated water systems. The value and volume of NRW can be staggering, especially when water scarcity is so dire, and so many people are without access to reliable water at all. Reducing non-revenue water should, in theory, improve water access and spread costs of water system maintenance more fairly, capturing water "already" in the system, and adding it back, without more water drawn.

In 2018, the International Water Association, a global network of professionals and experts in the water sector, published research on NRW based on data collected from 109 mostly urban water utilities in 28 countries. The study concluded that worldwide, "the cost/value of water lost amounts to USD 39 billion per year" and that the overall volume being lost was equivalent to half the annual flow of the Ganges River in India, or 30% of input to water systems worldwide. The report observed, "Not only is this an enormous financial concern but elevated NRW also detracts from water utilities in a time of increasing scarcity and climate change reaching their goals of full service coverage at a reliable level of service at an affordable price."

The researchers concluded that in most situations, payback periods for investments in NRW recovery would be 7–10 years, adding that they found it "difficult to understand why water utilities and governments are so reluctant to invest in NRW reduction."

Advances in technology, especially AI, can cut into the NRW loss, high technical digital techniques to "listen" underground and locate leakages quickly at least cost, chasing down every wayward water drop. According to the US EPA, about 1 trillion gallons of water leak away each year in US households, equivalent to the annual usage of 11 million homes—water gone through dripping faucets and worn-out toilet floaters, treated to drinkability standard but then never used, valued, or paid for.

Fortunately, as water scarcity and costs become more evident, investments in water efficient technologies are fashionable and growing in appeal. For example, the city of Cleveland, Ohio, on the shore of Lake Erie, one of the US Great Lakes where 20% of the world's freshwater collects, developed the Cleveland Water Alliance, a business group specifically targeting water technology companies. The alliance is "focused on growing the region's water economy by providing innovators from all over the country the ability to conceive of, test, scale up and demonstrate innovative water technology directly with customers." The initiative was new in 2022 and promising. The alliance said, "This Initiative bridges the gap in bringing new water technologies to market . . . accelerating the impact of innovation on an increasingly water-stressed world."

Ultimately, only capturing the pricelessness of water as a public asset can adequately reverse waste and drive efficiency. Surely, though, the public good value of every water drop would argue that public budgets bear the lion's share of the costs of plumbing maintenance and upgrade as essential social, physical, and economic infrastructure.

If water stewardship were valued even close to what wastage and NRW costs, water infrastructure maintenance could more easily raise capital by justifying the financial and actual water savings, using the GAIP concept recommended by Sir Ronald Cohen where financial accounting finally turns its eyes to the negative-positive environmental impact balance.

Also, at some point, given increasing water scarcity and drought pressures, water pricing approaches may have to include what is known as "virtual water" or embedded water costs. Put another way, this is the invisible value of water that travels with a product produced using that water. Embedded virtual water is as invisible as carbon emissions, and carries similar hidden costs, such as transporting water-rich products by truck, air, and ship.

In short, water travels globally through the virtual water concept, so how do we track that transfer of value so it supports efficiency of use, and not profit alone? For example, according to the California Water Impact Network, about 70% of the almond crop raised in California is exported. If we were accounting for virtual water, water used to grow almonds would amount to water export, indirectly subsidized by residents of California. Perhaps, though, they might have preferred the water to be used in other ways?

On the other hand, perhaps enough value from the embedded-water almond export market reverts to the state in business revenue, sales taxes, employment, and agricultural profile to compensate for the water that will never return. Who can keep these esoteric but perhaps inevitable ledgers to political, civil, and economic satisfaction?

How do we arbitrate the affordability of water, and who will do it?

Water neutrality, similar to carbon neutrality, has a role to play in adding value to water without putting the cost of water out of reach. Water neutrality draws on the carbon market offset model—reduced water use here offsets other water use there.

Direct financial compensation, however, is perhaps the best inspiration for water savings, especially if water use is cheap to begin with in a given location and water waste is not economically punitive.

Using a "software as a service" model, Kilimo, based in Argentina and operating in seven Latin American countries, piloted a compensation system that connects farmers who save water with companies willing to pay for those savings. According to Kilimo, companies pledging to be "water neutral" or more water efficient generally have increased 34% since 2020.

The innovative Kilimo model goes beyond fixing a given pipe or faucet to reduce leakage, and instead treats invisible underground aquifers as visible overground lakes. The model conceptualizes disparate underground resources as if they all flowed into one, meaning that a water savings in section A of an aquifer serves the well-being and water use needs of users in Section B, and vice versa.

The brainchild of four enterprising and motivated young Argentinians concerned with climate change, Kilimo aims to insulate Latin American farmers from the ravages of increasing drought, and protecting farming as a viable economic livelihood in a water-stressed world.

Agriculture uses about 70% of the world's freshwater, with a high degree of inefficiency in irrigation, caused especially by evaporation of water once it is applied to crops. Costs of reducing that water waste, however, can be prohibitive. Kilimo cuts the cost of water scrutiny, however, by using real-time satellite technology and AI to feed information straight to a farmer's mobile phone, no field hardware needed.

Kilimo has set up an Irrigation Academy, and contracts with farmers to dispense information on irrigation techniques. Farmers sign up for Kilimo's services, and each year together they plot out planting plans, field by field, crop by crop, and analyze the "initial water state" of the fields—a water baseline, as it were.

Kilimo then integrates current weather information and satellite technology to better predict evaporation rates, also field by field, helping the farmer move irrigation to places where it is likely to evaporate least. In certain cases, farmers received placement feedback in less than 10 minutes.

However, in many situations, especially in Latin America, water costs are low, and so chasing every drop of savings is not particularly cost-effective for farmers, whose margins are tight in any case. Kilimo adds value to these water savings by pairing farmers with large water users who are also drawing on local or regional aquifers. Kilimo presubscribes companies with substantial water needs operating locally, such as Intel, Coca-Cola, and Microsoft. The water-using companies sign multi-year contracts with Kilimo, committing to pay for water savings from farmers. The basic premise for these commitments is that all water users are served well by more healthy and rich aquifers, and companies drawing on local aquifers for major industrial uses can "recharge" a bit of their own withdrawals by compensating farmers for water saved, no matter where.

During the year, farmers track their water savings by cubic meter, verified by Kilimo annually as "verified water savings." Using a formula combining water charges and going product prices, Kilimo arrives at a fair market "water savings price" and transfers the payments paid by companies directly to the farmers who achieved water savings, retaining a percentage to cover Kilimo business costs.

In 2023, Kilimo was the world's first company to match water savings from farmers with corporate water efficiency strategies and has returned US$2 million to farmers in its network in the 2022–23 operational year.

Kilimo monitors 44 crops for water use, including cherry, avocado, citrus, walnuts, corn, wheat, and soybeans, and also keeps its subscribing farmers updated on going market prices. Applying water to its highest, most remunerative use is the fundamental objective.

By integrating the latest climate and weather information from the sky with water needs on earth, Kilimo creates value for both buyer and seller of water savings. Gradually, the compensation Kilimo secures for farmers offers a price signal, and eventually translates the value of water up through the whole agricultural planning process, giving voice and substance to the priceless nature of water that makes the whole chain possible.

Perhaps, at some point, rationale pricing of water will require a virtual water footprint calculation label on every product for every purchase, perhaps also charged to every digital transaction, since so much water is needed to cool data centers and enable the instantaneous result of a URL click.

Desktop or quantum computing, streaming or TikTocking, data centers require vast amounts of electricity to run and water to cool. Through use of solar and other renewable sources, energy use can be "greened" but water itself cannot, other than by more efficiency. According to breakthrough research in 2021 on the water demand of data centers conducted in the United States at Virginia Tech and the Lawrence Berkeley National Laboratory, IT data centers "are among the top-ten water consuming industrial or commercial industries in the US" and "data centers disproportionately utilize water resources from watersheds experiencing greater water scarcity than average."

Like non-revenue water, the water footprint of data should command attention. According to the 2022 Data Center survey by the Uptime Institute, an international advisory service for the IT industry, "even in relatively non-water-stressed environments, water use is becoming a concern. Only 39% of respondents currently report their water use . . . most operators that don't track water use say it is because there is no business justification, which suggests a low priority for management (in terms of cost, risk or environmental considerations)."

Also, like bitcoin mining operations, data centers are likely to meet growing public resistance if they compromise increasingly limited water supplies. According to the Uptime Institute, "a growing number of municipalities will permit data center developments only if they are designed for minimal or near-zero direct water consumption. These types of rules will heavily influence facility design and product choices in the future, mandating cooling equipment that uses water sparingly (or not at all)."

Perhaps, we can envision a day when virtual water costs will be tracked across data screens as data itself. Perhaps, as well, atmospheric scarcity will converge with water scarcity in the pricing sphere and accelerate appreciation of the environmental and financial value of both. New technologies tantalize.

For example, in November 2022, a pioneering firm in irrigation efficiency, Netafim, based in Israel, made news by announcing an advance in its "dripper" systems that deliver water and nutrients only precisely where needed by a crop at the right time, similar to the Kilimo approach in Latin America.

For rice, Netafim's drip approach can mean saving 70% of water used, critical savings since the cultivation of rice, truly a global staple, consumes about 40% of the world's freshwater globally.

Netafim's technology also connects with mitigating climate change since rice production produces 10–15% of all emissions of methane, the nasty greenhouse gas. Netafim's drippers, the company claims, reduce methane emissions to zero.

To verify this reduction, Netafim aims to put flux chambers in the rice fields using its dripper technology to measure methane emissions in real time from the ground up. Verified, these reductions can qualify in carbon markets as bona fide methane emissions reductions, a carbon market variation on the Kilimo system of translating water savings to direct compensation payments.

Farmers who use Netafim's technology can then recover some costs of the water efficiency investment with the sale of carbon credits.

Just another angle on the inescapable.

That water belongs to everyone and no one presents its most urgent challenge, drop by shimmering irreplaceable drop. Water as a commodity is truly a currency of the clouds.

10

Wildlife and Wonderment: The Rhino Bond

The Okavango Delta of Botswana transforms time. There is only one real moment here—the moment when you connect with the sight before you, before it changes. Human dynamics count for nothing. Wildlife rules—and the value of the reign is surely the value of the original diversity of life on earth and its preservation somehow.

At Kanana Camp, in the heart of the Delta, the land awaited seasonal rains and southerly water from Angola, and the measure of time was set by the young male leopard we watched sauntering and tracking, then springing up a tree to get a finer viewing bead on the trio of impala within its sight, and to be above their scent line, according to our guide, O.T., who seemed to have vision so acute he could tell leaves apart as they fluttered.

It was the second leopard we had seen since arriving a day earlier on a 12-seater Cessna on an airstrip of hardened mud in the middle of nowhere, some might say, but actually it is the middle of everywhere and everything. "Everything here makes one full shape," said O.T. "And we all stay within it."

We waited and watched the leopard for 20 minutes, as it crouched and took the measure of the wind, head turning, sculpted and regal, the predator's golden eyes so luminous, I imagined them reflecting the sky. The leopard arched its back and raised on its haunches again as, meanwhile, the three impalas stood transfixed in our direction. O.T. said the impala were still unaware of the leopard but had a sense of us. This was the morning drama, our piece of the morning shape.

I had known of the Delta in abstract terms for quite a while and resolved to visit one day, attracted, like countless visitors before me, by the prospect of seeing Africa's storybook animals in the wild and the magnetism of experience that exists first in the myth of the mind. But I repeatedly postponed.

Then COVID-19 rampaged in the world, negating not only the notion of interplay across borders, but also issuing a stark reminder that life tosses dangerous and unpredictable slings; one day you can be in charge and the next day not. I resolved that as soon as COVID calmed down, I would take the trip, shelving my resistance to being a tourist, as if I could ever be otherwise in Okavango. I gave myself over to planning and set out, inviting my nephew to join me.

UNESCO declared the Okavango Delta its 1000th World Heritage site in 2014, recognizing Okavango's extraordinary biodiversity derived directly from the unique landscape feature of being an inland delta with no outlet to the sea. In Okavango, internal water flows dictate patterns of settlement, human and animal, annually rearranging riverbeds channels, ponds, islands, and streams, and influencing temperature patterns across the region.

Okavango is the essence of priceless, a bestowal to the world, and yet the task, even the burden, of keeping Okavango intact falls mostly to the nations that share it, and so Botswana and its neighbors cultivate tourism and wildlife viewing, striving to meet the socioeconomic needs of their people while providing wild animals enough room and protection to thrive.

Almost all countries in biodiversity-rich Africa face this balance. Wildlife viewing and preservation have been mostly an activity pursued by elite foreigners, especially where colonial powers long dictated economic emphasis, mostly extracting resources out. Human suffering and poverty persisted, while the leisure class philosophized about how the tapestry of wildlife should remain.

Certainly, that tapestry is visually and sensually mesmerizing. To come upon even a single giraffe nestling high among branches is startling, like spotting a sudden single orchid in the woods; to come upon a family of giraffes takes the breath away. Add zebra, and the mind takes on the lightness of feathers, as the zebra group, known as a dazzle, truly do, walking together often in such a scripted harmony of stripes that a few zebras can appear as if one animal.

Elephants bathe and gorge on water lilies, twist, rip, swallow, shaking their trunks to be sure there are no snails in the water and grass being pulled in. (Imagine a snail crawling up your trunk!) Mother elephants instruct their young, who follow, rolling in the water against the heat. Other times elephants took up the trail just ahead of us, packed together as closely as taxis in a traffic jam. We could get close enough to count the veins behind their ears or study the giant globes of their eyes, each sighting a privileged chance to take a long look at a specific aspect.

Slate-gray hippos bubble water into the air like whales, and scatter in pools like stepping-stones, speaking in tones of tuba and trombone, their ears twitching and serving as acoustic periscopes to keep one male from another. Baboons groom each other, picking off each other's pesty insects and seeming even to kiss some away, tender and constant.

Birdsong too is constant, in early morning and evening, then dead silent as the sun sinks. There are 500 or so bird species in Botswana alone, about half in the Delta—so many you can patch together a full sighting from the constant instant flits, like the photo the mind catches of the stunning tiny malachite kingfisher and its fiery blur of blue-red-orange-green.

A lion sighting launches an inner whoop of astonishment, as a lioness nuzzles a cub on a branch, downed trees and weaving wood a lion cub playground. Or the lion king himself (*Panthera leo*), ambling along, every footfall a command, the signature golden mane tracking with a breeze.

Then, in the evening, all the creatures and the land itself tune into falling night, blades of grass like feathery spears, and even when clouds obscure the sun, light both enters and leaves, pink like a skyrocket, as the sun sets.

The Okavango system is a living blueprint of earth, as biology combines with the dynamic water forces of the Delta, driving the animals to hunt, scavenge, eat, hide, mate, nurture, and even play, all to get to the next day. The natural system both excludes and includes humans, those who get close and those who never set foot in the wildlife world. The Delta describes itself in timeless rotation.

And so, what is this all worth, the essence of the tapestry and all that derives from it, directly and indirectly, the scores of animals left alone to be there?

This question takes us back to the core of the Dasgupta Review, "The Economics of Biodiversity," which says that to "imply that the biosphere is valuable because it can be imputed a large monetary value . . . is to get things backward." Furthermore:

> Drawing on analogy with human society, we could say biodiversity in an ecosystem resembles the extent to which people trust one another. A further analogy would be the diversity of human talents in an economy needed for it to thrive. From a financial perspective, just as diversity within a portfolio of financial assets reduces risk and uncertainty, so biodiversity increases Nature's resilience to shocks . . . biodiversity provides ecosystems with spare parts; it enables ecosystems to be resilient, to be able to adapt to changing circumstances and to be productive. Reduce biodiversity and the health of ecosystems generally suffers.

When it comes to the rate of species extinction, Dasgupta presents data suggesting that if extinction continues at the same rate as observed and reported in 2020, "the population of terrestrial vertebrates will halve in about 40 years."

Moreover, says Dasgupta, these declining trends track with the drop overall in the stock of broader natural capital, which fell per capita by 40% from 1992 to 2014, while produced capital per capita doubled during the same period. In short, we used up a lot of natural capital in favor of production we both need and do not, but are willing to pay for, free riding on the fact that for underpinning natural capital use, we pay relatively nothing. But, according to Dasgupta's figures, that stash of natural capital is eroding like beach sand under our feet.

In addition to intrinsic value, Dasgupta speaks of the "amenity value" of nature, and "asking people to state their willingness to pay for" a feature of nature they value, recognize, or enjoy. But we have no organized system for those questions and collating the replies into coherent financial actions.

So far, when it comes to such striking and visible attributes of nature as the wildlife of the Okavango Delta, tourism revenue has been the main way to suss out what people—mostly foreigners—will pay to support wildlife protection. Local people, too, increasingly tour at home, proud of their national natural endowments and further supporting wildlife protection by paying taxes and often foregoing use of their own national territory for other than off-limits wildlife domain.

Botswana, considered one of the most well-governed nations in Africa, has set aside a generous 38% of its territory for wildlife protection in a mix of land management arrangements, including public national parks and private concessions. In general, Botswana chose the model of high charges–low density for foreign visitors, to maximize tourism revenues while minimizing the number of actual tourists, using price to keep access low and demand high. It helps that the country also enjoys revenue from its diamond mines, and enlightened leadership has meant that the country's spending on basic human needs such as public health and education greatly exceeds the regional averages.

But tourism inevitably creates haves and have-nots, a servant class, and often resentment among local people, to whom the revenue benefits from foreign tourism do not necessarily trickle down. Asking people to pay to preserve wildlife may never be enough to preserve it. The tourism model is double-edged, vulnerable, and perhaps forever inequitable.

New financial forms are needed urgently to move beyond tourism dependence, especially given the 2022 UN "30x30" agreement to head off further biodiversity loss by setting aside and permanently protecting 30% of earth's natural systems, a very short turnaround in international governance terms.

In the face of such a challenge, how do we transfer commensurate value to what we hope to, and must, conserve? The question is as elusive as the horizon but, like the horizon, we can keep trying to approach.

For example, enter the rhino bond, officially known as the Wildlife Conservation Bond, a world first based on the "pay for success" model, issued by the World Bank in March 2022 for a face value of $150 million, with basic financial guarantee provided by the Global Environmental Facility (GEF). Success is defined as measurable increases in the black rhino population, the rarest rhino in Africa.

We hadn't seen rhinos in Botswana, so when we arrived in South Africa, which is home to the largest populations of black and white rhino on the continent, rhinos were a topic. Like most novices to the African rhino story, I thought color gave the name black or white but not at all. There are two distinct species, found only in Africa, and both are dusky gray. "White" is thought to be a mistranslation of an Afrikaans word for "lip," to highlight a key feature of the species with the squarish flat lip, as compared to the pointier lip of the black rhino. The white rhino tears food from the ground, while the black rhino pulls food down from trees and branches.

Europeans hunted the black rhino relentlessly in the 19th century, and populations plunged from hundreds of thousands to about 65,000 in the 1970s to barely 6,000 in 2022, according to the nonprofit Save the Rhino.

The white rhino fared better, and though the northern white rhino subspecies was declared extinct in the wild in 2008, in 2022, southern white rhino numbered about 20,000. Relative to the original populations and the distribution over extensive land requirements, today's rhinos seem in the same relationship to their habitat areas as a few plums left on a tree as plum season wanes.

When we arrived at Thornberry reserve in South Africa's vast Kruger National Park and mentioned rhino sighting, our guide, Bryce, and his long-time colleague, Sam, both gracefully tamped down our hopes, emphasizing the rarity of the rhino. So, duly dosed with realism, we set out on our first evening game viewing.

Still, even with lowered expectations, we had learned anything could be out there in the bush, and so it was. Plops of rhino dung appeared early on the road, to the surprise of Sam and Bryce both. We kept on, rocking and rolling in our jeep, with birdsong all around, and other constant appearances, including the flash of nyala, an antelope new to us, the handsome male with coloring on its lower legs like yellow socks.

We began losing daylight, but then, as if conjured by our will, two shadows appeared on our right. Sam had spotted them and pointed silently. I could make out moving gray and whispered "elephant?" before I lifted my binoculars. No. Two rhinos, about 100 yards off. My mind reeled.

Bryce moved the vehicle to where he thought they would cross, and they did, ships of state. Two white rhino, amazing prehistoric masses of flesh walking, a mother and calf, armored in leathered skin folded and caped, a page from the Jurassic book, and I was speechless.

It is one thing to see a massive elephant, so much higher, but in the rhino, all that weight is lower to the ground, and it is almost impossible to imagine how the animal can move. But we heard not a rustle or scrape. The rhino walked with a whispering lightness. The calf was 1 or 2 years old, the mother about 10, according to Bryce, and the diagonal marks across the mother's flank meant that "she recently had a good scratch."

The pair came within 20 yards of us, indifferent. Rhino have very poor vision, but they would have had to be blind not to see us. Apparently, though, we were of no concern. We just kept watching—the eyes, the hide, the gigantic feet. Night closed in, and I squinted for as long as I could to follow, as the rhinos lumbered off into the descending dark, until there was nothing left but the aura that rhino had once been there.

With the final plush of sunset, the sky seemed on fire, a red band flickering on the skyline of trees. An elephant had entered the tableau, its enormous steps soft as cushions on the grass. The clouds of the late afternoon had moved out and Orion popped its stars.

Biodiversity is the stuff of magic and children's tales, and the evening had been my own living bedtime story. But reality came in the morning.

As we set out again, I mentioned to Bryce how sensational it had been to see the rhino the night before. He then asked me if I had noticed the horn on the adult, and only then did I realize I had not seen it at all, fixated as I was on the mass.

Poachers poach for rhino horn, taking the horn by killing the rhino. So to thwart the rhino horn market, conservation authorities dart rhinos every few years, sedating the giant creatures. While the animals are out cold, their saviors drill down the horn, made of keratin, until it grows back, and the cycle starts again.

The female rhino we'd seen had had her horn drilled down to a nub, and I had not noticed. What a horror, I thought, like having a dentist work on your nose but, as Bryce put it, "we have little choice because local people who are hungry and have no income also have no choice." He added, "a rhino is poached in Africa every nine hours."

Statistics back him up and convey the history. South Africa has made extensive efforts to protect and expand both black and white rhino populations, but the highest poaching rates are also there, with 1,000 animals killed a year between 2013 and 2017, the peak poaching years, when poaching increased an unimaginable 9,000%. Most of that took place within the expansive and closely protected Kruger National Park, where rhino populations declined 59% since 2013. Poaching soared in South Africa because poaching gangs drifted over from neighboring Zimbabwe, where easy poaching had already significantly eviscerated rhino populations as governance fell apart under the Mugabe government, and people were in dire economic straits. Higher rhino concentrations in South Africa raised the chance a poacher would score.

South Africa tackled poacher encroachment with increased patrolling and enforcement, but poaching rates took off again during the peak of the COVID-19 pandemic, when patrolling shrank due to labor shortages. Capacity weakened further due to loss of tourism revenue that would normally be dedicated to paying anti-poaching police—tourism dropped to near zero all across Africa due to COVID-19. Urgent social services had to be prioritized, and conservation budgets postponed.

Poaching networks operate worldwide, shadowy and uncowed by universal condemnation—some rhino poaching even occurs in the highly guarded Okavango area—with the biggest demand for rhino horn still in China. Horns are ground into exotic powders believed to be aphrodisiac or carved into elaborate trophy cups to signal wealth. Before the global ban on rhino horn trophies, Christie's auctioned off a 17th-century rhino cup for about £300 sterling.

Poor local people are pawns in the horn market near Thornberry. They risk arrest to earn about 10,000 rand per rhino, we were told, just about $500 and higher than the street value of cocaine, and who knows what markups occur along the way. Mysterious "friends" may or may not bail out the perpetrators.

If we agree that the value of a thing is what it will bring, then by crass market standards, to value the rhino horn is to tote up what the horn is worth to the poacher, then up the whole supply chain, from impoverished local farmer to overindulged foreign potentate drinking from the polished rhino cup. Of course, that ladder of value is absurdly petty.

The rhino's horn is the animal's essence, vital to its every habit, the key to survival to fend off predators. Removing the horn de-rhinos the rhino—this radical intervention is what we have come to in the name of protection.

The new invention of the rhino bond is a transformational alternative.

The World Bank, officially known as the International Bank for Reconstruction and Development, was formed in 1947 in response to WWII destruction and economic catastrophe. The bank issues bonds to raise capital, bought by national governments and private investors, to finance bank projects aimed at alleviating poverty, stimulating economic development, and increasingly confronting mounting environmental problems that threaten the planet and human welfare.

World Bank bonds enjoy AAA rating, meaning very likely to pay off, but what distinguishes the rhino bond is that a "pay for success" premium payoff ties to progress in protecting rhinos, though investors also accept the risk of no progress.

How does it work? Instead of receiving annual interest coupon payments in proportion to their stake in the bond, as in a classic World Bank bond structure, investors in the rhino bond receive a "conservation success payment" after five years, meaning they have agreed to wait five years for their money. Financial underwriting from the GEF guarantees that investors will recoup at least the principal regardless.

In the meantime, the interest coupon payments that would normally be distributed each year to investors are sent instead as cash infusions earmarked for intensifying rhino conservation, including anti-poaching monitoring to the conservation teams of South Africa's Addo Elephant National Park and the Great Fish River Nature Reserve. Both are noted for their substantial rhino populations and solid track record in rhino management.

If during the life of the bond, rhino populations increase between 2% and 4%, verified by the verification agent, namely the Zoological Society of London, depending on the rate of increase, investors could reap a premium on basic interest if populations rise to the maximum.

In sum, private investors postpone return to allow for credible conservation efforts, taking the gamble those efforts will succeed.

The obvious direct innovation of the rhino bond is that it eliminates the risk to the investor of no payoff. But the bond also captures the intangible value of time. First, the "rhino bond" in a sense recovers time. It was 10 years in the making, between design, conception, and subscribing investors, so that the bond actually came into existence to vindicate and recover the value of all that painstaking effort.

Second, the bond speeds time, by providing critical funds to the parks in South Africa in advance of proof of success in raising rhino populations. Funding upfront is the sole pathway to secure that success, as pressure on existing rhino populations builds. Increasing rhino populations would be unlikely without direct and timely support, all the more since the revenue setbacks of the COVID-19 pandemic and domestic budget cuts.

So, over the five-year life of the rhino bond, while investors defer annual coupon payments, by inference the verified growth of rhino populations stands in for financial growth, and biological interest, in the form of thriving rhino populations, stands in for financial interest.

The bond brings conservation forward and, we can hope, soon enough to get ahead of poaching. Private capital is the lubricant in the race.

So what's the cost per rhino? We can do the simple division—funds spent, rhinos born. But this is too simple, as Dasgupta would say. Recall, "to imply that the biosphere is valuable because it can be imputed a large monetary value . . . is to get things backward."

The rhino bond structure conforms as closely as possible to classic bond structure, but it rests on entirely unconventional underlying variables, like the invaluable biodiversity wealth of thriving rhino populations. The bonds offer relief on domestic budgets to focus mostly on urgent social problems in the towns and villages around the parks, including creating jobs to take pressure off the need to hunt and kill rhinos for the pittance poachers pay.

In the process, South Africa, deeply chastised for corruption and outright "state capture" under the regime of President Jacob Zuma that ended in 2018, gains credibility for fiscal management, which can only help overall creditworthiness and public confidence.

All that benefit may be asking too much of a rhino horn to bear but, on the other hand, that curved pyramidal facial feature conveys the singularity of the rhino and its mythic status vibrating through worldwide imagination for centuries. Still, breeding success will not be easy, and the rhino bond prospectus is long on additional risks—biological, social, and financial—many of which remain outside control of the beneficiaries of the bond.

For one thing, the bond could trigger the irony of the seesaw—too few rhinos, too many rhinos. Successful expansion of rhino populations depends on sufficient habitat. There is concern that even with the bond, South Africa could be de facto running out of habitat for rhino. More living rhino will forage more land, adding perhaps conflict with human occupation and use, and also the need to patrol and strengthen security services will only increase as rhino territory widens.

Also, despite the additional funds used to patrol, poachers might work faster than rhino birth rates. Or introducing rhinos might backfire, creating competition for food browsing rights and roaming space with other large mammals, especially in fenced areas, or if droughts worsen and so forth. Disease poses further risks, along with bush fires and other habitat disruptions. Risks also include that local communities may cease cooperating with conservation work if their land needs go unmet or if new jobs in conservation do not last.

Then, the ultimate potential operational failure: that accurate monitoring of rhino population growth will prove impossible. Success could be hard to verify, meaning that the conservation success payments might be lower than expected or not materialize, undermining the conservation bond concept overall. Also, the unusual terms of the bond may limit an investor's ability to sell its stake on the secondary market and what the bank calls "uncertain tax treatment" of proceeds from such a bond in a given national tax jurisdiction.

So, even though basic financial return on the rhino bond itself is guaranteed, there are no absolute guarantees. Stipulated risks are also a measure of the elements of value, more or less announcing to investors and the world all the intangible factors that could influence tangible gains. Nature could default, in other words, and be unable to keep up with the framework humans establish. All best efforts may just simply implode.

Perhaps, to save biodiversity by assigning it a semblance of tangible value, we must swallow the risks of default just as we swallow the risks that cities may default on municipal bonds. One may not be worse than the other.

Duly warned, significant investors subscribed to the rhino bond early, such as Alliance Bernstein, Blue Bay Asset Management, and high-networth individuals from the private banking rosters of Citi and Credit Suisse, which jointly manage the bond's payment calendars.

Five years will tell if the pieces make the puzzle. The rhino bond is an experiment, with a narrow focus, and like all valuable inventions, a best faith effort for all involved.

I gave information about the rhino bond to the manager of the lodge where we stayed, thinking that perhaps the Thornberry area too could one day access the mechanism since the World Bank is keen on its replication. Perhaps too one day soon, where the Okavango Delta is concerned, why not a World Heritage Okavango Bond that generates conservation success payments in return for the global service of keeping the Delta intact?

It was not yet daylight when we had to depart, and we heard the crested franklin's call under the waxing crescent moon sparkling in a lightening blue sky. The bush was as we left it, as if we had slept in a distant parallel envelope. Time remained vanished.

11

Premiums to the Coral: Coral Reef Insurance

In clear blue water, divers glide at first like arrows shot from a bow. Yet instead of losing propulsion and falling, they flow on, their fins propelling them as if they were simply riding the force of wanting to, free of any sense of struggle.

The goal of the diver is, above all, to blend, especially among coral reefs, those wildly colored underwater structures found in coastal temperate zones, built over millennia by countless microscopic living coral polyps that leave their skeletons behind when they die for the next generation of polyps to build upon. Coral reefs redesign themselves each day, in fantastically shaped plates and pinnacles, feathery fans and fingers, astonishing the eye. To float among healthy coral reefs is to wish never to leave them.

The more skilled the diver, the more supple, for among reefs the goals of movement are simplicity, grace, and compromise, with no harsh kicks or flailing arms that could break off a coral branch; the cardinal rule of the diver is do not touch. Fragility permeates everywhere in coral reefs, even if the underlying reef foundation is calcium carbonate, a basic ingredient of limestone and cement.

High winds whip ocean waves into raging surges, tossing raw force against the coral in an uneven match. Yet reefs absorb sea punches, breaking the power of waves before they reach the shore. Like mangroves, reefs play a vital buffering role in protecting the coasts. Normally, even

189

if damaged, reefs remain hearty enough to rebuild to face the storm another day.

At least, reefs could hold their own in bad weather until the expected increasingly steady stream of extreme typhoons and hurricanes due to climate change, which leave coral reefs as if hit with explosives.

According to the US National Oceanic and Atmospheric Administration (NOAA) in a July 2022 review of increasing ocean storm activity, "Concerning future changes, a number of climate modeling studies project that climate warming will cause Atlantic hurricanes in the coming century to have higher rainfall rates than present-day hurricanes, and that they will be more intense (higher peak winds and lower central pressures) on average. All else equal, coastal inundation levels associated with tropical cyclones should increase with sea level rise."

Coral reefs cover less than 1% of the shallow seafloor, and their mass is only about 125,000 square miles worldwide spread across 100 countries, from Australia to Brazil, the Red Sea to Samoa, Mozambique to Mexico, Hawaii, Belize, and beyond. Intricate reef folds, contours, and colors, so visually mesmerizing to humans, shelter and nurture a staggering 25% of all marine species.

Yet, according to "The Status of Coral Reefs of the World, 2020," a comprehensive report by the intergovernmental International Coral Reef Initiative (ICRI), at least one-fifth and maybe one-half, some scientists say, of the world's coral reefs, are dead forever, killed off in the last 30 years, thanks to reef bleaching and acidification resulting from warming seas, direct pollution such as toxic pesticide runoff from land, and numerous other detrimental influences.

If projected global temperature and polluting trends continue, and many effects of climate change are definitively locked in, regardless of best efforts, coral reefs could be entirely gone from the earth by 2070—only about half a century away from the study that said so. Increasing battering from intensifying ocean storms can only hasten this demise.

This is both an environmental and a financial disaster.

Putting coral reefs into such exacerbated vulnerability defies not only environmental conscientiousness, but also financial logic. Perhaps because reefs seem so fragile to the eye, lost in this perception is the reef as a formidable economic force, a phenomenon of nature for which we must be economically grateful and on which we are economically dependent.

While the science of ecosystem services calculation is imperfect, the economic value conveyed by intact coral reefs is indelibly known and economically staggering. According to the 2020 report of the Global Coral Reef Monitoring Network (GCRMN), the world's leading partnership of governments and organizations aimed at tracking reef status and trends:

> The value of goods and services provided by coral reefs is estimated at US $2.7 trillion per year, including US $36 billion in coral reef tourism, as well as:

- Human health and well-being: 70% of the protein in the diets of Pacific Islanders comes from reef-associated fisheries.
- Shoreline protection: a healthy coral reef can reduce coastal wave energy by up to 97%. Globally, USD $6 billion of built capital is protected from flooding by coral reefs.
- Food security and livelihoods: Coral reef fisheries support as many as 6 million people and are worth USD $6.8 billion per year, providing an average annual seafood yield of 1.42 million tonnes
- Tourism: Coral reef tourism contributes USD $36 billion to the global tourism industry annually.
- Biodiversity: Coral reefs support approximately 4,000 species of fish and 800 species of hard corals. Globally, about 830,000 species of multicellular plants and animals are estimated to occur on coral reefs, of which an estimated 13% are unnamed and 74% are yet to be. discovered. Most of these species are cryptic, small, and relatively rare.
- Medicines: Coral reefs are the medicine chests of the 21st century, with more than half of all new cancer drug research focusing on marine organisms.

Even allowing for vagaries in the ecosystems modeling, ignoring these values and potential makes a mockery not only of our good sense and our modern systems of situating worth, but also of nearly all of planetary history.

Solitary corals, living microscopic animals, appear in the fossil record 400 million years ago, according to NOAA, generally attaching themselves to rocks and land outcroppings through geological upheavals and advancing seas, converting into reef-building systems about 25 million years ago. Found where sunlight is ample and seawater warm and clear, according to NOAA, coral reefs are "the largest structures on earth of biological origin."

Soft coral creates swaying sea fans and other diaphanous shapes, but coral reefs are created because stony polyps, or hard corals, secrete the critical calcium carbonate skeletons that become foundations for new layers of polyp colonies. Each living coral links to the next as no day before, from micro to macro and back.

The average hard coral polyp size is 1–3 millimeters in diameter, most with the same cuplike anatomy—an opening at the top, akin to a mouth for taking in nourishment and releasing some waste, ringed by defensive tentacles that also capture plankton and other tiny bits of food that might pass by.

Key to hard coral dynamics, though, if any single element can be isolated in such intricacies, are the zooxanthellae, microscopic algae resident in the gastro-dermal cells of the polyp, agents of the photosynthesis that keep the polyp alive. Not at all the smeary parasitic algae that can coat and choke coral, zooxanthellae interact with sunlight to create the proteins, acids, and carbohydrates that nourish polyps and permit the calcium carbonate secretion. Coral algal photosynthesis, by the way, also absorbs carbon dioxide from the atmosphere, making the ocean also a formidable sink for drawing greenhouse gases out of the air, as long as the zooxanthellae survive.

Stressing the zooxanthellae spells coral reef disaster. Higher sea temperature can instigate that scale of stress, inducing polyps to self-destruct by expelling their vital algae residents, literally spitting them out. Without zooxanthellae, the polyp loses color and withers to a ghoulish grayish white. This infamous coral bleaching wipes out once rapturous rainbow hues and leaves the reef looking like a baked undersea sidewalk. The massive coral bleaching under way also weakens reefs even further structurally, and these warm-water feedback loops could damn coral reefs forever. A dreaded cycle, true, but we can try to break the chain on at least the physical front when storms smash reefs, while we also hope to get ahead of the cycle of other ongoing threats.

That is a gamble in managing risks—just the task for an insurance product, the truly new and possibly transformational parametric coral reef insurance.

By definition, an asset worth insuring is valuable, and insurance tables and actuarial analyses express and book that value in financial and accounting terms. Insurance policies price the risk of loss relative to an asset's measurable value and replacement, especially if replacing the asset exceeds the means of the policyholder.

Generally, the insurance industry operates on the principle of "we will pay if it happens," or indemnity insurance, such as the familiar plans with high and low deductibles and coverages for insurance for cars, homes, jewels, and artwork. Collecting on insurance for these familiar assets usually requires an inspection—the tree did fall on the house, for example—followed by claims adjustment, often dispute resolution, and waiting time. In sum, indemnity insurance kicks in after the fact.

Parametric insurance, on the other hand, kicks in right away, releasing payouts quickly to offset losses as they occur, without a referee, if a prespecified mutually agreed trigger event occurs. Payouts can be activated within days of the trigger.

Using the parametric model to insure coral reefs, wind speed is an ideal triggering event, since wind speed is indisputably measurable in real time, and highly predictive of the extent of reef damage. For example, according to a 2021 report on risks facing the world's coral reefs by the Nature Conservancy, the government of Canada, and other partners, a Category 5 hurricane is likely to damage 51% of a reef, especially its living surface layer, as compared to 20% damage from a Category 2.

Ecosystems as complex and ancient as coral reefs build in some inherent resilience to disaster, and coral reefs can recover naturally from typical storm damage. But reefs reduced to rubble by superstorms will stay in ruins forever, unless physical repair takes place soon after the storm's wreckage, a combination of reef biology and arduous underwater manual labor.

Coral reef insurance underwrites the costs of urgent painstaking repair work. Where the usual golden rule for divers is do not touch, coral reef reconstruction requires the contrary: gently touch all you can and put it back in place as fast as possible.

In a race against time, coral restoration teams of divers and snorkelers hit the water. Specially trained for coral reef reconstruction, the rescuers slip among the damaged coral like an expeditionary force, maneuvering underwater in full diving regalia, balancing mesh baskets of repair tools. Divers gently pick up pieces of coral knocked off by the storm and relocate them to stable spots on the reef where the bits might fuse anew, even using underwater drills to etch out new crannies where broken coral might relodge. Divers carefully brush suffocating silt churned up from the storms off the living polyp layer, at times using toothbrushes to clear the tiniest crevices. Divers tie meticulous bows in thin line to anchor broken coral arms in optimum position to reconnect, hoping to restore some semblance of what was torn apart.

But how do we pay for outfitting and mobilizing such coral reef repair brigades, worldwide, perhaps over and over? The tactic is new, both desperate and promising, and an operational imperative for which no commercial or governmental budgets have ever planned.

Uniquely blending science, logistics, and human love of the sea, the Mesoamerican Reef Rescue Initiative (MRRI) incorporated parametric insurance in a fantastic experiment in covering reef repair costs. The model captures a semblance of the value of reef reconstruction in the Mesoamerican project pilot zone, a series of reefs that stretch across more than 1,000 kilometers of sparkling tropical sea from the Yucatan Peninsula in Mexico to the Caribbean coast of Honduras.

The MRRI insurance program began in 2021, the first pilot year, pooling damage risks among four first pilot reef sites during the 2021 Atlantic hurricane season, expanded to seven in 2022. Willis Towers Watson, the global insurance advisory firm and a pioneer in understanding environmental risks as insurance risks, co-funded the project and serves as central broker to the MRRI concept. The firm designed a parametric index and payout table correlated to windspeed, to determine where payouts would be most needed and pay or guarantee them as soon as possible. Sites are divided into a "cats-in-nested circles" map, radiating out from each reef site.

For example, wind speed reaching 64 knots per hour (about 70 miles per hour) triggers a 10% payout for Zone D of a given reef site, the area closest to the reef itself, and zero percent for Zone A, on land and farthest from the reef. If windspeed hits 96 knots per hour (about 110 miles per hour), Zone D payout rises to 40% and Zone A payout to 10%, recognizing that Zone A on land would then also need funds to ready, mobilize, and dispatch additional teams or support equipment as storms worsen. If windspeed climbs to 137 knots (157 miles per hour), Zone D payout climbs to 100% and Zone A to 20%. Payouts are managed by the MAR Fund, an international and intergovernmental umbrella group set up in 2004 to raise and steward funds to protect the Mesoamerican reef system.

MRRI also provides training, coordination, and inspiration to restoration teams, not usually drawn from among industrial divers summoned from gigantic offshore industrial rigs far away, but local recreational divers, dive masters, and boat captains who make themselves available. "*Participar y conviertete en un guardian del arrecife,*" solicits MRRI in various recruitment materials. "Participate and become a guardian of the reef."

MRRI offers frequent free classes and casts its staffing net widely. As an MRRI training video in Honduras promotes, "If you live in the Bay Islands, are a certified diver and want to help take care of the reef, this class is for you!"

Reef rescue teams practice reef reconstruction teamwork in classrooms and underwater, studying the basics of reef biology and physical restoration techniques, as basic as learning to tie knots while wearing diving gloves. With training accomplished and payouts guaranteed to cover costs, reef restoration teams can go quickly to work.

Diving materiel needs to be tiptop ready to go as well—dive boats, tarps, tanks, masks, weights, floats, regulators, clamps, clips, measuring tapes, regulators, boats, ropes, drills, and even ordinary land-based construction materials. Because coral reef skeletons are mostly calcium carbonate, coral is not allergic to the common construction cement that restoration teams can use to hold broken coral in place while it heals.

According to a 2020 MAR Fund report on an emergency reef restoration effort after Hurricanes Gamma, Delta, and Zeta, "2152 coral colonies were stabilized, 5143 fragments were cemented, and 8428 fragments were propped."

This script of tiny tasks could unnerve even Sisyphus, but the science of coral reef restoration advances rapidly. Worldwide, coral reef specialists are developing coral types resistant to mounting ocean acidification, also adding to their resilience against storms. Coral reef nursery scientists are also busy developing biodegradable reconstruction materials, as well as "micro-fragmentation," where live coral pieces are taken from the sea to a laboratory and cut into smaller pieces to reproduce in stable laboratory conditions, then replaced in the ocean, stronger.

By paying off quickly so that local, regional, or national governments—usually the entities in charge of reef protection in marine parks or other designated areas—can preposition trained rescue teams and their trappings, the reef insurance program makes the hope of coral restoration possible.

As of 2022, the dream was still in proof-of-concept phase. The critical pilot phase payout pool in 2022, for example, of US $2.5 million was provided by the InsuResilience Fund, whose mission is to encourage financial innovations to meet climate change challenges, and was seeded largely by development funds from the government of Germany. Parametric policies were not yet commercially sold.

Including another earlier restoration project in Quintana Roo, Mexico, coral reef insurance has been live-and-learn. However, the scope of coral reef problems requires innovations such as coral reef insurance to scale worldwide, truly establishing value at the level of what is at stake.

Out of sight of most people on earth, reefs exist mostly in our common imagination, fantastic natural features out there somewhere.

However, the answer to what is worth doing would seem self-evident, given the overall annual value of nearly $3 trillion worldwide by the GCRMN, excluding the immediate additional costs in human lives and well-being and repairing physical coastal damage when our natural coral seawalls no longer hold. Also, according to the MRRI based on analysis by the Inter-American Development Bank, the Mesoamerican reef alone "delivers benefits of USD 4.5 billion every year to key sectors," a value that, minus the coral reef insurance concept, is literally cast to the winds.

Coral reef restoration funds seem a logical first step in the ultimate goal of insuring reefs overall as national assets, kept and protected on a nation's books like any other infrastructure capital. If, according to the GCRMN overall estimate, global reef value can be estimated at US $3 trillion, should we not try to insure the world's reefs for that amount? Could we create a special global reef insurance policy, with premiums paid a bit by all world governments?

Where reef restoration specifically is concerned, so laborious and dangerous, and intensifying ocean storms may never end, it can seem madness to imagine constantly rebuilding reefs wrecked by the waves. Is the effort worthwhile? This is a public policy decision, of course, and even though national boundaries may include coral reefs, reefs have no explicit owners, but many users and beneficiaries. Given the multiplicity of interests, decisions on what is worth investing in may bounce around, but it can hardly make sense to value coastal structures more highly than the reefs that protect them.

For perspective on investment flows, the first *Avatar* film cost US $237 million to produce, and its box office gross was $2.8 billion, as of 2022. *Avatar* sequels were projected to cost about $250 million each, about $10 million for each million years it took coral reefs to form. Coral reef plates and colors are just as phantasmagorical, but Hollywood could never have created them.

Coral reef insurance has created funds for rescue where none were before, so that divers become reconstruction workers, a reef a reconstruction site. In this way, diving is no longer mostly a tourism industry, but a planetary survival industry.

The very wind that churns the sea and crushes coral glories also triggers a system to undo its damage, reef finance to underwrite fragility and perhaps restore to coral reefs a value that respects their timeless role and origins.

12

Forests as Infrastructure: The Forest Resilience Bond

Flames lick and crackle the same the world over, but while we know Arctic ice is melting, the Arctic is not supposed to be burning too. Science says it may, though, as climate disruptions find their way to every longitude and latitude of our beloved planet.

Wildfires perhaps express the nightmare of renegade climate change most visibly. Flames turn skies orange and shock the eyes of the world as drought-dry brush and forests crack into flame like popcorn, leaving behind charred wreckage and smoldering scenes.

"Spreading Like Wildfire: The Rising Threat of Extraordinary Landscape Fires," a 2022 UNEP report, projects that fires will spark where they've been previously unheard of, or burn more intensely where they've been known, including in "tropical savannas and tropical and temperate grasslands, which are predicted to be altered by increased burning in some areas and decreased burning in others."

Satellites too keep an eye. Europe's Forest Fire Information System (EFFIS) tracks wildfire closely, and the heartbreak of loss that falls away from the headlines say that in Kazakhstan in 2022, where in less than a week, wildfires displaced 1,800 people, more than 2,200 firefighters battled the wind-whipped flames, using almost 200 pieces of fire equipment, aircraft, and even specialized fire trains. How to picture so many firefighters mobilized?

Or in Algeria, where wildfires in the country's dense northern forests resulted in at least 43 deaths: "Near the town of Setif, firefighters raced through raging fires to evacuate villagers, including what one local video shows of a firefighter clutching a screaming infant and running to safety."

Or in the Algarve in Portugal, where the extensive fires raged through the Leiria and Santarém districts in July 2022, a pilot died when a fire plane crashed, 135 people were injured, and over 800 people had to evacuate. Smoke from a fire in Portugal's Serra da Estrela national park that began on August 6 was carried for miles to "envelop skyscrapers in the Spanish capital of Madrid."

In Spain itself, dozens of fires burned that same month, and "In one of the most dramatic scenes to emerge from the fires, a train from Madrid to Ferrol stopped for a few minutes because of fire on the tracks around Zamora-Sanabria on Monday, July 18. Two people died in Zamora's fire—a firefighter and a 69-year-old farmer."

Horrifyingly, "The dramatic train scene repeated itself almost exactly a month later as a train in the Valencia region stopped to reverse course as a wildfire advanced on its position. When the train stopped, a number of people fled after breaking windows in the carriages, and ten were injured as they fled."

Or Sweden, where climate change upends fire surveillance statistics. Aviation 24 reported that in 2022, pilots "discovered 105 fires in forests and land . . . aircraft worked 3,441 hours in the air." A year earlier, aircraft spotted 74 fires with just about the same flight time."

Or Scandinavia in general, where many weather records were broken in 2018, according to US National Aeronautics and Space Administration (NASA), with fires as far north as the Arctic circle, with all-time-high temperatures recorded in Norway, "where temperatures hit 33°C (92°F), as the southern part of the country was peppered with fires in 100 localities."

Or almost anywhere we might want to put a finger on the map.

It can be tempting to think of climate change as an external destructive power, visiting negative impacts on us as receivers, but we too are actors over and above the greenhouse gas emissions rise caused by human industry.

It was one thing when, forming itself, the earth inhaled and exhaled carbon dioxide over eons. However, in 2023, with 8 billion people living across every planetary climatic zone, the impacts of climate change cannot be isolated from our own behavior, settlement patterns, inherited economic structures, and individual habits.

In fact, humans cause roughly 90% of wildfires, either through outright arson, accident, or negligence. Sparks can fly from railroad tracks or utility power lines, the careless tossing of a match, or the failure to douse a cooking fire. Catastrophe occurs when climate change exacerbates these human failings and proximity to woodlands with intensifying tinder conditions due to drought and heat waves.

In the United States, all states face some wildfire risk, but California stands out. Tables have turned since wildfires were once a bearable occurrence. California's legislative analyst's office summarized the shift in its overview of the state's 2022–23 budget:

> Historically, significant parts of the state would burn annually, especially during the warm, dry months of the year. . . . These regular fires played an important role in keeping the state's forests and landscapes healthy. . . . However, in recent decades, California has seen some of the worst wildfires in the state's recorded history. For example, the 2018 wildfire season included the Camp Fire in Butte County, which became the single most destructive wildfire in state history with nearly 19,000 structures destroyed and 85 fatalities, including the near-total destruction of the town of Paradise.

Traditional liability, insurance, and credit ratings systems creak under the weight of mounting costs of wildfire devastation and loss, especially as the causes of fires emerge. For example, California's largest utility, PG&E, also the nation's largest, admitted that faults in its transmission lines triggered wildfires in some cases, then filed for bankruptcy to shield itself from potentially thousands of 2017–18 wildfire liability claims.

The utility reported to the US SEC foreseeable liabilities as high as $30 billion, towering above only $1.4 billion in insurance coverage. Setting the scene for further debacles, the utility added: "PG&E also expects to face increasing difficulty securing liability insurance in future years due to availability and to face significantly increased insurance costs."

True to prediction, in 2022, PG&E settled with California's Sonoma County for $55 million in connection with the 2019 Kincade fire, in part to avoid criminal charges tied to negligence that caused injury to firefighters, destruction of roughly 300 buildings in California's wine country, and evacuation of about 200,000 people, plus the burning of 120 square miles, including vineyards.

Credit agencies such as Moody's, Fitch, and S&P Global dropped credit ratings to junk status for PG&E, Southern California Gas, and Southern California Edison, other California utilities, in view of brewing massive liability claims from various wildfire and power disruptions.

Rounding out 2022, PG&E took a $100 million charge in anticipation of likely losses related specifically to a single fire, the Mosquito fire near Sacramento, which proved to be the largest in California that year.

All in all, in 2022 alone, Cal-Fire, California's state agency charged with prevention and protection against fire, estimated it had drawn $1.17 billion from its emergency fund for fire suppression costs in 2021–22, in addition to having tapped it for $1.23 billion in 2020–21. The 2021 Dixie fire alone burned nearly 1 million acres and cost over $600 million to suppress.

Adding to the worrying picture, according to a December 2022 "US Wildfire snapshot" by Karen Clark and Company, an international advisory service based in Massachusetts that pioneered catastrophe modeling for economic and insurance purposes, "Climate trends are encouraging larger, more frequent fire events. Each year around 15 fires larger than 10,000 acres are likely to occur, which is triple the number that could be expected in 1980. All ten of the highest loss-producing wildfires in the last 35 years occurred in California, and Wildland Urban Interfaces— where wildlands meet developed lands—are most affected."

Then there are the billions in uninsured wildfire losses, as with extreme hurricanes, that bounce around the economy with no place to land except on the victims, who are left to fend for themselves with little recourse, or on public budgets and taxpayers through disaster relief programs, limited and inadequate over time. For example, in the United States, the Federal Emergency Management Agency (FEMA) advised residents with houses still standing that the best FEMA could offer was support to make the dwellings "livable."

Surely such an unremitting mountain of likely costs warrants a radical revamp of allocation and application of public and private to prevent losses, especially as legacy forms of insurance and reinsurance repeatedly sound the alarm that they cannot or will not cover catastrophic claims.

In the familiar calculus of cost-benefit, perhaps the best long-term tactic to neutralize mounting wildfire costs is to dramatically advance the benefits of the counterweight—healthy resilient forests better able to survive the onslaughts of climate change extremes. Against forest conflagration stands forest restoration, though restoration can seem quaint by comparison.

Restoration is a tender-loving-care process, gateway to forest benefits, almost tree by tree, costly and endless, as long as we expect to need or want forests. Restoration amounts to forest gardening with a menu of techniques, including controlled burns, although as human settlements spread closer to forests, controlled burns are limited to avoid danger of wandering smoke and flame. While some ecological theory suggests that the best forest management is to leave forests to their own devices, a hands-off approach becomes less viable given human encroachment on forests and as climate change introduces vulnerabilities that natural processes cannot overcome.

Active restoration means strengthening resistance to fire overall, by regular thinning, trimming firebreaks, meadow burning, removal of parasitic species that overly suck water, and, importantly, clearing combustible felled branches and brush from the forest floor. Restoration work also generates jobs, of course, for climbers, foresters, drivers, hydrologists, and others, especially the collecting and transporting of underbrush and putting it to other uses, including biomass energy.

Despite the benefits, restoration budgets chronically fall short.

In 2018, the US National Forest Service, which is also responsible for managing fire risk in California on federal lands, estimated that 6 to 9 million acres needed "treatment to increase their resilience to the impacts of disturbances such as wildfire, climate change, invasive species and human population growth." The Forest Service tried its best, restoring 200,000 acres per year, but admitted that "even at this aggressive rate of treatment, it would take 30 to 45 years to treat the number of acres needed to make the difference."

In the face of these decades of backlog, the novel Forest Resilience Bond (FRB) took shape in California, a financial tool that shares costs and benefits of forest restoration among a mixed group of beneficiaries and investors. Investors stake the bond and beneficiaries of future forest health agree to pay it off, with a reasonable premium.

The explicit goal is to advance funds to speed up and expand forest restoration, beginning with large swaths of vulnerable forest in the Lake Tahoe area. The breakthrough "bet against fires" structure of the FRB situates private investors to make money the less fire-prone risk to a forest. The bond's design explicitly values the differentiated tangible and intangible benefits of healthy forests well ahead of when the benefits will be realized.

If we walk in the woods, benefits of a healthy forest fall first on all five senses, the pleasure of birdsong and breezes, the drumstick snap of a twig underfoot, the fragrance of pine, or the intrigue of wildlife tracks leading off into dense bush and bramble.

Sonnets and symphonies rhapsodize forests, and contemporary scientists even speak of forest systems as social networks, each tree in touch with the others through roots and branch messaging humans can barely contemplate.

Resilient forests retain water, invaluable protection against dryness, made more prevalent and severe by rising average temperatures, catching rainfall throughout the tree, and gradually guiding it down to refresh the water table. Keeping soil in place, trees prevent dust-ups and siltation of streams. Wildlife teem in healthy forests, from beetle to bear, not to mention plant-based products of every sort, and lumber too, obviously. In the United States, forest products of all kinds account for nearly 5% of US GDP, exclusive of ecosystem services.

Regarding tourism, according to the US National Park Service, "In 2021, 297 million park visitors spent an estimated $20.5 billion," visiting national parks, including forests, and "these expenditures supported a total of 323 thousand jobs, $14.6 billion in labor income, $24.3 billion in value added, and $42.5 billion in economic output in the national economy."

And of course, forests are critical carbon sinks sequestering greenhouse gases across the entire planet, as is now indelibly known.

Forests never cease to serve, but they disperse their services on a clock slower and less explicitly than conventional finance and public budgets planning requires. As a result, allocating public budgets to forest protection can be timid. The California overview analysis of 2022–23 budget expressed the conundrum: "Many of the activities proposed for funding are widely considered good practices to reduce wildfire risks. . . . However, the available information on the cost-effectiveness of many programs is somewhat limited—making it difficult for the Legislature to know whether the Governor's proposed package represents the most effective way to allocate funds for wildfire prevention and mitigation."

As an antidote to uncertainty, the FRB bond closes the time gap, reckoning on the benefits, and attracting private investors willing to advance capital based on projected value to beneficiaries. Beneficiaries can include hydropower utilities, for example, which benefit from improved rainfall retention and therefore groundwater replenishment and stabilized water flow to their dam systems. Better flow means fewer costly service interruptions when water is sapped by dry conditions. Tourism operators also benefit, if wilderness-seeking vacationers do not stay away for fear of fire. Budget-beleaguered public forest management services benefit from saving funds spent on fighting fires that are preferably spent on preventing them.

Considering that healthy forests—giant redwoods, sequoia, high Sierra chapparal—are inseparable from the image, economy, and livability of California, investment in healthy forests is an investment in the veritable future of the state.

In the FRB arrangement, investors gamble that fire prevention will eventually yield the expected positive outcomes—invest cash now for financial reward later. By committing to pay off the bond, beneficiaries gamble that the intangible benefits will accrue and become tangible on their books in revenue or dollars saved. In sum, the FRB is based on environmentally idealistic financial speculation, on behalf of standing healthy forests.

The FRB was conceived by four MBA students at the Haas School of Business at the University of California at Berkeley. The idea won them the Morgan Stanley Sustainable Investing Challenge that year, a contest posed to business school students globally to design a financial product that could meet a significant social or environmental problem while still providing market return.

The FRB team brought diverse personal and professional experiences to their graduate school stints: Zach Knight had worked at investor firm Merrill Lynch in structured finance; Leigh Madeira had been in investment banking; Nick Wobbrock was a water engineer who had also been a Peace Corps volunteer; and Chad Reed said in a presentation on the winning project, "I started my career in the intelligence community . . . operating primarily in the Middle East."

Perhaps these varied starting points helped the group envision a financial product that would meld differentiated needs and interests. Success of the FRB model depends on forging alignment of financial advantage to confront a common threat. As Wobbrock put it, without the FRB, "the disparate stakeholders had no mechanism to share the risk or the costs."

When the FRB was conceived, 94% of California was in a state of drought, and the 37% of the rest of the United States was officially considered to be in moderate drought conditions. Snowpack in California was at 5% of its historic average, a frightening situation from the point of view of water availability because California's snowpack would have typically held as much water as all of the state's reservoirs. Due to water shortages and dry conditions, 23,000 agricultural jobs were predicted to be lost, at a cost of $16 billion to the state's economy.

Convergence, a network of investors focused on blended finance, summarized the dire shortfall in public forest funding in a 2020 case study on the FRB:

> Despite benefits associated with forest restoration, this work is not being done at the pace or scale required to solve the growing challenge of overgrown forests in the western US. To make matters worse, progressively severe and costly wildfires have forced the USDA Forest Service to divert funds from prevention (e.g., forest restoration) to fire suppression. The result is a growing financing gap, while an estimated $60 billion is needed to restore forests within the US, the Forest Service had an annual budget of less than $500 million allowed to restoration in FY 2019. Public dollars alone cannot address this issue at scale.

To meet the likely persistent funding gap, and illustrate an alternative model fit for future purpose, especially accelerated forest maintenance, the FRB arrayed farsighted investors with here-and-now beneficiaries.

In the FRB structure, various benefits cross-subsidize each other, an interrelationship that would not occur without the FRB as a convening platform. For example, in conservatively calculating the benefit to water utilities of improved water retention and water availability, the FRB found that water costs to utilities could drop from the average of $1,300 per acre foot to $200, since costs of improving water supply through forest restoration would be shared with other beneficiaries.

Yuba I, the first FRB, was established as a special purpose vehicle, debt issuer, and wholly owned subsidiary of Blue Forest Conservation, a nonprofit set up by the FRB founding team to manage and design FRB projects. Blue Conservation aimed to strike projects in high-fire-risk areas ranging from $25 million to $50 million, as well as aggregate smaller projects for efficiency and eventually raise rolling capital to create an ongoing pipeline of projects across the United States, with possible international adaptations.

Yuba I had a modest face value of $4 million to protect roughly 15,000 acres within the Yuba Watershed in the Tahoe National Forest. Dense with undergrowth and significantly fire prone in dry weather, the selected area was an apt candidate for the FRB structure.

Original commercial investors were Calvert Impact Capital, an investment firm with environmental and social interests; and CSAA

Insurance Group, a regional AAA insurer that invested out of recognition that forest fire prevention in turn reduces forest-fire-caused insurance claims. The FRB structure provides a 4% annual return to commercial investors, who receive principal and interest on a quarterly basis.

Several philanthropic foundations also invested in Yuba I at concessional return rates of 1% per year, recognizing the FRB's potential to scale its innovative financial structure. An anchoring beneficiary is the Yuba Water Agency (YWA), a water and hydropower utility set up in 1959 to reduce flood and manage water supply. YWA sells water to eight irrigation districts, water companies, and other water users, and operates the New Bullards Bar Dam and reservoir and hydroelectric facility. A major portion of the watershed on which YWA depends lies within the Tahoe National Forest. YWA committed to $1.5 million in repayments to the FRB, payable in annual $300,000 installments for five years, based on its assumption of benefits from having more water retained in the watershed for throughput to hydro plants and to supply water users.

Cal-Fire, California's agency charged with managing and preventing fires and fire risk, also enrolled as an FRB beneficiary, committing $2.6 million in grant funds to the FRB to reimburse restoration funds paid to forest restoration contractors authorized by Cal-Fire or the National Forest Service to provide restoration services.

Drawing on its upfront FRB investor capital pool, Blue Forest advances costs of restoration work that must be done in real time and without delay. The state's reimbursement process runs more slowly and falls behind. By smoothing out payments and enabling advance planning for consistent restoration work, the FRB projected a remarkable reduction in restoration time for the Yuba I target area—ten years cut to four.

To avoid conflicts of interest and ensure that neither investors nor beneficiaries overly influence choice of projects, priorities, or contractors, the FRB team undertook significant academic and scientific research, including in collaboration with the World Resources Institute (WRI) to identify target projects before seeking investment and structuring the bond.

The US EPA's Water Infrastructure and Resiliency Finance Center summarized the promising impact of the FRB in a 2021 report: "The FRB represents a new direction for collaborative forest management, as the debts and revenues pledged for repayment are provided by different parties. . . . If the collaborative model can improve project scale and create repetitive pathways for private capital investment, the pace of restoration work can be accelerated to address the national forest restoration investment gap. . . . Additionally, the Yuba Project is expected to produce approximately 35,000 green tons of biomass for processing at the nearby Loyalton Biomass facility. Increased forest restoration activity could prompt multiplier effect investment in rural communities with the promise of more stable supplies of biomass for energy production and timber products."

Of course, as with any prototype, the FRB structure presents hazards for all parties. For investors, this is the fundamental risk of the inventive model: will the multifaceted financial structure keep disparate parties together or become too unwieldy to scale? Will the administration costs of that process rise too high? Also, as with the rhino bond in its original iteration, there is no secondary market for FRBs, so investors cannot easily exit or sell.

Another signature risk is that the environmental benefits of forest restoration envisioned are exaggerated or do not materialize. Or that legal disputes arise over ownership of water rights, for example, if as predicted more water enters the catchment area over time. Or what if another pandemic like COVID-19 hits and logger teams cannot get to work and lose a whole year or longer? The risk list can be daunting, including the most obvious: default by the payor beneficiaries.

The FRB built reasonable assurances into the investor and beneficiary contracts, firsts of their kind, after all. The critical risk mitigation, though, is the open-mindedness of the upfront investors to accept unknowns and unknowables for the sake of demonstrating financial innovation as a path to greater good. Designers of the FRB hope it becomes a standard market instrument that stands on its own financial feet, and as it seeks to move to a fully commercial phase, risk mitigation will have to be crisp.

All things being equal, though, investing in standing forests and avoiding deforestation, in which wildfires play a significant part, would seem to be attractive to private capital, riding high on the ESG list. An MSCI report on "ESG and Climate Trends to Watch in 2023" implied that only well-managed forest companies might be investable, especially in the EU where anticipated rules "require that all products sold in the EU be deforestation-free."

Tightening forest-related regulations will drive demand then for more forest care, such as that the FRB structure encourages. Also, considering the clamor for financial instruments and investments to protect biological diversity, especially the "30x30" land-and-sea off limits pledges made in 2022 in Montreal at COP 15, the FRB concept could well attract global investor attention.

In fact, Yuba II, launched in late 2021 with a face value of $25 million, brought in several new investors, including Hall Capital, Impact Assets, and RSF Social Finance, with CSAA as a repeat investor.

Yuba Water Agency returned as well, committing $6 million to Yuba II. This second FRB supports forest resilience work and post-fire restoration on 48,000 acres in the North Yuba River watershed in collaboration with the North Yuba Forest Partnership, a consortium of government agencies, environmental and community organizations. Ultimately, the partnership hopes to conduct critical wildfire prevention work across the whole 275,000-acre North Yuba watershed, and Yuba II is a first step.

In February 2023, the FRB principle of aligning current and future benefits of forest restoration received a $25 million further vote of confidence, in the form of a seed investment by CSAA Insurance Group to create the California Wildfire Innovation Fund, to be managed by Blue Forest Asset Management. Zach Knight, CEO of Blue Forest, said the fund "is specifically tailored to create strategic value for insurance company investors by aligning wildfire risk reduction outcomes with compelling financial returns."

The fund would focus on investment opportunities in key forest resilience activities, including direct restoration, utilization of tinder wood as biomass, and potentially revenue from carbon markets and forest and land sequestration of CO_2.

The fund claimed to be the first of its kind, and could significantly help showcase advantages of more capital investment in forest preservation.

Investment gaps in preventing wildfires seem inexplicable, considering how the intensity and frequency of wildfires rise in frightening recitation. That Cal-Fire deemed the 2018 California wildfire season the "deadliest and most destructive wildfire season on record in California" meant the 2019 season could be deemed "relatively mild" by comparison even though the season included the Kincade fire.

Then 2020 boomed back, supplanting 2018 as a new "record-setting year of wildfires that burned across the state of California as measured during the modern era of wildfire management and record keeping . . . including the state's first 'gigafire' as the area burned exceeded 1 million acres. The fire crossed seven counties and has been described as being larger than the state of Rhode Island." The year 2021 saw "an unusually early start" to the wildfire season in California, while in 2022 acreage burned was below average, even though "a number of significant fires burned."

And then 2023 unfolded in terrifying meteorological counterpoint as the skies of California erupted into raging rainstorms fed by nine consecutive "atmospheric rivers" over three weeks. Major cities, waterways, and rivers were inundated, with rainfall overwhelming catchment areas so most of the desperately needed rain ran off to the sea. There were 700 landslides, 500,000 people left without power, and 20 dead. Moody's estimated total economic losses from the flooding at between $5 billion and $7 billion, and said, "insured losses are anticipated to be between $500 million and $1.5 billion, including losses to the National Flood Insurance Program and the private flood market."

In the United States, fearsome costs of weather disasters multiplied beyond wildfire. According to the database that tracks US Billion-Dollar Weather and Climate Events of the National Centers for Environmental Information (NCEI), in 2022 there were 18 events with losses exceeding $1 billion, the eighth year in a row with more than 10.

Summarizing recent years, NCEI said, "After adjusting for inflation, the U.S. experienced more than twice the number of billion-dollar disasters during the 2010s than the 2000s decade: 119 versus 59. . . . In addition, the two most destructive and costly wildfire seasons in U.S. history have taken place over the last three years, with losses exceeding $40 billion, with much of this damage in California."

NCEI wove in further perspective, stating, "The total costs for the last five complete years ($788.4 billion) are more than one-third of the disaster cost total of the last 43 years (1980–2022), which exceeds $2.295 trillion (inflation-adjusted to 2022 dollars). This reflects a 5-year cost average of nearly $157.6 billion/year—a new record." In the scheme of billion-dollar events from 1980 to 2022, NCEI calculates wildfires at "an average cost of $6.3 billion per event."

Reinsurers, the underwriters of last resort, tally and worry. In 2023, leading reinsurer Munich Re reported that costs of global natural disasters that year carried "overall losses of around US$270 billion . . . and insured loss of US$120 billion . . . 2022 joins the recent run of years with high losses."

Thomas Bluck, a member of Munich Re's management board, headlined, "climate change is taking an increasing toll," adding that the 2022 figures were "dominated by events that . . . are more intense or are occurring more frequently. In some cases, both trends apply."

Can reinsurance catch up? Bluck said, "Another alarming aspect we witnessed time and again is that natural disasters hit people in poorer countries especially hard. Prevention and financial protection, for example, in the form of insurance must therefore be given higher priority."

Against this waterfall of billion-dollar costs, the FRB seems a tossed pebble. Also, the argument could be made that regardless of size, the FRB merely leverages preexisting public money that would be spent eventually and that no "new money" is created.

However, climate change rattles all presumption, and we may have to rethink our definitions in the face of heightening environmental dilemmas. By illuminating the invisible priceless benefits of a resilient forest, and consolidating them in a credible financial instrument, the FRB liberates new value formerly locked away out of sight. The more that value is made visible, the more new investment it can attract—new sightlines, new money.

Also, undeniably, at least regarding wildfires, the FRB lubricates the movement of existing public money to accelerate forest resilience, meaning that the FRB model neutralizes the costs of delay. The FRB's acceleration of Yuba I restoration time from 10 years to 4 could be said to have created a dramatic quantity of "new time," an asset that no monetary measurement can accurately capture.

Perhaps the most important long-term contribution of the FRB is its treatment of healthy forests as essential infrastructure that requires maintenance—natural infrastructure to fend off wildfire and all destruction that can follow.

Once recognized as infrastructure, forests acquire the financial profile of physical capital, desirable capital assets enumerated in capital budgets and deemed to embody and return long-term value. Capital assets also may be borrowed against and paid for over a presumed lifespan, adding to the options and financial stamina of the asset holder. By extension, capital assets demand stewardship and that depreciation be held at bay. Forests listed as capital assets means the more environmentally robust the forest, the more financially robust the asset and the balance sheet of the asset owner, namely, in the case of public forests, the public itself. Booking forests in capital budgets endows them with a level of forward-looking attention consistent with keeping forest value as high as possible, as compared to operational budget planning whose main goal is to keep costs as low as possible.

If forests are natural assets with capital value, their conservation becomes an essential matter. By focusing on the urgency of restoring forests, the FRB directly confronts the malaise and mindset that allow timely maintenance of classic infrastructure, especially in the United States, to be postponed, underfunded, and ignored.

Like coral reef insurance that generates cash quickly so fractured reefs can be reassembled to provide coastal infrastructure support, the FRB model also advances cash to secure the future benefits of forest resiliency.

As we insure bridges, we can insure reefs. Are we not obliged to maintain forests as we are obliged to maintain bridges, tunnels, grids, and highways and other built structures deemed indispensable to economic and social well-being?

By making visible the invisible benefits of natural infrastructure, both coral reef insurance and the FRB offer to move natural infrastructure from the margins of public budgets to the center, as strategic public assets. For example, in 2022, the US Congress passed the Jobs and Infrastructure Act, allocating US $1.2 trillion to upgrade America's crumbling physical infrastructure, such as railroads, water tunnels, roads, and broadband, the largest federal expenditure and ambition of its type since the 1930s New Deal investments to rebuild America. A good deal of the money in the act aims to accelerate maintenance, the same goals as the FRB.

So, what is the logic for not investing as much in nature as hard-built infrastructure? Forest maintenance and rebuilding coral reefs are nowhere mentioned in the Jobs and Environment Act, comparatively starving for funding.

At the same time, the annual report card on US infrastructure by the American Society of Civil Engineers (ASCE) reports on the persistently dismal state of US infrastructure, trying to spread a bit of cheer on otherwise inexcusable facts: "For the first time in 20 years, our infrastructure GPA is a C−, up from a D+ in 2017." Yet, of the 17 infrastructure categories graded, 11 were "stuck in the D range. . . . Maintenance backlogs continue to be an issue, but asset management helps prioritize limited funding."

In the United States, investment gaps stagger all prospects of reaching even the second rate grade of B: "We're still just paying about half of our infrastructure bill—and the total investment gap has gone from $2.1 trillion over two years to nearly $2.59 trillion over ten years. . . . By 2039, a continued underinvestment in our infrastructure at current rates will cost $10 trillion GDP . . . and will cost the Average American household $3300 a year."

This is a sorrowful situation for a 21st-century society.

Additionally, if the physical infrastructure in the United States is in such poor condition, though visible and essential, why make the economic assumption that our natural infrastructure is in any better shape? Concomitantly, if the US hard-built infrastructure is worthy of $1.2 trillion in public funding, and a hard-won sweepingly funded Jobs and Infrastructure Act, why not create a similar monumental effort for natural infrastructure?

Far from far-fetched, the question may have an evolving answer. In 2021, the International Institute for Sustainable Development (IISD), a leading think tank, along with the GEF and others, formed the Nature-Based Infrastructure Global Resource Center, precisely to examine the unrealized but key economic and infrastructural role played by natural systems such as wetlands, reefs, forest, peatlands, and mangroves, as compared to the concrete, steel, and macadam of conventional building, referred to as "grey." The center assesses natural infrastructure value and potential worldwide.

The center's founding report in 2021 claims to be first in the world to estimate how much global infrastructure need could be met by natural systems, with bold result: "Our research shows that nature based infrastructure (NBI) can be a game-changer in meeting some of the world's infrastructure needs. . . . Over the next 20 years, the level of infrastructure needed to support development needs would cost USD 4.29 trillion annually if only grey infrastructure is used . . . in practice some of this infrastructure can instead be built using nature. We found that 11.4% of this need could be met effectively using NBI."

Investing in NBI also generates major premium, according to the report: "The argument in favour of NBI gets even stronger when looking at what other benefits come from using nature instead of a built solution. We found that NBI's added value is 28% greater than grey infrastructure."

The report postulates an unbooked additional value of NBI of US $489 billion annually from ecosystem services provided by NBI, noting, "Traditional valuations . . . focus only on a narrow set of financial indicators that have not been adjusted to integrate the value of nature or the value of its loss . . . Continuing to use traditional valuations means that investments flow disproportionately to grey infrastructure."

The report concludes that favoritism to grey infrastructure is a "missed opportunity to tackle the twin crises of biodiversity loss and climate change, which will lead to far greater environmental, social, and economic costs down the line." The line, yes, between taking action and not, profit and loss, assets and costs, near-term and short-term, imagination and none, leaders and followers, mainstream and vanguard, crisp courageous vision to radically question conventional finance, and the cloudiness of systems built long ago for purposes now faltering—prosaic perhaps but simply put, the line between grey and green.

Nature is a public good, functioning day and night as essential infrastructure for all the rest of human endeavor and aspiration—the centerpiece, to be booked as an asset and carefully tended, not an expense to be evaded or minimized.

No matter how we rhetorically exalt the magnificence of nature and its importance, when it comes to restoring, protecting, and cherishing nature not only for its services today but for all future generations, we treat the protection of nature as a financial cost center and financial burden to bear.

Innovations like the FRB do not privatize public goods but elevate the value of their public purpose. The FRB brings and holds together stakeholders who might otherwise never have perceived their common interests, and surely never pooled those interests via a financial tool that credibly prices that which will always defy price. All priceless elements we value can command that unity, for the essence of pricelessness is its differentiated yet universal recognition.

Whether the FRB model can realize its potential remains to be seen, but such is the wager of creativity. To an extent, the FRB reconfigures disparate self-interest as a vision of mutual benefit and understanding, to protect what must be held as one. In short, a common capture and cherishing of pricelessness in the here and now and, we can hope, always.

13

Off Limits: The Value of Do Not Touch

When an overcast sky breaks on the Kerry coast in Ireland, sun falls on the sea like pent-up love, as if that day's particular heat and sparkle had been waiting behind the clouds for years. It is mostly misty in Kerry, but a sunny day can blind the eyes with the crushed-glass glisten of the Atlantic Ocean as it rolls into wide beaches or tiny coves of sand. A narrow road winds in and out of the craggy fingers of land, famed as the Ring of Kerry, a ribbon through one of the most breathtaking landscapes in the world.

However, despite the awe, the global climate change crisis plays out in local expression not far from the sea, in an emblematic clash between the constant imperative to reduce emissions from all sources and the impact of an unexpected war. Russia's invasion of Ukraine in 2022 triggered energy price upswings throughout the EU and set off nettlesome trade-offs over long-standing local practices and local regulation, such as in Ireland, the burning of bogland and peat for home heating in rural areas, known there as "cutting turf" and a rural practice for centuries. Turf cutting was so common that unique Kerry bog ponies were domesticated in the 17the century to work the peatlands. Their stocky low height and heavy weight gave the docile ponies sure footing in the soft, soddy terrain, and farmers depended on them to haul the heavy chunks of peat to be dried and then burned or sold as fuel.

Found on every continent, peatlands—also known as bogs and sod—are generally dismissed as unproductive for cultivation. Spongy plant and mossy material mostly, peatlands are chronically saturated with water or dampness. Oxygen deprived, they only partly decompose and so hold in the gases of normal organic soil decay, namely carbon dioxide and others such as methane. In polar regions, a sealing layer of permafrost above keeps peatlands from exposure to the air. Peatlands, therefore, are formidably saturated with carbon and greenhouse gas but, for the same reason, cuts of dried peat are living bricks of fuel, though giving less heat when burned than coal, with more emissions.

Peatlands formed over thousands of years as the earth cooled and warmed in natural geological cycles, but through deliberate burning or melting of usually frozen ground due to warming temperatures, the motherlode of peatland packed-in gases can be liberated in mere weeks.

Asia holds 33% of the world's peatland stock, with 32% in North America; 13% in Latin America and the Caribbean; 12% in Europe; 8% in Africa, notably in the Congo River Basin; and 2% in Oceania and Antarctica.

Peatlands statistics punch out warning. According to the UN's 2022 Global Peatlands Assessment (GPA), even though peatlands cover only 3–4% of earth's surface, they "contain up to one third of the world's soil carbon. This is twice the amount of carbon as found in the entirety of earth's forest biomass. Keeping this carbon locked away is absolutely critical to achieve global climate change goals."

"Locked away" sounds so simple, but such renunciation is the heartbeat of the global climate challenge and the dilemma of value. By definition, keeping peatland carbon locked away means forsaking its energy potential—actually giving up and turning the eyes away from its tempting presence to, in best case, restore peatlands where possible and above all not to disturb or burn peatland still intact. To "lock away" needed energy sources asks much of people, who hear a constant refrain about environmental issues that are "absolutely critical," and puts the need to address climate change in an unworkable dependency on a surrender to sacrifice, begging the question for what is forsaken, what will be given?

Ireland presents a vivid case, a developed country in the European Union with an environmental leadership profile, squeezed between best intentions and complex imperatives. Though representing just one-twentieth of a percent of earth's land surface, Ireland hosts nearly 3% of earth's blanket bog, the peatland type found at shorelines and in uplands, and about half of the EU's raised bog, a peatland type found more midland. Peatlands once covered nearly 17% of Ireland, but gradually bogs were drained for planting or cut and dried into fuel blocks, literally the energy of rural Irish village life.

According to the GPA, as of 2022, 50% of Europe's peatlands degraded in one way or another, mostly for agriculture, and "this makes Europe the second largest current greenhouse gas emitter from drained peatlands at close to 600 MtCo$_2$e per year." For perspective, this total just about equals the annual emissions of Germany or the combined emissions of France and the UK, meaning emissions released from degrading peatlands can wipe out any near-term emissions reductions these nations might make.

To protect peatlands and cut down on smoky air, the EU set restrictions on peatland use, and Ireland issued an outright ban on turf cutting and burning in October 2022. The ban, though, was widely flouted and taken as an unfair demand on rural families struggling to make ends meet, especially as household energy costs rose due to the energy disruptions that came along with the war in Ukraine.

According to the *New York Times,* at the time of the ban, one in seven Irish families burned dried peat at least partially for heat. An average household could cover a winter's heating needs for roughly €500, a pittance compared to costs of other fuels and electricity. "People are glad to have turf. It's like having an oilwell in your own backyard," Michael Fitzmaurice, chair of Ireland Turf Cutters and Contractors Association and an independent member of Ireland's Parliament, told the *Guardian* in December 2022.

Turf burning persisted and Ireland faced fines from the EU in fall 2022 for failing to sufficiently halt it, while Irish legislators battled over the ruling and argued over lifting the ban temporarily to provide families fuel cost relief. The government of Ireland also embarked on significant peatland restoration and bought back private titles to peatlands in protected areas, a bit caught between peatland coming and going in a sense, as is the rest of the world.

According to the GPA, 12% of global peatlands are degraded due to draining, deforestation, drought, and other intrusions. These degraded lands, as of 2022, "emit about 2,000 Mt of Co$_2$e, by microbial oxidation, which is 4% of all anthropogenic emissions, fires excluded. Fires on drained peatlands are particularly serious as they can lead to very substantial emissions of greenhouse gases."

The ideal of peatland-rich nations voluntarily locking up their peatlands drew sharp geopolitical attention in 2022 at the annual UN climate conference, COP27, in Egypt. US Special Presidential Envoy for Climate John Kerry made a personal plea to President Felix Tshisekedi of the Democratic Republic of Congo (DRC) to halt plans to offer oil drilling concessions in the DRC's enormous rainforests and peatlands. The DRC hosts two-thirds of the Congo Basin's peatlands, the largest store of tropical peatland area on earth.

According to Nature Geoscience's updated spatial and field research published in August 2022, Congo River Basin peatlands remain mostly intact, mostly covered by rainforest, holding about 28% of the world's tropical peat carbon. This makes the basin a royal palace of locked-up climate danger that should never hit the air.

Hydrocarbon exploitation in the basin would flout that reality. According to Nature Geoscience research, oil concessions "cover almost the entire peatland complex. Mining, logging and palm oil concessions 'overlie . . . about 26%' of the peatland area." However, the research adds, "only 8% of this peat carbon lies within nationally protected areas, suggesting its vulnerability to future land-use change."

So between oil-rich allure and global climate change urgency, a burning fuse, almost literally, or as Nature Geoscience calmly concludes, "keeping the central Congo Basin peatlands wet is vital to prevent peat carbon being released to the atmosphere."

Keeping the peatlands wet means minimal disturbance to overlying rainforests, ecologically invaluable in themselves. Protecting peatlands also obviates most extractive concessions because cutting down trees, building roads, digging pipelines, and drilling itself can tear peatlands and forests apart. Nevertheless, despite local protest, the government of the DRC opened 30 oil and gas bids for permits in July 2022, of which several overlap with peatlands, insisting environmental protections would be required for any concession granted.

Justifying the oil concession auction, Eve Bazaiba, deputy prime minister and minister of environment of the DRC said, "DRC continues to import oil at high prices and with poor quality, and yet we have oil under our feet."

How to weigh the balance? According to the GPA:

> The situation is critical but not hopeless. It is imperative that the 88% of the world's peatlands that have not been drained and not been heavily degraded be urgently protected to prevent their immense carbon stocks from being mobilized. . . . Conservation and restoration of tropical peatlands alone could cost $40 billion US Dollars but could

reduce global greenhouse gas emissions by 800 million tons CO2e per year (equivalent to 1.5% of annual global emissions). Such action would simultaneously support biodiversity, improve water quality, reduce flood risk, reduce air pollution from peatland fires and enhance the protection of important cultural heritage. The benefits are enormous.

Conservation and restoration would seem an unmitigated bargain compared to the climate change costs unleashed otherwise and a likely undervaluation of the contribution to atmospheric balance of protecting the world's peat.

However, how does this compare to the value to the DRC of selling oil? Climate science and the Paris Agreement would argue that, in theory, most of the oil held in the Congo Basin is a "stranded asset" because little, if any, fossil fuel can be added to the world's energy mix if the Paris schedule of emissions reductions is to remain within reach.

Stranded, though, by whom, for whom, and at what price for renouncing the price per barrel, to benefit whom? According to the World Bank, in the DRC as of 2021, 60% its 60 million people struggled to live on less than $2.15 per day. When the DRC put the oil concessions on the auction block in July 2022, Bloomberg reported they would be worth potentially $650 billion based on estimated reserves of 16 billion barrels at roughly $107 per barrel and a recovery rate of 35%.

Scandal on logging concessions erupted in the DRC around the same time as the auction, after the nation's General Inspectorate of Finance (IGF) issued an audit exposing the granting of illegal logging concessions going back to 2002, poor monitoring of logging overall, and failure to book logging royalty fees to the public budget, the implication being the fees were diverted to private pockets, if paid at all. Minister Bazaiba suspended contracts determined illegal by the audit, and set up a commission to further examine the allegations.

Rainforest protection braids into peatlands issues, obviously, and the audit had been required by the Central African Financial Initiative (CAFI), a coalition of donor nations, including Norway, Germany, and the UK, that jointly provide development funds in the central African region aimed mostly at preventing deforestation. In November 2021, CAFI signed an MOU that would grant $500 million over five years to the DRC, which committed to use the funds to cap forest loss and address socioeconomic cause of deforestation, mostly related to the need for agricultural land and fuel among the DRC's rural people, still a paltry sum compared to possible oil revenue.

Gifted with rainforests and peatlands, the Congo Basin falls into the tightening vice of geopolitics, persistent wealth inequality, and climate change. According to the World Resources Institute (WRI), as of 2023, of the world's three largest tropical rainforests, the Congo Basin remains the last on earth that still had "enough standing forest left to remain a strong net carbon sink—meaning to continue to absorb more carbon than it emitted through deforestation. The Congo's tropical rainforest sequesters 600 million metric tonnes more carbon dioxide per year than it emits, equivalent to about one-third of the CO_2 emissions from all U.S. transportation."

The Congo Basin's negative emissions balance, though, derives mostly from its poverty, absence of industrialization, and low levels of consumption and use of fossil fuels by the many people in the region living at barely subsistence level.

Ironically, the stringent urgency of addressing climate change could offer routes to overcome that destitution at last by yet another irony—placing a commensurate value on fossil fuel assets locked away and converting that asset value into revenue flows to meet socioeconomic need. Pricing locked-away assets for greenhouse gas mitigation value, for example, in pricing and paying for the rainforest and peatlands ecosystem services, would amount to an intergenerational national asset portfolio, and its earnings to a form of national annuity for the DRC.

Without transformative approaches to valuing and pricing the Congo Basin's priceless natural resources, the ongoing push to alleviate poverty remains dependent on carbonization, and so, no doubt, extensive exploration of its rainforests and peatlands will occur, the extractive model of the 20th century damning most of the 21st.

In this business-as-usual scenario, the last remaining tropical carbon sink on the planet will become by default merely a "consumption sink," absorbing the emissions of fossil fuel waste and excess in faraway industrial countries. In the "consumption sink" model, the poor of the Congo Basin look on, expected to willingly guard their natural assets for almost only the sake of general global welfare.

Gabon, with 2 million people and a territory that occupies 18% of the Congo River Basin, has attempted to avoid being sucked into the consumption sink trap by emphasizing forest protection as a money-maker. As of 2022, the nation maintained one of the lowest rates of deforestation in the world. Its conservation-minded second president, Omar Bongo, who took office in 1967, established an extensive system of national parks and reserves, and his son, who followed his father in office, imposed a ban on export of raw logs in 2010.

Gabon was also the first nation in the world to commit to the "30x30" off-limits pledges made at COP15, committing to meet that schedule of protecting 30% of its land and ocean territory by 2030. Though Gabon still exploits its fossil fuel and ore reserves, its conservation-weighted economic direction is a hedge against the fact that oil and other extractive industries will inevitably reach a point of diminishing returns and instead elevates Gabon's rainforests, covering nearly 90% of the national territory, to a kind of exalted economic status.

The shift requires delicate counterpoint, since income from oil, manganese, and other extractive industries made up 98% of Gabon's exports in 2021, according to the World Bank, with a majority to importers in Asia, especially China, India, Singapore, South Korea, and Malaysia. In the meantime, a third of the Gabonese people live below the poverty line of $5.50 per day, worsened by job loss and economic crash when exports collapsed during the COVID-19 pandemic from about US $6.5 billion in 2019 to $4.3 billion in 2020.

To treasure forests and still earn from them, Gabon's Minister of Forests and Water, Lee White, introduced reforms when he took office in 2019. White established special economic zones so Gabon could develop a home-grown forest product industry and gain the value-added revenue of limited production, imposing strict guidelines on what trees may be cut. Carved tables, bookcases, shelving veneer, and other products drawn only from ecologically well-managed forests can command high export value, and a made-in-Gabon wood industry recognizes that even the strictest logging bans cannot be 100% policed and controlled, especially given the need for local jobs and export earnings. White set up special economic zones to centralize the monitoring, manufacture, and export of Gabon's forestry products, including jobs training.

According to White, this insistence of local value-added flipped the forest value pyramid, so that where raw wood export had added only about 8% to Gabon's economy, with a value of about $250 million per year, processing wood products in Gabon earned US $1 billion a year. Overall, according to White, Gabon's forest industry created roughly 30,000 jobs, employing about 7% of the workforce. "This way we made the forest more precious," White said at the spring meeting of the International Monetary Fund in May 2022.

According to the African Development Bank, Gabon's forest industries contributed 3–5% to national GDP, excluding, of course, value of ecosystem services the GDP does not capture.

Gabon demonstrates that careful processing of forest products can enable the opposite: leaving most of the trees alone so their value as carbon sinks can be monetized, to then also capitalize on carbon pricing and other financial innovations and investments in forest protection.

Threading between competing pressures, still contemporary Gabon could illuminate a pathway to pricing the priceless value of standing trees at a national and even continental scale. That journey, though, is incremental.

In June 2021, Gabon became the first country in Africa to receive a direct payment for the value of reduction of CO_2 emissions from deforestation. The "results-based" payment of US $17 million that Norway contributed was the first installment of a $150 million 10-year agreement between Gabon and CAFI, certifying that Gabon's emissions from deforestation fell in 2016–17 compared to 2008–15.

Despite low historical rates of deforestation and forest degradation, Gabon has been able to reduce CO_2 emissions even further. White said the payment would "finance projects that preserve Gabon's forests. It also paves the way for Gabon to finalize the systems that will be required to enable the country to formally sell carbon credits in the future." True to White's prediction in October 2022, the UNF-CCC validated Gabon's claims to forest protection credits for forest protection and emissions reductions from 2010 to 2018, to be held in Gabon's national account, and eligible to be sold and retired from the ledger as "sovereign credits." White said, "I expect . . . Gabon will generate 100 million tonnes of net carbon sequestration credits per year and sell them for $20 to $30 per tonne." Prices could also possibly climb well above White's estimate as carbon markets integrate globally, adding more financial weight and visibility to the value of standing trees. Gabon stipulated its planned use of proceeds from any credit sale, applying revenue earned from standing trees to meet diverse needs across the whole national budget:

- 25% for improved education, health and infrastructure to increase climate resilience
- 10% to manage and conserve biodiversity including through financial contributions to the Gabonese Foundation for Biodiversity
- 10% for contributions to environmental and social NGOs working in communities and with rural populations
- 25% to the Gabonese Sovereign Wealth fund as reserve capital to further investments in sustainable development practices
- And notably, 30% to service Gabon's debt or to create carbon-backed bonds

As of 2022, according to the World Bank, Gabon's debt amounted to 65% of its GDP but was projected to decline gradually to 37% in 2027, assuming post-COVID economic recovery. Instead of cutting more trees to sell for cash to cover debt service, using carbon credit revenue to meet debt service breaks the regressive pattern of spending down natural capital of the future to catch up with deficits of the past. It also dramatically illustrates the direct use of financial benefits from protecting forests.

Use of proceeds to enhance education and public health also converts the value of standing trees into socioeconomic benefits and social capital that people need and can appreciate. Additionally, applying 30% of carbon credit sale proceeds to debt service also endows Gabon's forest conservation effort with augmented financial strength, changing the pendulum swing to question who, over time, is the debtor and who the lender.

In the classic development paradigm, high-income countries loan funds to lower-income countries, whose inherited income streams, often postcolonial, rarely suffice to meet debt and even the concessionary interest payments of multinational institutions, such as the World Bank and the IMF.

By saving its trees, Gabon contributes their sequestration power and value to the rest of the world, lending them in a sense to industrialized nations short on emissions reductions options and craving sequestration sources. Also, as carbon prices rise, so will proceeds applied to debt reduction, meaning that, over time, Gabon's standing forest could become a permanent counterweight to what is owed to public creditors.

Gabon's magnificent wildlands should be an asset that only rises in value, able to serve as indisputable collateral to secure further national investment, or securitize development funds received. Overall, could forest protection eventually fully nullify Gabon's external debt, based on what such a trove of standing trees and their carbon absorption is worth to the world every year, formerly nature's unpaid labor, now fairly remunerated? If carbon market credit prices were truly commensurate with the value of fending off dramatic climate change, would Gabon's creditors not owe Gabon for its service?

Many question whether the debt burden of developing countries is fair to begin with, but gradually retiring debt through forest protection and other acts of environmental "locking away" seems a formidable transfer of wealth back to countries still well endowed with natural resources on which all nations increasingly depend.

Green trees wiping out red ink—a power of the priceless. The dynamic is based on the inherent and intrinsic power of nature itself, increasingly referred to as "nature-based solutions."

Given that climate change could easily outrun technical solutions to direct emissions reductions, the profile of "nature-based solutions" (NBs) becomes more vivid. Endowed with their own acronym, NBs are generally any actions or policies that protect, manage, or restore natural ecosystems, leveraging nature's own capacity to redress the harm inflicted on it and resolve environmental imbalances it did not create.

Direct reforestation is a flagship NB, and there is almost no limit to the benefits of planting or protecting forests and sharpening the value-added of limited forest products, as in Gabon, or reforestation of deforested areas. Some estimates are that in the past 300 years, 1.5 billion hectares of forest have been removed from the planet for countless reasons, an area roughly one and one-half times the size of the United States.

Or, for example, an intentional planting of trees along a riverbank to hold back soil runoff or shade the river to cool its temperature so the river remains hospitable to the myriad fish and other creatures whose life cycles are being disrupted by warming waters. Exactly that has occurred in Scotland to create conditions more conducive to salmon spawning. There are numerous other examples—mangrove, wetlands, and all forms of land restoration; coral reef restoration; reserves and land use planning—biodiversity protection of all sorts.

Of course, as acronyms proliferate, we would be wise to remember that the main "solution" we are after is addressing climate change. That is the bull's-eye, the process that must be undone, slowed down, and ultimately arrested—either directly by cutting emissions right at their source or by sopping them up elsewhere, through the amazingly resilient and widespread options provided by NBs.

Nature is the ultimate "carbon sink," and its ecosystem value can be expressed in carbon markets, notably cap-and-trade. In that the goal of the cap-and-trade is to visibly tag the price of emitting a ton of CO_2e into the dwindling atmospheric space not yet crammed with greenhouse gases, that price can also nominally attach to a ton absorbed up by nature, the basic concept of offsets.

Carbon budgets calculate clearly dwindling atmospheric space, and we also know that as carbon markets become more integrated globally, with tightened and stricter rules, compliance prices can only climb and so value of nature-based solutions should climb too.

However, as long as nature-based solutions remain under the "offsets-are-a-free-pass" cloud and hold second-class status, we are at risk of squandering their immense suite of broad environmental benefits, and especially their key carbon sink role.

Estimates vary, but research by the Nature Conservancy and 17 various institutions, published by the US National Academy of Sciences, found that "natural climate solutions can provide 37% of cost-effective CO_2 mitigation needed through 2030."

The odds that nature-based solutions could do that job seems high. According to the research, the NBS suite has "a greater than 66% chance of holding warming to the scientific limits stipulated in the Paris agreement," and at tantalizingly low cost. The research concludes that a third of nature-based mitigation would be achievable at costs at or below $10 per ton, well below the allowance compliance costs in the EU ETS, expected to average roughly between €75 and €95 in 2023–24.

Obviously, given the costs of EU allowances, investments in nature-based solutions are well below compliance costs in the world's leading mandatory market. Yet investment gaps in nature-based projections are yawning.

A 2021 key report by the United Nations Environment Programme (UNEP), the World Economic Forum (WEF), and the Economics of Land Degradation Initiative (ELD) stated, "investment in NBs ought to at least triple in real terms by 2030 and increase four-fold by 2050 if the world is to meet its climate change, biodiversity and land degradation targets. This acceleration would equate to cumulative total investment of up to USD 8.1 trillion and a future annual investment of USD 536 billion." The same report found that, in 2020 as a base year, only US $133 billion was directed to NBs, of which 86% was public funding.

Nature's needs have been invisible to markets since markets began, and the projected $8.1 trillion need does not automatically equate to a $8.1 trillion market opportunity just waiting for capital to flow to it, public or private. The funding gap fills with mixed messages.

The Association of Financial Markets in Europe (AFME) and EY published a bullish report in November 2022 called "Into the Wild: Why Nature may be the Next Frontier of Capital Markets," enumerating numerous opportunities. Yet the report also cited the fallback caveat, that a main barrier to "investing in nature at scale is that the risks outweigh the returns."

If markets replete with capital shrink from lesser returns or plausible risks, why shouldn't poor nations too? Why should countries with desperate populations and extensive virgin natural assets renounce exploitation of those assets for the world's greater benefit, without expectation of financial return ample enough to meet domestic needs and aspirations?

If conventional capital market accounting does not shift soon enough to confer sufficient value on natural assets left alone, or at sufficient scale, what is the remedy for holders of those assets? A highest bidder always tends to appear.

Minister Eve Bazaiba of the DRC crystallized the inescapable when she spoke in November 2022 about oil concessions in the DRC competing with peatland protections, saying, "If the world wants Congo to preserve the peatlands, where is the compensation? That's a question of ethics and morals."

Her remarks recalled provocative comments I heard at the 1992 UN Earth Summit in Rio de Janeiro, when an energetic Brazilian activist posed a pointed question at a citizen's forum outside the official government meetings. To a crowd gathered under a sweltering tent, she confidently asserted, "if the North says it is so important for us to keep our rainforest standing, why don't they rent it from us?"

We can only wonder with regret how far along the world would be in wrestling runaway greenhouse emissions as well as socioeconomic progress in Amazonian countries if major emitting nations then had calculated and willingly paid such rent. In fact, according to WRI, the future of the Amazon as a net carbon sink fell into doubt due to high rates of deforestation in the Brazilian Amazon, the bulk of Latin America's Amazonia. Brazil's Amazon region metamorphosed from net absorber of CO_2 to net emitter from roughly 1980 to 2020, with extremely high rates when Jair Bolsonaro was president from 2019 to 2022. He resented measures to protect the Amazon, and according to INPE, the national space agency of Brazil, deforestation increased 9.5% in 2020 alone, the most since 2015, meaning an area seven times the size of the city of London had been lost during just one year of Bolsonaro's tenure.

Loss of trees also means loss of rainfall, as rainforests both draw and evaporate rain in the constant water cycle that sustains them. Deforestation breaks that water feedback loop, worsening the interruption in rainfall pattern caused by climate change itself. As a result, according to research in 2022 by a consortium of Brazilian and Portuguese researchers, droughts from 2003 to 2020 in the Amazon were double the 10-year frequency rate of the prior 100 years.

Amazonian drought is truly unimaginable, so much does—or did—water reign when I spent a year in Amazonia well before the study period. Rain bursts were constant, with raindrops like jackhammers for hours on roofs and falling in sheets through the trees and pinging off leaves as large as tabletops. During rainy season, the rivers flooded so, as we rowed along in inflatable dinghies, we could gradually reach the tree-tops, entirely unaware we had been traveling a silent graceful lift of water.

What does the horror of a thirsty drying Amazon portend for Congo basin trees and peat? Certainly their fate as unpaid laborers could be the same.

Minister of Environment Arlette Soudan-Nonault, for the Republic of Congo (ROC), also a major Congo Basin nation rich in rainforest, peatland, and oil, made the connection crisply in a BBC interview in June 2022 on the fate of Congo peatlands, saying, "Now that the Amazon has lost its role as the regulator of the world climate due to deforestation . . . the Congo Basin acts as the lungs of humanity."

For that service, the question is the same whether rent, compensation, or transfer of funds by any other name. What is the price and value of environmental assets undisturbed and unexploited, left alone to do the work so long taken for granted, for which there is no compensation truly sufficient, especially as environmental stakes intensify?

The question transcends the long-running "loss and damages" debate—on whether industrialized countries whose greenhouse gas emissions powered their economic growth, but brought on the climate crisis, owe legal settlement or reparations to nations whose emissions have been far lower, who had little or no role in creating the problem but who suffer its consequences just the same.

A general agreement was reached on loss-and-damages at COP27 in Egypt in 2022, and an international fund was created to collect payments, but loss-and-damages is a classic liability claim framework to address the past. Knotty as the negotiations became, loss-and-damages does not grapple with the ongoing dynamic of the future—expressing the value of resources locked away.

Using carbon prices as a gauge, at the Climate Leaders Summit convened in April 2021 by US President Biden, DRC President Tshisekedi said a $100 per ton carbon price would be the least that would be "fair" to the DRC if other financial "opportunities" were to be foregone. The EU ETS compliance allowances did hover at that price until disruption of the energy-carbon price balance in 2022 due to the Russian cutoff of fuel supplies to Europe, so the $100 "if we forego" price is not untenable.

In August 2022, the DRC also announced that environmental groups and even cryptocurrency companies lobbying the DRC to keep its peatlands oil off the market were welcome to join the auction for oilfield concessions as long as the bidders could meet the tender offer financially. Referring to letting outsiders bid and the proposed plans to earn "carbon credits" from leaving oil in the ground, the DRC's Minister for Hydrocarbons, Didier Budimbu Ntubuanga, said in an interview with the *Financial Times,* "if it can help our economy and the country, why not?" He also said the DRC's goal in exploiting its oil was not to destroy its rainforest, but rather, "We're doing it for economic gain . . . with or without oil, what's important is that we earn [money]."

As climate science marches on, the debate over leaving Congo Basin oil in the ground rings with the deafening echo of decades passing. In 2007, oil-rich Ecuador presciently and vividly framed the value of oil left in the ground in its ill-fated Yasuni-ITT Initiative, a boldly original proposal that foresaw the future and tragically, we can appreciate, glanced like a skipping stone off most of the environmental and financial assumptions of the time. The Ecuadorian idea failed not because it came on the scene too early, though truly avant-garde, but because the rest of the world opened its eyes to the inevitability of its premise too late.

In 2007, then president of Ecuador, Rafael Correa, in a far-sighted plea before the United Nations, beckoned the entire world to essentially buy oil in Ecuador that would never leave the ground. At the time, 20% of Ecuador's known oil reserves lay beneath the Yasuni National Park in Ecuador's Amazonian forest, in the Ishpingo-Tambococha-Tiputini (ITT) concession block. In 1989, UNESCO declared the Yasuni area a unique Man and Biosphere Reserve, given its staggering tree, plant, animal, and insect biodiversity.

The charismatic but volatile Correa launched a rousing challenge at a High-Level Dialogue of the General Assembly:

> Madam, Co-Chairs, Ladies and Gentlemen . . . Climate change knows no borders, but we must point out that its distribution and impact are inequitable. . . . Ecuador is a marginal country in terms of emissions (less of 1% of the world-wide total). . . .
>
> Nevertheless, Ecuador is prepared to make enormous sacrifices, with a sense of justice and creativity, to counteract global warming. The initiative of the Ecuadorian Government to maintain crude oil ITT underground . . . entails a commitment not to exploit nearly 920 million barrels of petroleum, thereby preserving one of the most bio-diverse regions of the world. Nevertheless, this means that enormous investments will be lost, nearly 720 million dollars per year, a very significant amount for a small country with 13 million habitants and around 6 million living in poverty . . . we need the international community to share the responsibility by providing a minimum compensation in recognition of the environmental benefits we will generate for the entire planet.

Correa stated that not burning Yasuni-ITT oil would prevent the emission of roughly 111 million tons of carbon, and that Ecuador would lose $10–$15 per barrel, leaving Yasuni oil alone. Yet Correa asked $5 per barrel in the name of his country to "preserve biodiversity, to protect the indigenous people who live in the area in voluntary isolation, and to prevent carbon dioxide emissions."

Ecuador sought a total "look away" payment of approximately $4.6 billion dollars. Correa also promised to create a Yasuní-ITT Environmental Fund to be administered by the UN's Development Programme (UNDP) that would support Ecuadoran socioeconomic programs such as health and education, ecotourism expansion, and diversification of energy sources.

Correa spoke from and to history: "For the first time an oil producing country, Ecuador, where one-third of state revenues depend on the exploitation of that resource, forsakes that income for the sake of all humanity, and invites the world to join in this effort through fair compensation, so that together we can lay the foundation of a more human and fair civilization."

To further break precedent, Correa proposed an unprecedented financial tool, the Yasuni Guarantee Certificate (CGY), a unique financial instrument issued by the Ecuadorian state in return for contributions to the Yasuni plan. The CGY also guaranteed the state would repay CGY holders in full, though without interest, should Ecuador renege and begin Yasuni oil exploitation, what Correa unashamedly termed Plan B. Ecuador's compensation schedule was to raise $100 million by end the end of 2011, then that amount incrementally each year, with the entire roughly $5 billion by 2024.

At the time, Ecuador could not issue or sell carbon credits for emissions avoided through the Yasuni-ITT plan—there was no precedent for issuing credits for oil left unburned, carbon markets were nascent, and Ecuador's proposal was too far ahead.

The boldness of Correa's challenge became a cause célèbre. Though he did not quite shut down preparations for Plan B, Ecuador promoted the Yasuni plan nationally and internationally. Ecuador sought contributions from international agencies, foreign governments, and eventually individuals in an early form of GoFundMe or crowdsourcing. Celebrities such as Leonardo DiCaprio and Bo Derek pledged funds. Within Ecuador, government polling showed public support for Yasuni-ITT reportedly reached 80%.

The government of Germany stepped up as an anchor contributor, whose coalition government pledged $50 million per year. Pledges also came from Italy, France, Belgium, Brazil, and others—even from subnational entities such as the Belgian state of Wallonia and a construction company in Korea. Nobel Laureate Mohammed Yunus, founder of the micro-lending concept; Ban-Ki Moon, UN Secretary-General; and Prince Charles of Great Britain also lent support, along with international organization such as the Organization of American States (OAS). According to a UN report, even the Organization of Petroleum Exporting Countries (OPEC) publicly endorsed the Yasuni concept.

Meanwhile, though, the 2008 financial crisis pressed global economies and Ecuador's record of default on paying debt on its national bonds chilled its credibility on CGYs. At the same time, detractors questioned Correa's environmental good faith, as Ecuador granted oil leases near to Yasuni, including to China, which was becoming a major lender and trade partner in Latin America.

In 2011, Germany's coalition government changed, and the new ensemble withdrew the government's pledge to the Yasuni Fund, though Germany did contribute directly to Yasuni forestry protection programs that were not contingent on paying for oil below ground.

By 2013, time ran out on the Yasuni-ITT idea and Correa bitterly cancelled the project, citing lack of international support. In 2012, media reported that Yasuni had received pledges of $300 million, but when the UNDP closed its books on the Yasuni fund in 2015, total actual receipts were only $10,583,801, mostly from Italy, Spain, Luxembourg, and Belgium, with a sprinkling of private donations and foundations.

Ecuador did undertake Plan B, ITT blocks were opened to drilling in 2016, and as of 2020, about 4.5% of Ecuador's GDP derived from oil rents, the difference between value of oil production at regional prices and costs of production. Temporary moratoria have been established concerning drilling in Yasuni, but concessions remained embroiled in legal battling as of 2023.

What happened to the plan to keep Yasuni oil underground? On the one hand, Correa compromised his credibility and sincerity by constantly dangling the threat of Plan B. Nor did local oil interests cease undercutting the plan, including Petrocuador, Ecuador's national oil company. Some donor nations also held back out of fear the Yasuni plan could eventually inspire a form of future environmental blackmail, where other oil-rich nations could propose their own Yasuni plans, ever more expensive, along with unmeetable oil price demands.

A network of Yasuni plans around the world could have indeed been an outright revolt against the oil economy of the time. Imagine if Yasuni triggered competition in oil pricing, so that barrels of oil burned were notably more expensive than those left in the ground? Would the need to avoid those extra-costly barrels have accelerated investments in alternative energies or, at the least, spurred significant energy efficiency policies?

Overall, however, Ecuador's proposal dug to the heart of the matter, as Correa said, the need for an economic system that rewards the production of value by nature, not "only the production of commodities."

Interestingly, a study of the ecosystems services value of Yasuni to Ecuador's economy and the world's, for that matter, was undertaken but did not receive significant attention. According to a UN report on the Yasuni project, "Using the benefit transfer approach, it was estimated that the value of the flow of non-market ecosystem services in Yasuní National Park is between $2 and $5.4 billion per year," meaning that the ecological value of Yasuni would surpass the value of oil exploitation after five to seven years. The study further concluded that the "total present value" of Yasuni's ecosystem services was a staggering $1.7–$4.4 trillion, which it termed "a likely significant underestimate of the total economic value of natural capital assets in the form of healthy resilient ecosystems."

Summing up and supporting Correa's vision definitively, the report concluded, "Oil extraction in the area would provide short-term gains at the expense of significant loss in ecosystem service value over time. It justified Ecuador for asking the international community for compensation for protecting and not drilling the ITT block." Correa had fingered precisely the paradox of pricelessness, but the world was not ready to lock away hydrocarbons, at any price.

It took science fiction, in 2020, to elevate the premise again, in Kim Stanley Robinson's popular novel *The Ministry of the Future*. Robinson put a savior tool called "carbon coin" at the heart of his climate change disaster tale, a new currency the world would use to pay oil producers not to exploit their reserves, and to reward businesses for sequestering carbon.

Robinson, though, tapped the idea from Delton Chen, an Australian civil engineer and self-proclaimed financial innovator, even working Chen and his research into the novel. Chen has said he became interested in carbon pricing in 2013, about 20 years after Rio, 15 years after the Kyoto Protocol, and the same year the Yasuni project closed down. After immersing himself in environmental economics, Chen founded the Global Carbon Reward (GCR) Initiative, intended to turn climate change mitigation into internationally sanctioned monetary policy in effect, and establish a commonly accepted new currency that would rise and fall in value as mitigating climate change succeeds or does not, issued and guaranteed by central banks without debt obligation attached.

One unit of Chen's "experimental carbon coin," tickered XCC in currency trading terms, would represent one metric ton of CO_2e mitigated for 100 years. Projects would be verified and graded by a national carbon exchange authority. According to the GCR prospectus and pricing theory, XCC would operate as a "representative currency," not a medium of exchange, but rather "it will be issued as an incentive and will behave as a financial asset" and a "store of value."

The GCR also envisions a carbon exchange standard that would "define the quality of the climate mitigation services that may be rewarded with CC and will determine the minimum economic value of the CC that is to be issued as the reward."

Chen's carbon coin mostly intends to support high-cost, high-stakes carbon mitigation, such as DAC technologies to reclaim existing greenhouse gas emissions from the atmosphere.

Most science suggests that direct air capture will be needed, truly akin to stuffing a genie back into the bottle, in order to reach the target of net-zero emissions by 2050, the ultimate goal of the Paris Agreement. This means no net emissions rise.

DAC technologies are literally far-out, aimed at greenhouse gases already resident up in the atmosphere in low concentrations, making them diffuse and difficult to suck back. Also, the returning gases would need a new home on earth, either back underground by massive injection or solidified into building cubes, or other as yet unimagined locations and products. Countless genies to stuff into countless bottles.

Conceptual challenges aside, technologies assumed to have significant climate change mitigation potential demand extensive research and experimentation imbued with significant financial and physical risks. That central banks would bear that risk is the primary benefit of Chen's carbon coin, or any similar approach.

In the carbon coin scheme, companies that may have promising DAC technologies would apply to the carbon exchange authority to present their plans, have the 100 year duration verified, and be issued carbon coin that would have a floor value assigned and guaranteed by the central bank. No debt or risk attaches.

DAC companies could then raise capital in open markets by selling their carbon coin as if government bonds to currency traders or other secondary buyers, on the assumption that carbon coin will climb in value. Since XCC carbon coin has no other transactional purpose or value, it could not be used for other than its stated purpose.

Carbon coin could also underwrite other high-stakes climate change mitigation technologies, such as running the internet on the sun directly, recognizing the untenably voracious demand for energy of the IT sector, an idea suggested but even more far-out than DACs.

Central banks, such as the Federal Reserve in the United States, Banque of France, and Monetary Authority of Singapore, and ideally all central banks, would issue their national version of Chen's XCC, and guarantee its redemption just as they guarantee national monies. This central bank issuance and guarantee would de-risk environmental investments that would be made by private and public investors who sought to earn and trade XCC and, in one fell swoop, mostly de-risk investments in nature overall. Central bank guarantee would add time to the cash-reward cycle, so that investment is more in sync with the pace of the ecological processes involved, a bit as the FRB structure guarantees investors payment for forest restoration benefits that come in slowly.

Removing financial risk from investments would substantially, maybe unimaginably, lubricate financial flows. If central banks issue XCC, they would be conveying the nearly inviolable premise that protecting nature generates public proceeds as credible as any other form of economic activity on which central banks bank. Central bank backup would also affirm that protecting nature is indispensable to a nation's economic fundamentals, its global trading status, and responsible economic planning and national accounting.

Carbon coin would trade as conventional currencies, enjoying the "full faith and credit" of the government issuer. Is this hocus pocus, a confabulation of high finance? After all, the XCC case would ask the world to accept a wholly new form of money, created from whole cloth and based on measures of invisible gases. Quicksand, hot air, financial balloons ready to burst?

Perhaps, on the other hand, XCC is not such a radical departure. All monies on earth sprang from zero, growing into familiar and credible use. Whether shell, coin, or paper money, all currencies begin with a common agreement of value, and a promise to pay, based on confidence among the users and an accepted unit of measurement.

Carbon markets already price invisibility, and themselves invented the currency of allowances and "credits." They are based on a universal measurement of emissions, and the value of an underlying asset, atmospheric scarcity, an interplay that did not exist before carbon markets asserted it so. Acceptance of allowances and credits attests to their increasing credibility and transferability, codified in market rules and governed with market oversight.

The "carbon financial instrument" (CFI) issued by the Chicago Climate Exchange (CCX) was also self-proclaimed, and CCX went even beyond that—creating a local version of sorts in lush Kerala state in India. There CCX brought a bank to the table to indemnify verified carbon reduction vouchers that local villagers could transact and redeem for cash.

In Kerala, many villagers used biogas cookers that burned dung and mud bricks for energy, but the cookers generated unhealthy smoke and smog within village homes, as well as emitting methane, the highly potent greenhouse gas. CCX worked with a local nonprofit group, Andhyodaya, and their team went house to house to help villagers improve maintenance of the cookstoves, in turn reducing dirt and methane emissions. Cleaner air was a welcome health benefit, but could the villagers also monetize the methane reductions they achieved, if the cuts could be measured and verified? No other carbon market at the time traded all six greenhouse gases as CO_2e, but CCX did.

Andhyodaya developed a credible verification method and aggregated reductions and issued vouchers to households to corroborate their methane reductions, that amounted to "methane credits." Then the Federal Bank of Kerala agreed to underwrite the value of the credits and absorb any risk they might not be sold or disallowed.

Villagers submitted their vouchers to the bank, where they received cash payment on the spot based on the going rate for the CFI, slightly discounted. The bank then registered the methane reductions with CCX, where they could be bought on a limited pilot basis by CCX members as offset credits, generally with a slight premium above the bank's cash outlay.

Through this system, methane in the air became rupees in the pocket. Villagers received needed cash they would never have earned otherwise, in return for achieving methane reductions, an economic boost for sure, but also demonstrating the revenue value of cookstove improvements to their communities.

A Kerala carbon currency of sorts resulted. Ultimately, the Andhyodaya Biogas aggregation program attracted about 15,000 participants from 12 districts in Kerala who, by the end of CCX Phase One had earned about $1.2 million in gross revenue. Phase Two, expanded to other parts of India, reached approximately 100,000 rural households, displacing nearly 500,000 metric tons of CO_2e, generating about $2 million per year.

As far back as 1991, the city of Ithaca, New York, also created a brand-new currency of its own, the Ithaca Hour, declaring a time value for the work of its residents and issuing a "store in value" currency like the XCC carbon coin, against it. Ithaca's objective was to increase the purchasing power of residents, especially the self-employed whose earnings were up and down. The stipulated base value of One Ithaca Hour was $10, the average hourly wage in the city. The city issued Ithaca Hours in denominations of one hour, half hour, and so forth.

At first, Ithaca Hours were used mostly in bartering, especially to remunerate manual work such as plumbing and carpentry, where services might be traded for goods. The Hours could cover costs or round out hybrid transactions also using cash. Gradually, though, the Hours could be used as easily as cash in local restaurants and other establishments. Hours were even accepted by Ithaca's public libraries to pay penalties for overdue books. As digital banking and debit card transactions become more popular than cash, however, use of Itaca Hours waned, though other communities worldwide had begun to issue versions of local money.

And what of the 100% intangible currency created by our presence on the internet, which pretty much free-rides and builds its value on us. We may not think of ourselves as currency creators, but the longer we rest our eyes or fingers on an app or an internet site, the more value we transfer to advertisers, who transform our every click, swipe, tweet, instant message, surf, and email into a sales result of some sort. The longer we pass over a page, the more value we transfer out, for free, to digital data gatherers.

So if, in the internet world, we ourselves can be monetized and packaged into data revenue, the underlying value being the time we spend scanning screens, Chen's carbon coin based on the immutable need to invest in greenhouse gas reductions and backed by central banks hardly seems fanciful. As with existing currency notes and government-issued bonds, anyone could buy, own, and hold XCC, but only the central bank could create and back it.

Chen's proposal can sound grandiose and heavy-handed, especially his notion of a "supranational authority" to manage demand for XCC and set a guaranteed minimum exchange rate or floor price. Weighting and reweighting the carbon reward price, according to the GCR prospectus, requires the price "be such that it can produce an amount of additional carbon mitigation (i.e. reduction and removal) that is sufficient to achieve a probabilistic climate objective."

According to Chen in an interview with the *Wall Street Journal* in 2022, "From the perspective of businesses, the carbon currency will be a debt-free revenue source with a predictable value, but it will also require that each business that wants to earn the currency must accept a long-term service agreement." That agreement would spell out the costs, technologies, and potential of a given proposed climate change remedy and "will ensure that one unit of the carbon currency is issued for one metric ton of CO_2e that has been mitigated for the long term."

Chen sums up XCC as the debt-free financial expression of a "positive externality," namely the otherwise unbooked value of containing a permanent and disastrous climate change problem. As of 2023, the GCR had a small team and was shopping its idea, as Rafael Correa and Ecuador shopped the Yasuni Guarantee Certificates. Chen hoped for rollout in 2025.

By valuing long-term climate mitigation, and rewarding it in transactable currency, carbon coin could also help resolve tough choice inherent in "locking away," faced by all nations, industrialized or not. Battles over what natural resources remain exploitable crop up everywhere, with trade-offs and compensation issues ever-present.

In spring 2022, the government of Sweden, a long-standing proponent of environmental stewardship, approved plans to open an iron ore mine in Lapland, despite protests that the mine would damage delicate northland ecosystems, especially from the local Sami population that the plant would disrupt the reindeer herding and migration patterns on which their livelihoods depended.

The government countered by linking the need for the mine with the evolving needs of a "green steel" industry and to generate jobs in remote areas as climate change and warming temperatures eliminated traditional occupations. Legal battles over the mine were likely to continue for several additional years—the plan first surfaced in 2017 and has been disputed ever since.

In the United States, Native Americans protest mining of lithium and cobalt across vast traditional lands, minerals needed for batteries and the electrification of transportation and other industries dependent on fossil fuel.

In Costa Rica, known worldwide for its far-sighted environmental protection and extensive system of national parks, announced in spring 2022 that it would explore for oil and gas, this despite having co-founded with Denmark, France, and other nations the Beyond Oil and Gas Alliance, which promised to set a date for the end of oil and gas extraction and leasing in their countries. In these and numerous similar cases, trade-offs stand between present value of exploiting natural resources, and compensation for the off-limits approach.

In bucolic Otsego County in upstate New York, a mixed economic mosaic with pockets of affluence in communities mostly of self-employed workers and farmers often struggling to meet their property tax bills, debates erupted in 2011 when hydrofracking to open seams of natural gas was proposed for the area.

Most of the community banded together to take legal action against gas exploration. Many residents simply rejected interference with the local home rule tradition. Many also feared contamination of ground water, on which most homes depended, by chemicals used in the hydrofracking process to split underground shale. Others just plain did not want to lose the landscape to extract gas that would mostly be piped away to other communities. Many Otsego residents turned their backs on cash for leases and received nothing in return.

In fact, hydrofracking was banned throughout New York State in 2014, while the value of the natural gas underground simmers. Perhaps the day will come when the people of New York will be paid in carbon coin for leaving it there.

It could be easy to dismiss concepts like Chen's XCC as esoteric and too truly science fiction to be workable, another catchy save-the-day disruption to become the teaser for podcasts, talk shows, and edgy insider conversation webinars.

However, the concept of a new environmental currency needs to be mainstream, if potential solutions to the climate crisis and planetary deterioration are to scale in time. In fact, it builds on decades of outsider economics that has knocked on the door of conventional finance without ever being truly admitted, trying valiantly to express "externalities" that are now undebatably internal.

It is also critical, however, that any environmental currency not be confused with cryptocurrency, generally rejected by banks, including central banks, as odd and untraceable. Nothing is crypto about natural assets, and the key to their protection is precisely to move that protection into the norms of financial thinking.

Developing a currency that underwrites and guarantees the value of nature is possibly the revolutionary step needed by societies and governments that claim to see climate change and other environmental insults as urgent priorities.

Environmental currency would harness price and pricelessness in every denomination issued, a new unit representing a new form of economic certainty, with nature as the benchmark.

What have been conventionally regarded as intangible would become tangible instantly, and all the elements of nature that have remained invisible to the eyes of economics, and therefore treated as unseen servants, would be irreversibly standing tall.

Carbon coin is no magician's snap of the finger conjuring thin-air value, but rather could be bona fide financial invention that creates indisputable tangible value long ignored. If social and economic equilibrium and fairness rest on long-term climate balance, shouldn't our money systems too?

Kim Stanley Robinson, whose novel injected Chen's idea into mainstream media, has commented that, given the inexorable need to remove and reduce greenhouse gases from the atmosphere, he imagines a day when "petrostates," oil producers whose national budgets and income rely on exploitation and sale of fossil fuels, will also have to be paid not to exploit that fuel, and compensated for the world's need to decarbonize.

For petrostates, in fact, their entire economies could be stranded, given the terms and schedule for emissions reductions enshrined in the Paris Agreement. What would petrostates live on then, given the demise of their known economies and their need to support their societies beyond the life expectancy of major oil production?

Robinson has said "money is not just public wealth; it is also a medium and instrument of public welfare." Robinson regards carbon coin as perhaps just a step in the evolution of currency: "in the same way that the gold standard was understood to be based on a physical amount of gold, the fiscal solidity of carbon coins could be backed by the physical amount of sequestered carbon."

Gold, of course, though no longer the irrefutable foundation of national currencies, remains exceedingly rare, coveted, and seen as never losing value. According to the World Gold Council in 2022, through all of human history, only about 205,000 metric tons of gold have been mined, most since 1950, and if all that gold is put together, it would yield a cube only 22 meters or so on each side.

However, a physical amount of gold may have a heraldic environmental vocation in the 21st century—to have a turn at its own form of carbon coin. If value accrues to keeping oil in the ground, value may also accrue to gold left in the ground as well. Nature's Vault, a blockchain fintech company, announced in 2022 the Legacy Token that, at proposed launch in 2023, will represent 1/100 gram of gold left unmined. Nature's Vault buys rights to gold mines, and then sells tradeable and investable tokens pegged to the value of the gold it never extracts—a surrogate gold and surrogate value. The objective is to secure and monetize the value of gold, without the financial risks inherent in gold mining operations, as well as eliminating the negative environmental impact of mining, increasingly recognized.

According to research in March 2022 in the *Journal of Cleaner Production* by Australian researchers, the gold mining industry worldwide produces about 100 metric tons of CO_2 per year, and the industry is highly carbon intensive. S&P Global calculated in a 2019 study that mining a single ounce of gold generates 800 kilograms of CO_2e, nearly a ton per ounce. In addition, gold mine pits gouge and ravage landscapes as well as societies. For centuries, gold mining depended on pickaxe and rope slave labor, especially in the Western European and British colonies in Africa and Latin America. Gold mining remains treacherous and frequently underpaid work, just like coal mining and other forms of extractive effort.

Doubtless, gold has numerous contemporary uses. Nearly indestructible, gold is a perfect filament to carry electricity, essential to semiconductors and most delicate motors and mechanisms. Still, beguiling since human eyes first beheld its glitter, much raw gold ends up as jewelry worldwide—about 95,000 metric tons of what has been mined. However, at present mining rates, extractable reserves of gold will be exhausted in about two decades. Then what?

Nature's Vault points out that about half the world's mined gold sits inertly in vaults around the world, either in secure government citadels or private safes and other undisclosed locations. Phil Rickard, who founded Nature's Vault and who worked formerly in minerals mining, including gold mining in Indonesia, commented to Impact Alpha in 2022 that for "vanity" materials like, gold, silver, and sometimes platinum, "There's not really much of a reason to dig it up and stick it in a bank vault anymore."

Based in Singapore, Nature's Vault planned to secure rights to about a million ounces of gold in the ground at the outset, ideally in areas with "undisturbed natural ecosystems" to date, with its first stakes in remote Ontario, Canada. The company would independently quantify and verify the existence of gold deposits and use blockchain to record token issuance against mining rights held, as well as track tokens as they change hands investor to investor.

Nature's Vault would hold 20% of its gold mine stake in reserve, in the event of litigation over title or other unexpected events that could dilute or jeopardize token value or keep Nature's Vault from keeping its end of the bargain.

In its 2022 white paper entitled "The Token with a Purpose," Nature's Vault explains, "As more legacy tokens are issued backed by a commitment to preserve unmined gold deposits, legacy token holds promise as a new ESG and natural capital asset class linked to the preservation of gold in the ground." The paper states that the aim of Nature's Vault is to "start a movement to change the way we invest in our planet."

We may need such a movement as staid intergovernmental processes proceed, providing legitimacy and animation for financial risk, still insufficient to keep pace with environmental imperatives. The December 2022 COP15 agreement in Montreal set its formidable ambition to put 30% of earth's land and ocean territory off limits to protect biodiversity, but the plan sounds impossible to realize.

The objective reflects voluntary and inspirational ambition, not binding commitment, and is contingent in practical terms on significant increases in funding at recommended levels of at least $200 billion a year. Considering the funding gaps in capital flowing to nature-based solutions at the time the agreement was signed, the additional funding called for must substantially defy history, unless true financial innovations occur.

As in nearly all international negotiations, tensions flared between have and have-not nations over how to cover the costs of the agreement. As for decades, developing countries held that developed countries should bear most of the financial costs of the off-limits approach, since so many countries rich in biodiversity are not rich otherwise.

Though the UN requires consensus for agreements to be adopted, the president of the Conference, Huang Runqiu of China, appeared to gavel discussions to a conclusion before delegates of various African nations had had a chance to weigh in. Many angrily dissented and said their views had been cut off, including Minister Eve Bazaiba of the DRC.

In the end, however, after the president of the assembly apologized for what had come across as brusque behavior, Minister Bazaiba withdrew her objections and at the 11th hour just days before the new year of 2023 rolled in, the Montreal agreement was adopted by unanimous vote.

"30x30" seems a heartbreakingly limited area of earth remaining to be set aside safely. Yet it is at the least a commonsense ambition, between idealistic voluntary commitments with no chance of being achieved, and draconian requirements that impose restrictions. Common sense should not need tokenization or sci-fi thrillers to speak, but innovations that express inexpressible values will be essential if there is any chance of meeting the "30x30" target on time as well as other interrelated environmental pressures.

We have perhaps reached the point where only locking away resources can save them, and locking away means compensation at a scale commensurate with the value of those assets, the benefits they bestow, and the cost of their loss. We know what calamity can lie ahead and the eyes of time pass upon us. What one generation takes from the ground, the next will likely have to leave alone, whether oil or gas or peat, or any other rarity long since overused.

All nations and peoples confront such dilemmas, from Canada to the Congo, India to Ireland. Irish Nobel Laureate Seamus Heaney wrote in his poem "Digging" of his father and grandfather and the prideful necessity of working peat he thought was over: "the curt cuts of an edge, through living roots awaken in my head. But I've no spade to follow men like them." Yet the need for digging peat returned.

Ecuador's Yasuni proposal cut to the essence, and, though it failed, its moment has come again as the climate change challenge mounts. The world needs energy, and not every source of fossil fuel can be renounced in the near term—at least such renunciation would likely be rejected at large if no coherent, reliable, affordable alternatives exist. Yet the burning of fossil fuels must be significantly curtailed. Only public-purpose finance can manage these seemingly intractable circumstances, perhaps.

In his original speech, Correa declared, "the Ecuadorian proposal seeks to transform old conceptions of economy and of value. In the market system the only possible value is exchange value, the price. The Yasuní-ITT project is based above all on the recognition of the value of use and service, on the non-economic value of the environmental safety and the maintenance of the planetary diversity. It aims to introduce a new economic logic for the 21st century."

14

Infinite Value: Return to Rome

Centuries melt in the Vatican, and on the morning of the papal audience, traveling light seemed in order. I left behind all distractions (phone and iPad for sure), taking along nothing but the basics of palm-sized notebook, pen, camera, and open mind. In the purge of efficiency, I also forgot the lace shawl "starter veil" I had purchased from a Catholic online supplier in case I needed to cover my head, once required of girls and women in Catholic churches.

I walked quickly up the street from my hotel, past the lingering homeless and the souvenir vendors yanking the metal grates off their stalls and hosing down their tiny patch of St. Peter's Square.

I was early through security, as a breeze rustled the silk-striped uniforms of the sardonic Swiss Guards, who barely smiled as they dropped the simple chain rope that weeds out the general tourists from those, like us, who had special pass of entry to the restricted areas of the Vatican. In our case, the laissez-passer was a simple card on a red string identifying us as attendees of the *Laudato Si* conference, third anniversary. One by one, we crossed the threshold.

In the private courtyard, we milled around chatting, the buzz rather like that before a graduation, when giddy students and faculty gather to put on their caps and gowns and prepare for the processional. I had to fight an urge to ask our priest escorts who irons their shirts so crisply, wishing the answer would be that they do it themselves but knowing it was likely the women around them, the nuns and secretaries. The all-maleness of the Vatican hits you bluntly.

As we stood around, I drifted into conversation with Henrik Ehrnrooth, a Finnish economist and apostle of reforestation, as well as chairman of the Climate Leadership Council in Helsinki, a network of Finnish and international companies that had long since recognized the urgency of the climate change problem. He told me that a tree should be understood as a mass of sequestered carbon, and that "if we were to use forestation properly, it would not mean the end of oil, but definitely the end of coal. . . . We could manage the climate problem and still use oil for what it's best used for."

He added, "That's why the oil industry is for a carbon price; they know it will not put them out of business." I reminded him the oil industry supports the lowest of all possible carbon prices, to which he quipped, "Well they also know they can tolerate more."

Cardinal Turkson of Ghana, who had fielded my original letter to the pope, with whom I had had my first Vatican conversation on carbon markets, and who as host had arranged my invitation to the conference, stood at the top of the Synod steps. He waited patiently for our motley flock to fully collect and settle down.

The conference had been a two-day affair, with attendees from all over the world, including Amazonian Indigenous people and Pacific Islanders, not to mention prelates and practitioners from a range of religious affiliations, such as, for example, the Catholic archbishop of Mauritius and the orthodox metropolitan of Pergamon.

After Cardinal Turkson's welcome, we listened to the litany of pending and present climate change problems, including a most eerie whistling chant by a climate activist from Greenland, seeming to both worship and lament the low rushing sound of melting ice. His morose hum was followed by Professor Hans Joachim Schellnhuber, then director of the Potsdam Institute for Climate Impact Research, who recited the latest disturbing scientific trends as clipped facts: "Greenland big ice melted from five kilometers deep to two deep as of then; serious possibility of shutdown of the Gulf Stream; warming seas eating into Antarctic ice sheet from below, with serious concern about surprise collapses"—on and on. Regardless of the cause, he added, the temperature trajectory increase is irrefutable and the interrelationship effects grave.

On the human front, Schellnhuber put forward what he called many "unspoken facts," for example, that there had recently been 4,600 premature deaths in Puerto Rico after Hurricane Maria that had only just been counted, all attributable to the long power outages in hospitals and homes.

Professor Nicholas Stern of the London School of Economics also spoke, having led the landmark Stern Review on "The Economics of Climate Change," commissioned by the UK government, as it subsequently commissioned the Dasgupta Review on biodiversity. The Stern Review framed the daunting negative economic impacts inherent in apparent climate change trends, and Stern was a sought-after guru on the topic.

Another key speaker was Patricia Espinosa, then executive secretary of the UNFCCC, her office charged with diplomatically pressing nations to keep their Paris COP21 promises.

Espinosa and Stern were luminaries and long dedicated to highlighting the complex urgency of tackling climate change. I knew them both, and we caught up a bit before they spoke. I mentioned the idea of a "carbon neutral" Vatican, and they each took the point. During Espinosa's prepared remarks, she added a sidebar in which she said, "We at the UN Climate Change Secretariat are committed to climate neutrality . . . it takes work yes . . . but we stand ready to support the Vatican if you would like to go into that challenge of becoming carbon neutral."

Stern, who has long called for taxing companies on their "free riding" of nature, worked into his remarks the suggestion that the Vatican "announce an early target to get to net zero," which would by definition require involvement in carbon markets.

I was pleased and proud of their reinforcement, since I had not had a chance to further lobby Cardinal Turkson on Vatican actions once I arrived at the conference. However, I saw Turkson smile and jotting notes at the ad lib suggestions from Stern and Espinosa, and later at lunch he said he thought I would have begun to sing when I heard the ideas I'd proposed to him again made public.

Before all that, though, as we stood around in the backstreets of Vatican City, my attention flowed to meeting the pope. Cardinal Turkson motioned, fell in step with the Vatican police, and we all began to make our way across the Synod's nondescript parking area and into the Vatican sanctum.

Across ancient piazzas and cobblestones, through the flow of the impeccable Vatican Gardens, under arch after arch, pathways narrowing, splendor heightening—the eyes take it all in while the mind remembers the slaughters of the Crusades and the Inquisition, the drumbeat of molestation of children hushed up for so long, the Vatican as repository for the highest achievements of the human mind, and the lowest. My skin felt like the skin of a bubble, about to burst from the contradictions.

Yet, all around, the sense of the burning religious beliefs of millions, expressed in the ecstasies of the Sistine Chapel so close, the Michelangelo frescoes I had cited in my letter to Pope Francis, now metaphorically within reach.

Across the Cortile di San Damaso, designed by Bramante, the first architect of St. Peter's Square, then finished by Rafael, the Vatican museums, the map room, invaluable objects gathered or commandeered from the four corners of the world to this, the heartbeat of Renaissance ecclesiastical art, unique and magnetic—all ineffably and permanently priceless.

Then, more astonishing footfalls, up the Scala Nobile to the Sala Clementina, where the pope receives presidents and other heads of state, calling the eye to the open sky frescoes above and covering every wall by the brothers Alberti, Giovanni and Cherubino, adding dimension and expanding the sense of the room, already immense.

Our group settled in and ushers in white ties brought in more plush scarlet straight-backed chairs, moving them around to ranking monsignors and archbishops, cardinals in the front row.

We, the secular, jabbered among ourselves, in a growing din. Cardinal Turkson stepped up to the microphone and whispered, "Hush." Every sound disappeared.

Before one other word could be said, the towering door on the right opened and hotter lights flicked on. Then one more step, and enter the pope. Universal jubilant clamor.

The pope shook hands with Cardinal Turkson and then took two short steps back up to a slight elevation, flanked by two priests. One handed him his glasses, and the pope hesitated ever so slightly to find the best position on his nose. There was no attempt made to hide this slight infirmity. The pope needs reading glasses.

He spoke in Italian. Around him, utter silence.

"I welcome all of you assembled for this conference marking the third anniversary of the encyclical letter *Laudato Si,* on care for our common home. I thank you for coming together to 'hear with your hearts' the increasingly desperate cries of the earth and its poor, who look for our help and concern. . . . Your presence here is the sign of your commitment to take concrete steps to save the planet and the life it sustains, inspired by the encyclical's assumption that 'everything is connected.' That principle lies at the heart of an integral ecology."

Then, a bit later, came a radical declaration: "Financial institutions, too, have an important role to play, as part both of the problem and its solution. A financial paradigm shift is needed, for the sake of promoting integral human development."

To Indigenous peoples, he said quoting from his own encyclical, "land is not a commodity" and to young people, "intergenerational solidarity is not optional but rather a basic question of justice."

Then up we went, one a time. To each, the pope smiled and appeared to be intently listening, with no hint of reproach or remove. The aides stood tightly at his side. There were no police, not even a Swiss Guard in the room. Most people were silent when they returned to their seats. Some were visibly shaken at the papal touch, some wept, and some simply sat down quietly and bowed their heads.

A woman in the row in front of me said "wow" aloud when she got back to her seat. She told me she was from Kenya, adding "we have no forests anymore because climate change and corruption go hand in hand."

As for me, I confess to having been transported by the whole event—to the point that for some time I had to retreat from my own thoughts so as not to admit anything extraneous to the actual experience. Who could forget the medieval rack, and the Vatican's tacit silence during the Nazi period, and the endless list of edicts declaring forbidden behaviors, notwithstanding "Who am I to judge?" But still, to ignore the moment of this particular pope's rallying call for the planet seemed to reduce something great.

There was definitely a sense of a man trying to break a yoke, and I had to admit to being a bit speechless in the face of what was happening, for it was exactly the sort of occasion to which the word "awesome" actually applies. Awe of space and place, of art and person, of the patience and the modesty of the man himself, given the surroundings and the banal bombast of our times.

Celestial and earthly at the same time. After all, what is the job of the pope but to put his power to good use? To take on centuries with a touch, and a critique of colonialism and economic lust in a few words that we could amplify.

And at a certain instant it hit me—that I had been here at all had always been unimaginable. Until it happened. Long considered, quickly over, as quick as the loss of what we think can never go away—nature's balance perhaps? Three years since I wrote the pope, a few hours today. The odd calibrations of time—a peony takes nearly a week to drop all its petals once the flower is cut from the garden, but some petals dry in place and never fall.

The moment was all reflected power, not the power of the man himself or the towering scene around us. What we felt is what we all, somehow, from the four corners of the earth, brought with us, what we need, what we sought.

Then, in June 2019, a year later, setting aside papal infallibility, the pope publicly endorsed that which he had formerly dismissed, carbon pricing, stating, "Carbon pricing is essential if humanity is to use the resources of creation wisely.

The failure to deal with carbon emissions has incurred a vast debt that will now have to be repaid with interest by those coming after us. Our use of the world's natural resources can only be considered ethical when the economic and social costs of using them are transparently recognized and are fully borne by those who incur them, rather than by other people or future generations."

In December 2020, the pope also committed the Vatican to carbon neutrality and to achieve net-zero emissions by 2050. While both commitments may be largely symbolic, they do immerse the Vatican in practical actions for all to observe and take example.

There will be other popes by the due dates, of course, and our world needs radical actions far sooner than that, with or without papal voices. *Laudato Si* was a formidable beacon, but beacons are far from enough anymore.

Worldwide, the faithful and the faithless understand and shudder at the uncertainties ahead, as tempests rage, species disappear, whole swaths of nations weep at unprecedented floods or droughts, and our common home of earth each day becomes a setting of common shock and unforgivable tragedies.

Still, threads come together, and indeed human commitment to solve environmental problems cannot be less resilient than our valiant planet itself, struggling against the detriment we visit upon it.

All human circumstances are laced with dichotomy and paradox, but the free ride on our planet's assets has run out of justification. Pricelessness is the currency to end it.

What needs to be done is not hieroglyphics. Money flows are upside down, and must be reversed to properly value what we can never recreate. Our books are out of balance and time is as fleeting as pricelessness is not.

We need nature only if we need infinity.

References

Advances in Atmospheric Sciences, https://www.springer.com/journal/376

American Society of Civil Engineers, https://www.asce.org/

Australian Competition and Consumer Commissions (ACCC)."Murray-Darling Basin water markets inquiry," https://www.accc.gov.au/focus-areas/inquiries-finalised/murray-darling-basin-water-markets-inquiry-0

Barefoot College, https://www.barefootcollege.org/

Beal, Graham W. J. (2010). "Mutual Admiration, Mutual Exploitation: Rivera, Ford and the Detroit Industry Murals." Berkeley Center for Latin American Studies, University of California, Spring, https://clas.berkeley.edu/mutual-admiration-mutual-exploitation-rivera-ford-and-detroit-industry-murals

Blue Forest Conservation, https://www.blueforest.org/

Capital Group. "ESG Global Study 2022," https://www.capitalgroup.com/eacg/esg/global-study.html

Carson, Rachel. (1962), *Silent Spring.* Houghton Mifflin.

Cohen, Sir Ronald. (2020). *Impact: Reshaping Capitalism to Drive Real Change.* Ebury Press.

Convergence. (2020). The Forest Resilience Bond Case Study, June, https://www.convergence.finance/resource/the-forest-resilience-bond-case-study/view

Correa, Rafael. (2007). "Ecuador President Rafael Correa to UN: We Offer to Forsake Oil Revenue, for the Sake of Humanity," https://climateandcapitalism.com/2007/09/28/ecuador-president-rafael-correa-to-un-we-offer-to-forsake-oil-revenue-for-the-sake-of-humanity/

Costanza, R., et al. (1997). "The value of the world's ecosystem services and natural capital." *Nature* 387 (15 May):253–60, https://doi.org/10.1038/387253a0

Costanza, R., et al. (2014). "Changes in the global value of ecosystem services." *Global Environmental Change* 26 (1) 152–58, DOI:10.1016/j.gloenvcha.2014.04.002

Dasgupta, Partha, et al. (2021). *The Economics of Biodiversity: The Dasgupta Review.* London: HM Treasury.

Dickinson, Paul. (2000). *Beautiful Corporations: Corporate Style in Action.* Financial Times/Prentice Hall.

Emerson, Jed. (2000). *The Nature of Returns.* Harvard Business School.

Emerton, L., and Min Aung Yan. (2013). "The Economic Value of Forest Ecosystem Services in Myanmar and Options for Sustainable Financing." Ministry of Environmental Conservation and Forestry, Union of Myanmar, September, DOI:10.13140/2.1.1896.0968

Environmental Protection Agency (EPA). Benefits of the SO2 program, https://www.epa.gov/acidrain/acid-rain-program

Environmental Protection Agency (EPA). (2021). "The Forest Resilience Bond: Structural Design and Contribution to Water Management and Collaborative Forest Restoration Partnerships," Water Infrastructure and Resiliency Finance Center, March, https://www.epa.gov/waterfinancecenter/forest-resilience-bond

Environmental Protection Agency (EPA). Water Infrastructure and Resiliency Finance Center, https://www.epa.gov/waterfinancecenter

Franzen, Jonathan. (2015). "Carbon Capture." *New Yorker,* April 6, https://www.newyorker.com/magazine/2015/04/06/carbon-capture

Fraumeni, Barbara, and Sumiye Okubo. "R&D in the National Income and Product Accounts: A First Look at Its Effects on GDP." US Bureau of Economic Analysis, https://www.bea.gov/system/files/papers/WP2002-1.pdf

Gates, Bill. (2022). "Need to eliminate global emissions of greenhouse gases by 2050," December 20, https://www.livemint.com/news/world/need-to-eliminate-global-emissions-of-greenhouse-gases-by-2050-bill-gates-11671556710983.html

"Global 2000: The Report to the President." Foreword by Jimmy Carter, https://www.cartercenter.org/resources/pdfs/pdf-archive/global2000reporttothepresident--enteringthe21stcentury-01011991.pdf

Global Carbon Reward, https://globalcarbonreward.org/

Global Coral Reef Monitoring Network (GCRMN), https://gcrmn.net/

Haber, Stephen H., et al. (2022). "ESG Investing: What Shareholders Do Fund Managers Represent?" Stanford Closer Look Series, Stanford

University, November 3, https://www.gsb.stanford.edu/faculty-research/publications/esg-investing-what-shareholders-do-fund-managers-represent

Henderson, Hazel. (1981). *The Politics of the Solar Age.* Anchor Press.

Hörhold, M., T. Münch, S. Weißbach, et al. (2023). "Modern temperatures in central–north Greenland warmest in past millennium." *Nature* 613, 503–507, https://doi.org/10.1038/s41586-022-05517-z.

Howe, Ben Ryder. (2021). "Wall Street Eyes Billions in the Colorado's Water." *New York Times,* January 21, https://www.nytimes.com/2021/01/03/business/colorado-river-water-rights.html

Institute for Climate Economics (I4CE). (2022). "Global Carbon Accounts in 2022," https://www.i4ce.org/en/publication/global-carbon-acounts-2022-climate/

Inter-American Development Bank. MRRI reef value, https://www.iadb.org/en/environment/natural-capital-lab

International Coral Reef Initiative. "Status of Coral Reefs of the World: 2020," https://gcrmn.net/2020-report/

International Water Association. NRW report, https://iwa-network.org/learn_resources/the-challenge-of-reducing-non-revenue-water-nrw-in-developing-countries-how-the-private-sector-can-help-a-look-at-performance-based-service-contracting/

Karen Clark and Company. US Wildfire Snapshot, https://www.karenclarkandco.com/models/us-wildfire

Karpik, Lucien. (2010). *Valuing the Unique: The Economics of Singularities.* Princeton University Press.

Keeling, Charles. (1970). "Is Carbon Dioxide from Fossil Fuel Changing Man's Environment?" *Proceedings of the American Philosophical Society* 114 (1):10–17, https://www.jstor.org/stable/985720

Kilimo, https://kilimo.go.ke/

Kornfeld, Robert. (2013). "Initial Results of the 2013 Comprehensive Revision of the National Income and Product Accounts," Survey of Current Business, https://apps.bea.gov/scb/pdf/2013/08%20August/0813_nipa-revision%20text.pdf

Laudato Si, https://www.vatican.va/content/francesco/en/encyclicals/documents/papa-francesco_20150524_enciclica-laudato-si.html

Liemberger, Roland, and Alan Wyatt. (2019). "Quantifying the global non-revenue water problem." Water Science & Technology Water Supply 19 (3, May 1): 831–837, https://www.researchgate.net/publication/326238463_Quantifying_the_global_non-revenue_water_problem

McCullah, S., et al. "Improved Estimates of the National Income and Product Accounts Results of the 2013 Comprehensive Revision," https://apps.bea.gov/scb/pdf/2013/09%20September/0913_comprehensive_nipa_revision.pdf

Metals Company, https://metals.co/

MSCI. "ESG and Climate Trends to Watch for 2023," https://www.msci.com/documents/1296102/35124068/ESG+and+Climate+Trends+to+Watch+for+2023.pdf

Munich Re. Annual Losses Report, https://www.munichre.com/en/company/investors/reports-and-presentations/results-reports.html

Mūsā al-Khwārizmī, Muhammed ibn. (2010). *The Compendious Book on Completion and Balancing.* VDM Publishing.

National Centers for Environmental Information (NCEI). (2023). "Billion-Dollar Weather and Climate Disasters," National Oceanic and Atmospheric Association, https://www.ncei.noaa.gov/access/billions/

National Research Council. (1999). *Nature's Numbers: Expanding the National Economic Accounts to Include the Environment.* Washington, DC: National Academies Press.

National Academy of Sciences, https://www.nasonline.org/

Nature-Based Infrastructure Global Resource Center, https://nbi.iisd.org/

Nature Conservancy, https://www.nature.org/en-us/

Nature's Vault, https://naturesvault.io/

Netafim, www.netafim.com

Robinson, Kim Stanley. (2023). "Paying Ourselves to Decarbonize." *Noema,* February 21, https://www.noemamag.com/paying-ourselves-to-decarbonize/

Ocean Tomo. (2015, 2020). Annual Study of Intangible Asset Market Value, https://oceantomo.com/intangible-asset-market-value-study/

Ostrom, Elinor. (2015). *Governing the Commons: The Evolution of Institutions for Collective Action.* Cambridge University Press.

Ostrom, Elinor. (2009). Nobel Prize Lecture, https://www.nobelprize.org/prizes/economic-sciences/2009/ostrom/lecture

Pacioli, Luca. (2010). *Particularis de Computis et Scripturis (The Rules of Double-Entry Bookkeeping).* CreateSpace Independent Publishing Platform.

Robinson, Kim Stanley. (2023). "Paying Ourselves to Decarbonize." *Noema,* February 21, https://www.noemamag.com/paying-ourselves-to-decarbonize/

Shiva, Vandana. (1989). *Staying Alive: Women, Ecology and Development.* Zed Books.

Smith, Adam. *The Wealth of Nations* and *Lectures on Jurisprudence.*

Stiglitz, J. E., et al. (2008). "Report by the Commission on the Measurement of Economic Performance and Social Progress," https://www.stat.si/doc/drzstat/stiglitz%20report.pdf

Sustainable Investing. Funds Directory, https://sustainableinvest.com/funds-directory/

Turenscape, https://www.turenscape.com/en/home/index.html

United Nations. (1992). Agenda 21, https://sustainabledevelopment.un.org/outcomedocuments/agenda21

United Nations. (2016). Paris Agreement, https://unfccc.int/process-and-meetings/the-paris-agreement

United Nations. (2022). COP15 Agreement, https://www.unep.org/news-and-stories/story/cop15-ends-landmark-biodiversity-agreement

United Nations. (2022). "Global Peatland Assessment: The State of the World's Peatlands," https://www.unep.org/resources/global-peatlands-assessment-2022

United Nations Environment Programme (UNEP). (2022). "Spreading like Wildfire: The Rising Threat of Extraordinary Landscape Fires," https://www.unep.org/resources/report/spreading-wildfire-rising-threat-extraordinary-landscape-fires

United Nations Framework Convention on Climate Change (UNFCCC). (2022). "Synthesis Report," https://unfccc.int/ndc-synthesis-report-2022

United Nations Global Compact. "Who Cares Wins: Connecting Financial Markets to a Changing World," https://www.unepfi.org/fileadmin/events/2004/stocks/who_cares_wins_global_compact_2004.pdf

Uptime Institute, https://uptimeinstitute.com/

Waring, Marilyn. (1988). *If Women Counted: A New Feminist Economics.* Harper and Row.

WestWater Research. (2022). "A down payment on stability for the Colorado River Basin: What large scale conservation looks like." Water Market Insider. October 26, https://waterexchange.com/a-down-payment-on-stability-for-the-colorado-river-basin/

Wheeler, Sarah, "Debunking Murray-Darling Basin water trade myths." *Australian Journal of Agricultural and Resource Economics* 66 (October): 797–821, https://doi.org/10.1111/1467-8489.12490

Wheeler, Sarah Ann, ed. (2021). *Water Markets: A Global Assessment*. Edward Elgar Publishing.

World Bank. "The Changing Wealth of Nations 2021: Managing Assets for the Future," https://www.worldbank.org/en/publication/changing-wealth-of-nations

World Meteorological Organization. "United in Science, 2022," https://public.wmo.int/en/resources/united_in_science

Xi Jinping, Communist Party Congress. (2022). "Report to the 20th National Congress of the Communist Party of China," http://my.china-embassy.gov.cn/eng/zgxw/202210/t20221026_10792358.htm

Zeitz, Jochen. "Environmental Profit and Loss Statement for the year ended 31 December 2010." PUMA, http://danielsotelsek.com/wp-content/uploads/2013/10/Puma-EPL.pdf

Acknowledgments

I would like to thank the Bellagio Center of the Rockefeller Foundation for innovation, early support, encouragement, vote of confidence, and inspiration; the center's staff in New York and Bellagio for impeccable commitment; and my fellow residents for such welcome animation and shared ideas. Also Leah Spiro and Herb Schaffner, who acted when inaction would have been easier. I would also like to thank and honor the memory of the great writer, publisher, and teacher Victor Navasky, who catalyzed my career by helping me publish my first professional article. All writers would be lucky to have the support of Bill Falloon and the excellent team at Wiley. Finally, I am grateful to many friends and colleagues who have tolerated my absence and contradictions, and to the daily gift of living common to us all and that this book tries to bring to bear.

Index